AN
AMERICAN
COMPANY

The Tragedy of United Fruit

AN AMERICAN COMPANY

The Tragedy of United Fruit

by THOMAS P. McCANN

edited by Henry Scammell

CROWN PUBLISHERS, INC., NEW YORK

Printed in the United States of America

Published simultaneously in Canada by General Publishing Company
Limited

Library of Congress Cataloging in Publication Data

McCann, Thomas P
  An American company.

  Includes index.
  1. United Fruit Company. 2. Central America—
History—1951- I. Scammell, Henry. II. Title.
HD9249.U6M23   1976   338.7′63′4   76-24811
ISBN 0-517-52809-6

CONTENTS

thing shiny in the *New York Times* · Elihu M. Blachowitz · The family business · "I would have made a good Pope" · An art event in New York · Channel 13 and the Eli Blacks of this world · End game

11 Transformations 181

12 What Happened Next 214

13 Last Thoughts 232

Epilogue 235

Index 237

Epigraph

"A dozen men with machine guns are no match for a single lawyer with a briefcase."

The Godfather, Mario Puzo

AN
AMERICAN
COMPANY

The Tragedy of United Fruit

Chapter 1

A TON OF BRICKS

THE LAST MORNING in the life of Eli M. Black—president, chairman, chief executive officer and principal architect of the two-billion-dollar United Brands multinational conglomerate—was Monday, February 3, 1975. It began with a cold dawn, typical for New York City near the end of winter. In his Park Avenue apartment, Black moved in the semidarkness from one room to another, preparing for his death. He was quiet, saying little to his wife, Shirley, who had slept beside him through the night, or his married daughter who had spent the night on a sofa bed in the living room. In the bathroom, he showered and shaved, then went back into the bedroom and dressed noiselessly in the half light by a window: conservative blue suit, conservative patterned tie—the familiar uniform. Next he opened a large, satchel-type briefcase, placed it on a living room chair and began to fill it to capacity with books taken apparently at random from the many shelves. All the volumes had in common was their size: they were unusually large. He snapped the case shut. There was a soft tap at the door. When Black opened it, the doorman, who had come up from the lobby, said, "Good morning," and passed him the early newspapers. That meant that Black's car was waiting at the curb outside. He said goodbye to his wife and daughter.

Jim Thomas, the driver, met Black a few minutes later on the sidewalk in front of the apartment building. Thomas had served as chauffeur for a total of six generations of the company's chief executives. Black nodded as Thomas held open the door to the Cadillac Fleetwood limousine. "Hello, Jim. How was your weekend?" The car pulled out into the light traffic on Park Avenue and rolled smoothly south, toward the Pan Am Building.

Thomas looked at Black in the mirror as they approached the building. "Will you be needing me, Mr. Black?"

"No, Jim," Black said. "This will be an in day."

The answer meant that Thomas would be parking the car in an all-day garage a few blocks farther south. He pulled the limousine to the curb, then jumped quickly out to open the rear door for Black. He reached for the brown leather briefcase at Black's feet. Black sometimes had a problem with stiffness and Thomas was used to holding his briefcase until Black was fully out of the car. "Careful, Jim," Black said. "It's a ton of bricks."

Thomas picked up the briefcase and smiled in surprise at its weight. When Black was on the sidewalk, Thomas passed it carefully back to him, closed the rear door, and returned to the driver's seat of the car. Black entered the lobby of the Pan Am Building as the car pulled away from the curb.

In the elevator, Black pushed the button to the forty-fourth floor. As usual, he was the first to arrive in the office that morning. He unlocked the double wooden doors to the outer office, entered the reception area, then locked the doors behind him by sliding the bolt on one door across to the catch on the other. Black then walked down the corridor to his own office, at the corner. That door, too, he locked behind him. He set down the briefcase on a chair in front of his desk, then took off his hat, scarf and coat and placed them on top of the satchel. Walking to the window he raised the venetian blind and looked out over the city—north up Park Avenue along which he had just been driven. Then he walked back to the chair and picked up the heavy briefcase; the coat, scarf and hat fell to the floor. Using the briefcase as a battering ram, Black smashed it against the quarter-inch-thick tempered plate glass of the window. The glass shattered. Some pieces fell outward into the air, and two or three large slabs fell inward and fragmented on the office floor. The room was filled with the high, sighing, alpine sounds of tall buildings and, far below, the noise of traffic. Black picked at the fragments of glass still hanging in the window and began to enlarge the hole. He cut himself on one or two of the pieces he removed. He then swung the briefcase in another arc, this time through the jagged hole, and watched it as it tumbled to the northbound Park Avenue ramp forty-four floors below.

In a drop from that height, an object the size and weight of Black's briefcase—or of Black himself—would be in the air for a full six seconds. It would be traveling at over one hundred miles an hour and still accelerating by the time it hit the ground. Black looked at the briefcase after it landed; it tumbled when it hit, finally coming to rest on a post office loading ramp.

Then Black climbed up on the windowsill and crouched low to pass through the opening in the glass. It was still a small hole— no more than four feet high and three feet wide. He stepped over the edge, and left a 180-degree pivot mark on the sill as he pushed away from the side of the building. Six seconds later he hit the street.

His body landed in heavy traffic on Park Avenue. Two policemen in a cruiser were on the scene in a matter of minutes. They made a search of the pockets, trying to keep their eyes from what little was left of the head and face. They found cash, some keys, a black notebook, a billfold. One of the policemen stood guard over the body while the other radioed his precinct, ". . . jumper . . . east side of Pan Am Building . . . on the ramp." Traffic was starting to back up, and more police arrived shortly to reroute it. Meanwhile, forty-four floors up, Jim Thomas, sensing something was wrong—thinking Black was ill—was now at the door of the outer office pushing against the bolt. Eventually he broke the lock, forcing the doors open. When the police arrived on that floor a few minutes later, they walked with Thomas to a window and asked him to look down and identify the body. Thomas nodded yes: even from that distance he recognized the suit. Another employee, G. Burke Wright, identified the body from closer range, in the street. By nine o'clock the morgue wagon departed with Black's remains in a thick, olive-drab, waterproof nylon bag.

Word of Black's death traveled quickly throughout his empire and around the world. People who had feared him, pitied him, loathed him, admired him, envied him, including many who were in Black's debt and many more who hardly knew him, felt moved to final words of tribute. They came from the worlds of business and the arts and education and politics and labor, speaking of Black as an intellectual, a philanthropist, a leader, a man of character and conscience, a gentle man who never raised his voice or hand against another, a man not of this world. Tributes came from César Chavez, Norman Cousins and the Chairman of Lincoln Center.

Rabbi Leonard Rosenfeld, a close friend of Black's for thirty-five years, flew from Jerusalem to be at the final rites. He called Black "a fiscal giant and a rabbi who remained searching for God all his life." Black was indeed a rabbi, having been graduated from Yeshiva University half a lifetime earlier. Rosenfeld asked, "How many persons pushed Eli to a desperate option—how many contributed to his untimely tragedy—and who called on Eli to choose the wrong door?"

The financial press was equally kind. They spoke of the many difficult times United Brands had gone through—hurricanes and floods, rising costs and extortionate taxes in the tropical countries where the company had its major operations, but they said that Black had steered his two-billion-dollar colossus through the worst of the storm and had apparently found smooth sailing at last.

Black's nephew, Phil Fuchs, was vice-president in charge of public relations for United Brands at the time of his uncle's death. "It was the one way," he said of Black's suicide, "to hurt everybody."

I heard of Black's death from a mutual acquaintance in New

York while the body was still lying in the street. I sat at my desk for a long time after the call, thinking back on what Eli Black had meant in my life, the demons that had driven him so hard and the demons he had unleashed—often deliberately, sometimes without knowing it—on others. I realized instantly that Black's death, like so much else in his life, was not what it appeared at the moment: it was neither the beginning of a new era nor the end of his effect on those around him. I was approached by an editor of *New York Magazine* to write "An Appreciation of Eli Black." I declined. A short time later, the unreal tranquillity would come to an end, and I knew it.

In the hour after Eli died, I tried to think of some of the ways his death would affect those around him: whose jobs would end, whose power would be cut off, whose varied allegiances would lead them now to disaster or reward. I thought of old friends, some who stayed and some of whom had left Eli's service when he had demanded too much for what he needed most: loyalty. And I thought of some of Eli's most dedicated enemies who had remained with him to the end.

I had no way of foreseeing the incredible chaos that lay directly ahead—suspension of United Brands stock from the New York Stock Exchange, charges of corruption and bribery that would unseat the president of a neighboring Central American nation and affect America's commercial relations with many others, the possible indictment of close friends of half my lifetime, the lawsuits against Black's estate by outraged shareholders, possible destruction of the very colossus Black had created.

And as I sat at my desk that morning, I kept coming back to the question of why Black had died. Had he been destroyed by the company he created? Did he jump as a final, desperate way of bringing into control a machine that had run wild? Or perhaps it was because he realized at last that he had become the one thing he hated most—a failure.

Chapter 2

NEVER BLUSH TO TELL AN HONEST BUSINESS

ELI BLACK first entered my life on an autumn afternoon in 1968. The announcement of his arrival was cryptic, a few words written in longhand on a page from a stenographic pad.

John Fox's secretary, Helen Collins, had opened the door quietly, crossed to Fox's chair, handed him the folded scrap of paper and then left the conference room without waiting for a response.

One of the men in the meeting had been reading some numbers, and he hesitated for a moment. Before Fox looked at the note, he nodded for him to continue. The rest of the eyes went back to the speaker, but I had sensed something in Helen's manner and I watched Fox as he unfolded the paper and looked down at the message.

He read it more than once. Then, still looking at the paper, he slowly raised his hand to the top of his head and began absently to massage his bald scalp. It was not the first time I had seen him make that gesture—thoughtful—the way another man might rub his chin or tug at an earlobe. It was a certain sign of bad news. In the months to come, I was to see him repeat that unconscious move again and again.

John M. Fox, then chairman of the board and chief executive officer of United Fruit Company of Boston, made an ideal

6

model for what a big businessman should look like: handsome, with a classically shaped head that was always bronzed by the sun, substantial, athletically trim, he dressed conservatively, but with an un-Bostonian style. On his left wrist he wore a gold Rolex with a heavy gold strap. He was a jogger, a sailor and had made his reputation as the man who got the Minute Maid Orange Juice Company off the ground. By the time of the meeting, I had worked closely with him at United Fruit for eight years—long enough to know him well and to trust him; I had liked him from the beginning. When Fox finally raised his eyes from the piece of paper, it was to look at the Rolex. I looked at my own wristwatch. The time was nearly 2:30 in the afternoon. The date was September 24.

Fox passed the note to me. It read: "Specialist office at NYSE advises that 733,000 shares of UNITED stock sold this afternoon. Third largest transaction in Exchange history. Buyer not known." I passed the note to Will Lauer, another old friend and a vice-president of United Fruit. Will read it and gave it to Ed Gibbons, the company's comptroller. The meeting came to an end.

The next two hours were chaos. There were two investment bankers on the company's board at that time: George Peabody Gardner, Jr., former chairman of the Fruit Company, was a general partner with Paine, Webber, Jackson and Curtis; and Stanley de J. Osborne, an old Latin-American hand and former president of Olin Mathieson, was a partner with Lazard Frères. But up until almost five o'clock, neither they nor anyone else in our entire organization, inside the company or outside, could come up with a single piece of useful information. This purchase, just under 10 percent of the company's stock, meant that our largest shareholder was unknown to us. A bomb had been planted; near the close of the business day we still had no idea who had put it there or how it was meant to go off.

Fox's phone finally rang a few minutes before five. The caller spoke very softly, pausing now and then to clear his throat. He identified himself as E. M. Black—not giving his first name—and said that he was "the new shareholder." He told Fox that he was coming to Boston that night, that he wanted to meet with

him, that he would then state exactly what he had in mind. Fox
agreed to meet Black at the Algonquin Club later that evening,
and ended the conversation.

Fox was still clearly angry, but when he hung up the phone
his face also had a look of relief: the raider had made contact,
had identified himself, and had agreed to meet with Fox on the
company's home ground.

After a brief discussion, it was decided that the company's
delegation to that meeting would be made up of Fox; Herbert
Cornuelle (pronounced Cornell), the president of United Fruit;
Victor Folsom, general counsel; and George Gardner. Whenever
I thought about the company's future in those days, it was inevitable that I would also think about Jack Fox: in many ways,
they were one and the same. I watched from my office window
in the Prudential Tower as the group crossed Boylston Street
on their way to the Algonquin Club, and I thought that whoever
E. M. Black was, he was in for the fight of his life.

They met with Black in the club library, a small, dimly lighted
room with Oriental scatter rugs on the floor and photos of several
generations of the club's presidents looking down at them from
between the shelves on the wall.

Black did not have the look of a very formidable adversary.
He was six feet tall—the same height as Jack Fox—but to the
others in the room he seemed shorter. He was balding, wore
thick dark-rimmed glasses and a conservative dark blue suit.
During the exchange of handshakes, his small, delicate hands
were soft to the touch, and he greeted the four men, with a
smile and a voice that went with the hands: soft, almost halting.
His full name, he told them, was Eli Black.

"I bought the stock," he said settling into a deep leather chair,
"because it seemed like a good investment." He smiled tenta-
tively, but the others did not smile back. "That is to say," he
continued, "I felt the stock is seriously undervalued –ah–that
there is an opportunity for some appreciation with little down-
side risk."

Black said he greatly admired the Fruit Company's management. It was clear that he knew a lot about Fox and Cornuelle,

including their respective records before they joined the company. He said he wanted to get to know United Fruit even better—of course, he would like a position on the board. He went on to suggest that maybe it would "work out" the way it had gone at the John Morrell Meat Company, where Black had bought a position in the company and had taken a passive role until the Morrell management had asked him to assume control. Black's own company was AMK Corporation; AMK had then absorbed Morrell.

Black was not at all what the four men had expected. Each asked some questions which Black answered agreeably and directly, but the meeting turned out to be very brief. Eventually, Fox suggested they all go upstairs for dinner.

In the next several weeks I was to hear that conversation cited over and over again, at first for reassurance and then in anger, until I was as familiar with the words as though I had been there when they were first spoken.

My immediate response to this story, when I heard it for the first time in Jack Fox's office at seven thirty the next morning, was to suggest that we plug in our contingency plan in the event of a raid. I was director of public relations and had drafted the plan that was approved the previous May. It called for releases, press contacts, notification of shareholders and directors and similar other moves to offset the impact of a surprise attack.

The management of United Fruit had good reason to anticipate an attempted takeover long before Eli M. Black appeared on their horizon. It was the era of the takeover. The company was free of debt and had almost one hundred million dollars in the bank with few attractive ways to spend it. Diversifying at that point in the late 1960s, even with all that money, was like arriving at Filene's Basement the morning after: there were still a few shreds left in the display bins, but they were picked over and unglamorous. The smart shoppers had come early and all the bargains were gone. So we were stuck with our hundred million, a huge lollipop hanging over the side of the corporate baby carriage.

It was Herb Cornuelle who pronounced sentence on the contingency plan. He said he thought that the worst thing we could do would be not to take Eli Black at his word. He repeated the words Black had used, such as "honorable" and "integrity" and "good faith." Not only was I told it would be extremely poor judgment to launch a campaign of outright resistance, there was no question that I was being chastened for having brought it up. But I persisted.

My point was that if Black had indeed bought the stock because it was such a good investment then we could put out a simple press release saying just that. If Black meant what he said that previous evening, why would he object to seeing it in print in the financial pages the next morning?

Herb Cornuelle was never the kind of man to clench his fist or bang the table. He simply lowered his voice and one eyebrow in about the same degree; I was certain everyone in the room was conscious of his restraint. He told me that the company was in the most delicate, vulnerable position in its history, and that to assume an adversary role with a man whose goodwill we desperately needed was to invite the very disaster he was trying to avert.

At the time, I had difficulty believing that Cornuelle was naïve enough to look upon Eli Black as a potential benefactor. I felt certain that the night before, in the familiar, elegant fastness of the Algonquin Club, Cornuelle thought that he had seen the first few letters of the handwriting on the wall.

A few hours later we issued a statement for the press which had been prepared by Black himself. It said that E. M. Black was the purchaser of the historic block of stock. It said that he had met with the Fruit Company's management, and that the meeting had been successful. It stated nothing of his intentions.

In his first meeting Black had met with no resistance—because we refused to see him as he doubtless saw us, as an enemy to be beaten. But by the end of that week, he had left no doubt in anyone's mind that United Fruit was in a struggle for its life. By that time we had already lost a tremendous amount of ground.

Seven years later, Herb Cornuelle told me that he had believed what Black had to say that first night at the Algonquin Club and he now felt that believing Black—instead of taking a firm stand and fighting him off—had been the biggest single mistake of his business career.

Ironically, the first time I heard of AMK Corporation was two months before Black came out in the open. A friend from New York called one day to tell me he had heard a rumor from his broker that AMK was planning an acquisition bid for United Fruit and that they were organizing their resources on the Street. I reported the rumor and asked our public relations firm in New York, Doremus and Company, to get me a copy of the AMK annual report for the previous year; the request appears on the Doremus monthly report for August, 1968. By mid-November, once the raid was on, Fox asked me for some background on how the rumor had got started. I checked and was able to trace it down to a man whom my source identified as a relative of E. M. Black. Fox and I were both surprised that Black would have an Achilles' heel in his own family, when so much of his success depended on confidence, secrecy and the element of surprise.

When I got the AMK report, the first words I read on the inside front cover were by Homer, "Never blush to tell an honest business," straight out of Bartlett's and straight out of context, with the meaning changed to fit the occasion. The next page was a quote from Eli M. Black, treated with the same typographical reverence accorded Homer. Something about the security of each of us depending on the performance of all of us. I looked at the numbers, which seemed big but not especially healthy, and forwarded the report to Tom Warner, our new financial vice-president.

That was the last I heard of AMK until they struck.

It was not until several months later that I learned that Tom Warner had known E. M. Black even before I had sent him the AMK annual report. Warner had been an auditor for Price Waterhouse at the time, and Black had been a director of one of Price Waterhouse's clients.

When Eli M. Black, the poet-raider, made his move, it gave rise to another Cornuelle phrase with which I was to become

increasingly familiar. If anyone suggested that we resist, that
we fight, Herb Cornuelle would say that kind of move would
"tear the company apart." This was five years before the same
defense was used, less successfully, as an argument against the
impeachment of President Nixon. The threat of impeachment
drove him from office, and the country survived.

What Herb was referring to, of course, was not the United
Fruit Company itself. His concern, and the concern of almost
all of the directors and managers of United Fruit who participated in those events, was for the price of the company's stock.
The price of the stock is a management's report card. And the
wrong moves could greatly affect the price of the stock and
reduce the value of their holdings and options. The right moves
could make them far richer men than most of them already
were. This is a conflict which raiders recognize, and which is
one of their strongest weapons.

During the next few weeks, in large measure through the
acquiescence of United Fruit's management, Eli Black was able
to accomplish what the management itself had been unable to
do for twenty years: to create an air of excitement, of expectation about the company. And the stock began to climb fast. By
the time United Fruit decided to look elsewhere for what it considered to be a more respectable bridegroom, Black had already
increased the value of the outstanding stock options held by
management, my own included, by millions of dollars.

In the following weeks, the rest of the management and all
but one of the directors (Vic Folsom) of United Fruit came to
the conclusion that rape was inevitable. A company in distress
emits a scent which is unmistakable to the practiced nose. Suitors
of all sizes and description assembled; some came by invitation
for a final, nervous dance; others crashed the party, their purposes transparently lustful.

With almost 10 percent of the company in his pocket, Black's
fortune was already assured. If United Fruit actually did produce a more compatible mate, Black was unlikely to part with his
stock for less than a 100 percent profit. And if not, he would
have the company in its entirety.

Eli M. Black limited his open moves during this period to watching quietly from the sidelines, and a curious transformation began to take place. The man who had started it all, whose single deft stroke on September 24 had so badly crippled the company that United Fruit would never again stand without help, simply by being patient and pretending to hold himself apart from the subsequent melee began to emerge as the politest boy at the party.

In 1968, the United Fruit Company was seventy years old. It had survived nearly every form of upheaval possible to imagine, including the chaos of its own beginnings. It had out-lived competitiors, survived thousands of acts of God such as hurricanes, droughts, pestilence, blights and floods. It had gone through several hundred political revolutions, two world wars, worldwide depression, expropriations, strikes, boycotts, muck-raking attacks, organized protests at home and abroad, management upheavals, dismemberment by the Department of Justice and the persistent aroma of its own reputation as "El Pulpo," the Octopus that strangled all it touched.

But it was not to survive much longer.

Chapter 3

MENOPAUSE

COMPANIES, like people, have most of their energy when they are young, and as they age they lose their potency; they become more rigid, their vision becomes narrower, their prospects fewer and they resist the kind of originality that marked their beginnings. While they still have the vigor of youth, the most important part of life is opportunity. As they age, and as their early labors bear fruit, they gradually change their priorities: habit becomes more important than innovation, and how things get done takes precedence over why. When I joined United Fruit in 1952—as an eighteen-year-old office boy at Pier Three in New York—the company was already well into middle age and its arteries had started to harden.

Companies have one great advantage over people: they can renew themselves. But they have to want renewal first, and that means that the men at the top have to recognize the signs of senility before the disease advances to the stage where it is incurable. In 1952, United Fruit was still thinking of itself and the world around it in pretty much the same way it had thought of those things at the company's beginnings. Many of the men who were running the company in the fifties learned their trade and methods from the men who had founded the company fifty years earlier. The rest of the world had changed and was changing, but United Fruit was already too deep in its rut to recognize the differences. In place of the innovations that marked its early years, the character of the company became imitative: it merely repeated earlier moves and tactics. The company had lost almost every semblance of invention. In the areas of production, sales and transportation, as in politics, United Fruit was doing business at the same old stand, but in fifty years the neighborhood had changed beyond recognition.

It was young men who gave the company its start. Three of them, Lorenzo Dow Baker, Minor C. Keith and Andrew W. Preston are generally regarded as having been the founders.

Baker was the captain of an 85-ton schooner, *Telegraph*, out of Wellfleet, Massachusetts, and one day in June of 1870 he pulled into the harbor at Port Morant, Jamaica, for a load of bamboo and a sip of the local rum. While sipping, he was approached by a local impresario who had several stems of green bananas to sell. Baker considered the proposition for the length of a second cup of planter's punch, then agreed to pay the man twenty-five cents a bunch. Eleven days later Baker sold those same bananas in New York for prices ranging between ten and fifteen times what he had paid for them.

Naturally, the next time Baker was in that part of the world he tried to do it again. On subsequent trips, however, he ran into problems. The transit time between Jamaica and New York could vary tremendously with the weather; it was the age of sail, and Baker ended more than one trip by dumping tons of rotten fruit into the harbors of Boston and New York. But he persisted, and in the 1880s he had a new schooner with an auxiliary steam engine which could dependably carry 10,000 stems of bananas from Jamaica to Boston in about a week and a half.

Once he had developed the volume, he turned to the task of building his own marketing organization. In 1885, he formed the Boston Fruit Company with a banana salesman named Andrew Preston and eight others. With Preston taking orders up and down the seaboard and Captain Baker filling them as fast as he could load his boats, the company grew big enough to make all the partners very rich men before the end of the next decade. By then, with eleven ships flying the company's pennants, Baker modestly named his shipping venture the Great White Fleet. The color was practical: it reflected the sun and kept the cargoes cooler, so they lasted longer.

Meanwhile, a man named Minor C. Keith had been following an equally successful career down in Costa Rica. Keith, once described by *Fortune* as "an apple-headed little man with the eyes of a fanatic," had started life in Brooklyn. All he ever wanted to do was build railroads and he went to Central America and began to make a good living doing just that. His most notable monument is the first twenty-five miles of track between Port Limón and the Costa Rican capital of San José. Keith had gone down to Limón in 1871 at the invitation of his uncle, Henry Meiggs, already famous as a railroad man in South America. That first twenty-five miles of track took root in somewhat the same manner that Massachusetts Indians had planted corn; only instead of dropping an alewife or codfish into the same hole with each seed, Keith came near to burying a worker with every tie. At least five thousand men died, including Keith's three brothers.

A lot of persuasion and ingenuity was required to enlist workers to that kind of commitment. One method, probably not used by Keith but employed successfully by a former Tennessee lawyer named William Walker, was to place an advertisement in the papers saying: "Wanted—ten or fifteen young men to go a short distance out of the city. Single men preferred. Passage paid." Walker's applicants would wind up in his mercenary army in Central America. Walker himself enjoyed a brief stint as president of Nicaragua, then made the error of borrowing some boats that belonged to Commodore Cornelius Vanderbilt without asking him. The Costa Rican army chased Walker into Honduras, Walker surrendered to the British Navy, the British turned him back to the Honduran Army, and he was placed in front of an adobe wall and shot.

Minor Keith preferred employing murderers and thieves from the jails of New Orleans. His first boatload numbered seven hundred, of whom only twenty-five survived the building of the railroad. He brought in two thousand Italians who took one look at the prospective working conditions and fled into the jungle; sixty of them died there before the rest decided that probable death in Keith's construction gang was a more cheerful prospect than certain death among the mangroves.

Once the railroad was built, Keith's next problem was finding people who wanted to ride on it. Both Keith and Costa Rica were deep in debt, and they were both surprised to discover that there was nowhere nearly enough passenger revenue to pay operating costs, not to mention the repayment of the money they had borrowed for construction. So Keith's next move was to take a page from Johnny Appleseed: he planted bananas in the jungles near Limón, within convenient distance from the tracks. By 1883 he owned three banana companies which shipped a combined total of five million stems each year to U.S. markets from four Central American countries. In addition, he was married to the daughter of one of Costa Rica's former presidents. Things were looking up.

Six years later, he unexpectedly incurred a debt of one and a half million dollars when a New York bank failure stuck him with a handful of short-term notes. The government of Costa Rica bailed him out, but he was still in trouble. Keith decided to go to Boston for a conversation with Andrew Preston. That trip resulted, on March 30, 1899, in the birth of United Fruit Company.

That was about as far as Minor Keith cared to go with bananas. After disposing of most of his shares in the new company, along with his million-and-a-half debt, he headed south again and soon reverted to his earlier ways. From the turn of the century until 1929, Keith built mile after mile of Central American railroad lines. He was responsible for putting together the International Railways of Central America, from Mexico to Salvador, from the Caribbean to the Pacific. In the process, he made the destitute little country of Salvador solvent, and perhaps did more than any other man to bring the nations of Central America together as an integrated economic entity. He died on the eve of the Great Depression.

During the same thirty years that followed the formation of United Fruit, the company itself prospered beyond its founders'

best hopes. The Great White Fleet grew to nearly a hundred
ships, and through a 1910 acquisition in England, United Fruit
gained an additional fleet to carry its bananas to Europe. In
1930, the company shipped a total of sixty-five million stems—
containing billions of bananas—from the jungles of the tropics.
It was never to equal that volume again. Preston, who had
acquired much of Keith's political clout in Costa Rica, par-
layed his advantages into a virtual banana kingdom. By the
time he died in 1924, he had ruled for the past quarter century
as "Boss of the Caribbean."

There is one more larger-than-life figure who played an important part in the company's beginnings, and that is Samuel
Zmuri, a Bessarabian Jew who anglicized his name to Zemurray
but never lost his Russian accent. He was known in the trade
as Sam the Banana Man. He entered the business in 1895 in
Mobile, Alabama, at the age of eighteen. His first venture was
the purchase of a hundred and fifty dollars' worth of "ripes and
turnings"—bananas which are already at their peak or approach-
ing it and have to be sold fast before they spoil. Within three
years he had a hundred thousand dollars in the bank; at the
age of twenty-one he was ready for the big time.

With a partner named Hubbard, Zemurray bought a bank-
rupt steamship company; United Fruit was in for a silent share
but soon sold out its interest to Zemurray and Hubbard. Zemurray headed for Honduras, arriving in the shanty town of
Puerto Cortés in 1905. In one important way, Sam the Banana
Man was different from almost all the other latter-day Con-
quistadores who had flocked to the tropics in that era: he had a
deep affection and understanding for the people of Central
America, especially Honduras; and to an extent he was guided
by those feelings throughout the rest of his life.

The attitude of the United States toward Central America
at the time was somewhat different. Perhaps the best illustration of that difference is provided by the events of 1910, when
Samuel Zemurray embarked on an adventure which would result in the conquest of Honduras.

In 1910, for two hundred thousand dollars, most of it borrowed money, Zemurray acquired a five-thousand-acre tract of land on the Cuyamel River in Honduras. The risks of indebtedness frightened Hubbard out of the partnership, so Zemurray renamed his venture the Cuyamel Company, plunging deeper into the tropics and deeper into debt. By the end of the year he owned fifteen thousand acres and owed most of the major bankers of New Orleans, Mobile and New York. He was also indebted to usurers who charged interest rates as high as 50 percent. But that was only one of his problems.

Zemurray knew he needed the assistance of the local governments if he was going to develop the company. He would require government concessions and permission to build rail lines, some certainty that he wouldn't be taxed out of existence and relief from import duty on the equipment his new venture needed to get started. At that time, it was not in the interest of the United States Government for Zemurray to receive that assistance. The reason was entirely financial. Both Nicaragua and Honduras were heavily in debt to Europe, and in order to meet their obligations they were considering a treaty which had been proposed by Philander C. Knox, then U.S. Secretary of State. Under the treaty, both countries would receive the money they needed, but with a novel plan for repayment: agents of the Morgan Bank, the underwriters of the loans, would actually sit in the customs houses of both countries, collecting revenues, authorizing concessions and in all other ways controlling the flow of currency and goods between those countries and the rest of the world. Secretary Knox called Zemurray to Washington, made it clear that there was no chance whatever that the Cuyamel Company would get any concessions or incentives with regard to either taxes or duties, and sternly warned Zemurray not to rock the boat. Zemurray replied, "Mr. Secretary, I'm no favorite grandson of Mr. Morgan's. Mr. Morgan never heard of me." He said all he wanted to do was protect his little business. And Zemurray, too, had a plan. He headed back to New Orleans.

Late that December, Zemurray met with three friends: Manuel Bonilla, a former president of Honduras; a famous soldier of fortune named "General" Lee Christmas; and Christmas's genial protégé, Guy "Machine Gun" Molony, a professional gun for hire. Although there was little the United States could do to restrain Zemurray's movements, Bonilla, Christmas and Molony were watched by the Secret Service night and day to keep them in New Orleans and to assure that they in no way influenced the course of treaty negotiations in either Honduras or Nicaragua. Zemurray's meeting with the three men was to thwart the Secret Service on both counts.

One cold night near the end of the year, clearance arrived from Washington for Bonilla's yacht, the *Hornet,* to depart for Guatemala; of course, Bonilla himself was not included in the release, so he watched his yacht's departure in the company of Christmas and Molony. At the pier, Bonilla made many signs of Latin regret and resignation, and then retired with his two friends to Madame May Evans's whorehouse on Basin Street. The Secret Service agent followed dutifully, taking his place across the street from May's front door where he listened to the revelry for about as long as he could stand it. At two o'clock in the morning he took one last look at the window of the parlor where he satisfied himself that Bonilla, Christmas and Molony were still just warming up for a long, long night. Then he headed home to write his report. Moments later, the laughter came to an abrupt stop, the door of Madame May's establishment flew open, and all three men came through it and started running for the waterfront. Within hours, Zemurray's fast launch had delivered them to the *Hornet,* which was waiting for them near Biloxi, and Bonilla was on his way back to power.

Lee Christmas and Guy Molony, equipped with a machine gun, a case of rifles and three thousand pounds of ammunition, swept through Honduras in a matter of weeks. The incumbent president stepped down, a new election was held, and Bonilla won an overwhelming victory. And Samuel Zemurray won his concessions, duly approved by the Honduran Congress, free for the next twenty-five years. His fortune was assured. In 1930, Zemurray sold his Cuyamel Company to United Fruit for stock worth $31,500,000 and decided to retire. In the course of acquiring Cuyamel, United Fruit made Zemurray their largest single shareholder.

The acquisition was a marriage of opposites. Zemurray's personal style, as well as his operating practices, was completely contrary to the traditions of United Fruit. Zemurray had lived in the tropics and had personally pioneered many of the practices in agriculture and engineering which became the standards for the industry. By contrast, the management of the United Fruit Company had been content, for the most part, to sit in Boston and count the money and watch bananas grow with the same detachment with which an actuary watches the growth and death of populations. Most of the directors and many of the managers had actually never even seen the tropics, and would not have known the difference between one banana variety and another. But they made all of the important decisions related to the techniques of land management, agriculture, engineering and transportation on which the company depended. By the end of 1932, Zemurray wearily faced the inevitable and headed for Boston.

He was greeted, frostily at best, by a board of directors which included Daniel Gould Wing, then chairman of the powerful First National Bank of Boston; former Massachusetts governor Channing H. Cox; direct descendant of two American presidential families, the Jeffersons and the Coolidges; the Lee half of Boston's most prestigious investment firm, Lee Higginson; and Bradley Webster Palmer, a leading Boston lawyer. Zemurray presented an incisive review of the company's mismanagement, backed by a bill of particulars which included the fact that the stock of United Fruit Company had declined by almost 90 percent since he had become as shareholder. He demanded to know what the board intended to do.

Daniel Gould Wing responded for the other directors. He smiled thinly and in a reference to Zemurray's accent, said, "Unfortunately, Mr. Zemurray, I can't understand a word you say." Zemurray just looked at Wing for a few seconds then at the other Brahmin faces around the room. The story goes that he muttered something under his breath as he left. He returned shortly with his hands full of enough proxies to make translation unnecessary. Slapping them down on the long, oval table at 1 Federal Street, and speaking, very clearly to avoid being misunderstood, Zemurray said, "You gentlemen have been fucking up this business long enough. I'm going to straighten it out." Wing and his clique were dumped from the board and Zemurray was back in bananas.

Samuel Zemurray was a different kind of man from anyone United Fruit met before or since, and for the next twenty years he shaped the company's operations to his own image: toughminded but fair, responsive and responsible. He dealt effectively with all problems including a banana disease called Sigatoka, which first appeared in 1936 and would almost certainly have wiped out the company's entire production within less than four years if not for Zemurray's daring in the use of the then-unproven Bordeaux Mixture.

Sitting around an old Cape Cod inn thirty years later, Dr. Vining Dunlap, the company's head agronomist, told me of the conversation he had with Zemurray in which the mixture was first mentioned. Dunlap reported that he had used it on a twenty-acre section, and the results were tentative but favorable, as far as he could tell. Zemurray heard him out, then said, "You put the medicine on the leaves and that cures the disease?"

Dunlap backed off. "It's not quite that simple. Sigatoka is an airborne spore. We think Bordeaux may arrest it—"

"Please, Sport," Zemurray called everyone Sport, "don't confuse me. You put the medicine on the leaves—"

"It's only an experiment," Dunlap protested.

"We'll spray five thousand acres," Zemurray said, and they did. It worked. The cost was half a million dollars. It saved United Fruit.

Equally important, Zemurray saw to it that the decisions in the company were made where they would be effected, and not at long distance by men who couldn't understand what was being asked of them. One of his best known epigrams was "You're there, we're here," and he repeatedly returned to the tropics where he could see the real United Fruit of men and machetes and machinery and vast plantations close at hand. He never confused that United Fruit with the company in Boston, the United Fruit of paper and proxies, meetings and numbers.

In his personal life, Zemurray was a private man, so reticent and mannerly that people often thought he was shy; perhaps he was . . . no one really knew him although a lot of people said they did. He gave away millions of dollars of his own fortune, sometimes in secret and often to causes that were considered radical and which even today appear innovative or unlikely. With a gift of $380,000 he was responsible for the opening of the New Orleans Child Guidance Clinic in the thirties. He helped back *The Nation*, a leading spokesman for America's growing liberal minority. He established a center for the study of Mayan art and Middle American research at Tulane, with donations of over a million dollars. And he underwrote a chair in Radcliffe's English Department for women only, with a grant of $250,000, at the urging of his daughter, Doris Zemurray Stone. He was even more generous in Central America, directing the United Fruit Company to establish an independent school for tropical agriculture (Escuela Agrícola Panamericana), of which the company has remained the principal benefactor for the past twenty-seven years. And he created the magnificent Lancitilla Botanical Gardens in Honduras, Central America's— and probably the world's—most comprehensive collection of tropical botany.

Despite all of Zemurray's advantages and accomplishments, despite his great personal fortune, despite his charities and his character and despite the fact that he was head of a company that may have been the most successful business in America, he was never accepted by Boston society. He couldn't get into any of the clubs. He was almost never invited to participate in Brahmin social functions. The WASP suburbs didn't want him either. For most of the years he lived in Boston, his home was a suite of rooms at the Ritz-Carlton Hotel. Over the years I have heard many stories about how this treatment galled Zemurray, but in most cases the tellers were Bostonians who had never even met him, and I came to believe that the stories were based on wishful thinking. Zemurray was too big a man to care. *That* must have galled the Brahmins.

Zemurray's reticence in private life was probably just another aspect of the unflinching self-control with which he governed himself in business as well. He was flamboyant when he had to be, and he gambled when caution would have meant disaster. His first meeting with Edward L. Bernays, the company's new public relations consultant back in World War II, provides an insight to his real character.

Bernays met with Zemurray to introduce himself and to discuss with him some of the projects which Bernays was recommending on the company's behalf. Before the meeting was very far along, the door opened, the secretary entered discreetly, and a note was placed in front of Zemurray on a folded piece of paper. Zemurray listened attentively while Bernays finished describing a particular idea, nodded thoughtfully, then excused himself and turned up the piece of paper and read the message. After only a moment, he returned his attention to Bernays and asked him to continue. The conversation went on for another several minutes, with Zemurray asking appropriate questions and carefully weighing Bernays' responses. Then the door opened again, the secretary entered with another note, and the same ritual was repeated. A few minutes later it occurred one final time. Each time, Zemurray's response was so self-contained, so private, that Bernays assumed the notes contained only the most trivial matters, perhaps to remind him of another meeting or to advise him of an unimportant telephone call. It was long after the meeting had ended and Zemurray graciously saw Bernays to the door without a single word of gesture about the messages, that Bernays discovered from someone else what the notes had contained. That day, within the space of only a few minutes, German submarines had torpedoed and sunk three freighters of the Great White Fleet.

Although United Fruit was a land-based company, it could be argued that its fortune owed at least as much to water; in fact, Captain Baker made his early living entirely by the sea without planting so much as a blade of grass. The Great White Fleet became more than a source of income: it was a symbol of the company's dominions—at home, in the tropics and on the seven seas.

The fleet went to America's defense in both World Wars.

Its ships served as troop transports and carried supplies; in the process, many of them—and their crews—were lost, and many were involved in great acts of heroism. The acts were rewarded by the government and by the company as well.

In some instances, the heroism took place before the war had been officially declared. Back in the mid-1930s, United Fruit entered into a barter contract with Nazi Germany. Then as now, the Germans loved bananas—today they are the highest consumers of bananas, per capita, in the world—but in those days their currency was even softer than their favorite fruit. The barter contract called for the building of a couple of ships in German yards in exchange for a certain number of bananas. The second ship was just about completed when the company got wind of a rumor that the Nazis were going to commandeer it "in the national interest." An American skipper was immediately dispatched for the sea trials, ostensibly to authenticate the shipbuilder's records and to witness the launching. As soon as the ship's engines turned over for the first time, the American captain took a gun from his pocket and jammed it into the stomach of his German counterpart. He forced him to order the ship onto the open seas, and a few hours later the still-incomplete boat pulled into a French seaport, changed crews, refueled, and headed across the Atlantic.

At the time of the sinking of the *Andrea Doria* in the 1950s, the first ship to arrive on the scene was the SS *Cape Ann* of the Great White Fleet. The captain and crew worked through the night and retrieved a lot of survivors from lifeboats and the open sea. It was the first ship to arrive in New York harbor with rescued *Doria* passengers. I handled the press relations. Captain Boyd, the *Cape Ann*'s skipper, looked gaunt and ravaged when the ship docked, and I imagined at first that it was from the horror of what he had seen at sea. Soon after, however, Boyd died of cancer; his disease was already in its terminal stages at the time of the rescue.

The Fruit Company was involved with another ship which achieved far greater fame for its role in the Zionist settlement of Israel in 1948. Sam Zemurray helped raise the purchase price and pushed through the registration of the *Exodus*, which carried emigrants through the British blockade into the Promised Land.

In March of 1953, Samuel Zemurray was still a director of United Fruit and still a powerful figure in the company. One cold, windy day he came down from Boston and walked into our offices on Pier Three. Ed Whitman, my boss of only a few weeks, brought me over and introduced us. I was nineteen and had been in the company less than a year. Zemurray was seventy-six and dying. The old man put out his hand and took mine, and I could feel the tremor of Parkinson's disease, a palsy that seemed to start in his feet or under the ground we stood on, the same feeling the building sometimes had when one of the freighters would shimmy along the pilings of the pier when there was a high wind or the pilot was careless. I don't have any recollection of what either of us said, but I'll never forget what I felt when I shook that hand. It was the first time in my life—and perhaps the last—that I was in awe. Zemurray acted as though what I said and thought really mattered. Before and for many years after, I was to be constantly reminded that I was an exception in a company of old men; even when I became a vice-president in 1969, I was told I was the youngest vice-president in the company's history. But for those few moments in 1953, Samuel Zemurray had greeted me as someone he cared about, someone who was his equal. It wasn't a knack or a gimmick. It was his character.

In thinking back on it, Sam the Banana Man represented the ideal I carried in my head of the whole company for almost twenty years, not because I imagined him that way from our brief meeting, but because at that time the company had really been shaped by his leadership. I remember Melvin Douglas in the movie *Hud*, saying to his young grandson that "the look of a country changes because of the men we admire." I believe that and I believe it sometimes happens in the case of companies as well; they eventually come to resemble their heroes. So, by the time Samuel Zemurray retired, his company and his character were almost exactly matched: both were tough, no-nonsense, quick to act. For many years, the similarities were to linger as well as to erode: as United Fruit took its direction and its identity from those who followed Zemurray, it seemed often to stumble into contradiction and paradox. It could be forceful one minute, indecisive the next, living as much off its own past as for its future. When the disparities between styles became too great, Zemurray finally sold out all his Fruit Company stock. He was too old to fight battles. Zemurray's career was bracketed by men who failed to grasp what United Fruit was about and who failed at leadership. There were exceptions, the most notable being Jack Fox, and of all the presidents to follow Zemurray, Fox certainly came closest to the old man's style. But by then it was too late.

There's an old poem about the Lowells speaking only to Cabots, and Cabots speaking only to God. I know that poem isn't true, because at one point a Cabot actually spoke with Samuel Zemurray—and in fact became his successor as president of United Fruit.

It did not last long. Thomas Cabot, son of the Godfrey L. Cabot of carbon black fame (who lived to be one hundred), was president of United Fruit for such a short time that the brevity of his tenure was a perennial problem in public relations, particularly when I was called on to provide a chronology of company presidents. Normally we would just say that Cabot had accepted the assignment on an interim basis. He lasted only a few months.

Legend has it that on assuming his new responsibilities, one of the first things Cabot did was go to MIT for a conversation with a professor of engineering. He accepted the view—Zemurray's view—that United Fruit operations in shipping, tropical agriculture and fruit handling all shared the common denominator of engineering: he planned a trip to the tropical divisions to appraise the level of competence with which the company's engineers were acquitting themselves. Cabot knew next to nothing about engineering himself, so he asked the professor at MIT to give him a problem by which he could conduct his test—a problem that any first-year engineering student should be able to solve in a few moments.

One can only guess at whether Tom Cabot's tropical tour proved to be a disappointment or a satisfying vindication of his worst suspicions, but he returned to Boston with a report which he felt sure would impress the directors: not one of the engineers in the company's tropical divisions could solve the MIT professor's problem. The directors were impressed, but more with the nature of the test than with the results. Most of them knew that the tropical engineers had either grown up in their jobs or their formal academic training was years behind them; either they would have had no practical reason to encounter Tom Cabot's Gordian knot, or they had simply forgotten how it was unraveled in the classrooms of their youth. But the test itself was to become a part of the brief dossier on Thomas Dudley Cabot's time in office, true or not. Unhappy with the ways of United Fruit, Cabot's resignation was at least proof of the severity of his discontent.

Prior to Cabot's appointment, Edward Bernays had been responsible for the founding of an organization called the Middle America Information Bureau, which was financed and run within the company and was intended to distribute information about that part of the world to anyone who wanted to know about it, from college students to the national news media. MAIB had very little direct connection with the company's business activities, but Bernays had conceived the organization as a reflection of Zemurray's attitude toward the company's tropical constituency: United Fruit had obligations beyond making a profit, and MAIB was one way of paying that debt. The MAIB budget was about a hundred and fifty thousand dollars yearly, which was a bargain in view of the scope of the job it was doing.

Tom Cabot did not see it as that much of a bargain for the Fruit Company, however, and one of his first acts was to question MAIB's existence. He used as his particular target an article which MAIB had recently published describing the wonders of a fish from Colombia which bore an unusual number of

eyes (I forget now whether it was one or four, but it was unusual), and he asked what possible connection that fish could
have with either United Fruit or the banana business. It was a
question, like the first-year engineering test, that required an
answer, and again like the engineering test I suspect Cabot
knew in advance that he alone was privy to the solution. MAIB
folded on the spot, and the hundred and fifty thousand was
redirected to things closer to home, perhaps the increasingly
difficult task, considering the huge payouts, of maintaining the
quarterly dividend.

As I say, both these stories were attributed to Cabot as among
his first acts as president. It could as accurately have been said
they were among his last.

During the Truman Administration, Cabot was director of
the Office of International Security Affairs in the State Department. He also served at one time as president of the Gibraltar
Steamship Company. Despite its name, this organization owns
no steamships. It leased land on Swan Island, a base for American propaganda in the Caribbean, last used during the time of
the Bay of Pigs. Cabot's connection with Gibraltar Steamship
Company and Swan Island became public knowledge during
the early sixties, when it received quite a bit of unwelcome
publicity. The Fruit Company's Tropical Radio and Telegraph
Company also operated from Swan Island.

Tom Cabot's brother, John Moors Cabot, was once Assistant
Secretary of State for Latin American Affairs as well.

A name that is less known in Boston but which was to achieve
an unwelcome windfall of free publicity for United Fruit was
that of Serafino Romualdi. Romualdi was a labor organizer for
the AFL/CIO in the fifties, assigned to Central America.
United Fruit was a reasonable target, being the largest employer in the area, and so Romualdi tried to organize the company's workers into a Latin-American union with the acronym
of ORIT. He was not well received by local management. The
division manager in the area of Panama where Serafino made
his move was an old-timer who felt that payday was about all

the recognition a worker deserved, and he wasn't too sure about even that. He got together with the chief of police, who was predictably sympathetic to the company's views in such matters, and Serafino was hauled off to jail in the Panamanian city of David. He would probably be there yet, if word had not somehow gotten out; as it was, it took the union about a week to get him released, and the damage that was done to the company's public image endured at least the length of Romualdi's lifetime. I heard him speak once a few years later in New York, and his hatred of the company was impressive.

United Fruit officially created a Public Relations Department in 1955; within a year it comprised a staff of twenty-eight—including me—with a budget of one and a half million dollars. The company was running an institutional advertising campaign in Spanish language publications, the theme of which was "The Living Circle." "The Living Circle" was essentially a great big wheel superimposed on a map of the Americas: from North America came an endless supply of all the good things that man—North American Man, that is—could make: cars, refrigerators, radios, TV sets, tires and other manufactured items. And from Latin America came all the materials and agricultural products one could take from the land: raw rubber, minerals, lumber and especially bananas. "The Living Circle" amounted to a graphic representation of colonialism and that's the way Latins viewed it. Not until the company had invested millions in the campaign did it make the discovery that it was the subject of great resentment and rancor in the Central American markets where the ads were running, in that it appeared to make a virtue of exploitation. But even the fact that Latin Americans choked on it was not enough to bring the program to an end. The company was so isolated from the impact of its actions and attitudes that the ads continued for almost five years in the tropics, inflaming Latins and working against any conceivable company interest.

Back in the middle fifties, United Fruit had a vice-president in charge of the Pier Three operations named J. Arthur Marquette. He came from New Orleans, and he was a movie buff.

Because of our waterfront location, we often got requests at Pier Three from various movie companies for permission to film on United Fruit docks. We had been approached in connection with *On the Waterfront* and had turned it down. Our reason in that case had been due to the company's delicate relationship with the International Longshoremen's Association: the ILA had opposed the filming of the picture and subsequently tried to block its showing in theatres. In the movie, longshoremen murder Rod Steiger, who plays Marlon Brando's big brother, and hang him from a hook, as well as steal from cargoes, beat up people and that kind of thing. Whenever we were given the choice, the company made a practice of being polite with the union. Besides, who really had heard of Rod Steiger, Marlon Brando or Karl Malden in those days? But when J. Arthur Marquette found out that we had turned down the producers, he felt the company had missed a great opportunity for publicity—which was probably true if you aren't too fussy about the kind of publicity you get. He set a policy by which all such future requests were to be brought to his attention. Naturally, he said yes to all of them.

It drove the operations people crazy. Whenever a movie camera would appear on the dock, work slowed to about half its normal rate, and the moment a star came into view—especially a female star—things stopped completely. Gangs and gangs of longshoremen, who even then were among the highest paid workingmen in America, would swarm over the scene, tripping on lights, knocking down props, whistling and catcalling—all at company expense. Meanwhile, the boats sat unattended at the docks, the bananas ripening in the holds, and orders from markets all over the northeast were not being filled. The ships' schedules were thrown out of whack, return cargo was not being properly loaded, and the Fruit Company's share in the production costs probably approached the price per minute of *Gone With the Wind,* although no one was ever enough of a spoilsport to sit down and try to figure it out.

We got a call one day from Columbia Pictures, saying they were making *Sabrina,* a movie starring William Holden, Humphrey Bogart and Audrey Hepburn. The company jumped at the chance, and I was assigned the job of Fruit Company liaison, which meant I was to take care of all the little details and amenities if any were required, and as an afterthought to write up the entire proceedings for the company magazine. I took along a camera in the hope of getting a shot to illustrate the story.

The scene they filmed that day called for Bogart to jump off the stringpiece of the pier (a parapet of concrete about six feet wide between the pilings and the pier shed) and on to a waiting tug which would take him to the *Ile-de-France* which was steaming downriver with Audrey Hepburn. I arrived at about eight o'clock in the morning, and the day already was off to a bad start with gray skies, a cold wind off the water and the threat of rain. Bogart and his entourage arrived at nine. The *Ile-de-France* was scheduled to leave by ten, but just as the filming was about to start we discovered that there would be a delay, caused, incidentally, by a strike by the longshoremen. This meant that the office personnel of the French Line were required to load on the passenger baggage, and it was going to hold back the departure.

Sabrina was the next to the last picture Bogart made before he died. He was terribly sick that morning. He had a persistent cough and at one point he coughed so violently that he began to vomit over the side of the stringpiece into the water. As the hours dragged by he seemed to fall further in on himself and he became very, very irritable. Before lunch, someone appeared with a pint of Scotch and Bogart began to gulp it down straight from the bottle.

There were further delays, the wind got worse, the light began to fail, but at about three that afternoon, the *Ile de France* finally sailed. By then, Bogart was in no shape to do his heroic jump off the stringpiece, so they faked the shot. All this time, I had been sitting in the stern of the tug; now and then Bogart would glare in my direction, and I decided it would be smarter if I just kept out of everybody's way. But as the shooting session neared its end, it occurred to me that my article for the company magazine should include a couple of words directly from Bogart himself. So I waited until there was no risk of interrupting the production and went over to where he was standing.

"Mr. Bogart," I started, "My name is Tom McCann. I made all the arrangements for . . ."

As I said, Bogart had been watching me off and on during the whole day; what he had seen was a kid in his twenties, obviously of nearly zero importance to either Columbia Pictures or United Fruit, who had taken a picture of him and who had run a few errands during the long, unpleasant day. He didn't let me finish my introduction. He did give me a couple of words, in the famous, raspy voice, but they were never to be passed on to the waiting readers of *Unifruitco*. He said, "Fuck off," and took another pull at the Scotch.

One of Zemurray's plans for United Fruit, near the end of his business life, developed from his awareness that a single-crop system was dangerous both to the company and to the countries in which we operated. At one time, when a plantation was exhausted or in the face of blight, the company's solution had been simply to take everything of value and put it on rail cars and move out to new land. When that was done they would usually come back and tear up the railroad tracks. Almost from the beginning this had proved impractical and costly for United Fruit—especially with competition and the growth of other industries forcing land values to new highs—and it had been disastrous for the workers. The idea of depleting and then abandoning land also resulted in a lot of unfavorable publicity for the company. Zemurray's plan would have avoided its repetition. He believed that the best solution to soil depletion and banana disease lay in crop rotation and diversification.

I still recall the first time I heard of United Fruit, back when I was in high school, and the image the name inspired was an amalgam of all the fruits grown anywhere in the world—apples, oranges, grapes, olives, peaches, pears, guava, papaya, mangoes. That image had been a mistaken one, but it was close to what Zemurray envisioned in the last years of his life.

Zemurray's hope for his company was never to be successfully tested. United Fruit was to diversify, but not in a way that would have any real impact on its agricultural programs in the tropics or on the economies of its host countries. Most North American consumers know little—and eat less—of the varied and delicious fruits that grow in such abundance in the tropics. The nonbanana crops with which the company experimented on its Central American plantations over the next few years—and even today— were doomed to failure for two basic reasons: they were expected to show an almost immediate profit (no one is more profit motivated than a division manager in the tropics); and the experiments were left to banana men whose full-time commitments were to the status quo.

For all that, there was something at once very exciting, very masculine and very romantic about the company in my early days. It was a mixture of John Wayne movie clichés and the legacy of an incredible period in history: gin and tonics and Dewar's White Label Scotch on tropical verandahs; endless miles of private jungle fiefdoms; natives who were variously brooding, surly or submissive; boots, khaki uniforms, horses and pistols; the Great White Fleet that was really the largest private navy in the world (and operated on the open-secret motto, "Every banana a guest, every passenger a pest."); the early morning produce markets and the colorful, crude men who ran them: longshoremen, traders, plantation managers, ambitious men, hard men, lazy men, rich men; and behind it all a tradition of enormous wealth and power and privilege that already was beginning to decay.

"Doc" Dunlap had been with United Fruit for about as long as any man can remember, and he remained active as a consultant to the time of his death in 1970. He was easily the company's most colorful relic and his stories delighted me for years, even when I heard them grow better with successive tellings. When he was well into his seventies he remained tough, romantic and alert; he loved Scotch whisky and a dance with a pretty girl, was the life of every party and the last to leave.

During the twenties, when the company was considering entry into the palm oil business, Doc was sent to Africa, he told me, to explore the fertile lands along the Niger River. After many weeks of travel, he came upon a primitive tribe of Nigerians who were ruled over by a beautiful black queen. The queen made him welcome, and he rested in the village for several days. One afternoon he heard some commotion along the bank of the river, and he walked down to see what it was all about. He found a small crowd of villagers gathered around a white man in a rumpled white suit who was just docking his dugout. Dunlap introduced himself, and discovered that the visitor was a German trader who lived downriver and who made a circuit of his territory several times a year. The German was a short, phlegmatic man who seemed reluctant to get involved in Dunlap's business, but it was obvious that he was taken aback by Doc's presence in the village. They talked guardedly for a few minutes, and gradually the German loosened up. He finally asked what Doc thought of the queen.

"A lovely woman," Doc allowed, wondering if the German trader had established some kind of prior claim which might now appear to be compromised. The German considered Doc's answer for a while, then visibly gathered his courage and asked the next question.

"Ven's der vedding?"

There was something about the way the question was asked that convinced Doc not to laugh in the trader's face. Moreover, in telling me the story years later, Doc admitted that the question did not sound quite as inane at the time as it might sound to someone who had never met the queen. Not only was she a beautiful woman, strong, tall, and with a regal pride such as Doc had never encountered in the more civilized world, but Doc had to admit that there had been certain signs—in fact, unmistakable signs—that the queen looked at Doc as something more than your average, run-of-the-mill palm oil promoter.

"To be very frank," Doc finally said to the little trader, "there *has* been some talk of a party this Friday, I believe some sort of a tribal celebration. The queen mentioned it, ah, last night."

The German grabbed at Doc's sleeve in horror, as though to pull him back to the river and escape. *"Mein Gott im Himmel,"* he said, "dot woman is ein *Menschenfresser*. She has married three udder men I know of, and der same ding happened to all three. You must go now, dis very minute."

"Well, now," Doc said, backing off. In all his travels, Doc had never developed a fondness for being touched by other men, and he disengaged the little German's fingers from his shirt. "For one thing, I don't think that would be very polite of me, on such short notice. And for another, what's a *Menschenfresser?*"

"*Ein Kannibale!*" the German said horrified. "Der queen is a man-eater. First she marries dem, und den she schticks dem in der pot!"

Doc weighed this new information for a moment. He was impressed, but there was still a loose end. "If that's so," he asked carefully, "then what are *you* doing here? You're a man."

"*Ja, ja,*" the little trader said impatiently, "but I never made der mistake of staying in dot hut." He pointed up the hill to the thatched house Doc had emerged from a few minutes earlier. "Every man on this river for ein hundred miles is not so crazy to stay in dot hut. Five nights of *liebe,* und den der pot. Guaranteed."

Doc Dunlap may not have been a perfect judge of the opposite sex, but he knew men and he knew the little German was telling the truth. Doc said he calmly walked down to the water, got into his boat, started the motor and pulled out into midstream without looking back.

Doc told me dozens of other stories, mostly about his life in the tropics, and most of them bordering on the incredible. I believed them at the time, and I believe them now; like Zemurray, Doc Dunlap was one of the handful of men who shaped United Fruit and whose early deeds were to flavor the character of the company for many years after.

One other story Doc told me, worth recounting here, is how the company selected the site of its present plantation in Golfito, Costa Rica.

Golfito is prime banana land on Costa Rica's Pacific coast. It is bordered by several miles of sandy beach and surrounded by hills that are almost high enough to be called mountains. The Fruit Company's plantation there represents one of its most substantial investments—in rail lines, in thousands of acres under cultivation, and in the town itself which United Fruit built to support its operation. When Doc Dunlap first saw Golfito, however, it was a very different place indeed: looking down from a small, single-engine company airplane, all Doc could see were the ocean on one side, the white ribbon of beach, the threatening mountains, and thousands upon thousands of acres of dense, inhospitable jungle. No landing strip, no town, and not a banana tree in sight.

Doc had selected the area as worthy of exploration because he knew from everything he had heard and all he had studied that the conditions at Golfito were just about perfect for growing bananas. The weather was ideal, the topography lent itself to our kind of operation, and it was convenient to transportation by sea. The fertility of the soil was abundantly apparent from the air; all that remained was for Doc to test the depth and composition of the loam.

That, however, would require that they land the airplane, and landing the airplane on a sandy beach several hundred miles from civilization was a prospect which neither Doc nor the pilot regarded with any enthusiasm. (Even today, the mountains continue to make Golfito a treacherous landing spot.) If they were to crash, there was no hope at all they would be rescued. If they merely got stuck in the sand on trying to take off again, the prospect of walking out through the jungle was nonexistent, and along the beach was only slightly better. Doc told the pilot to circle while he gave the matter some thought. He opened a quart bottle of Dewar's White Label Scotch whisky which all tropical agronomists carry with them for such emergencies; Doc took a long pull on it and passed it over to the pilot. For the next half hour the two men took turns drinking from it as they looked down at the endless jungle below. Finally Doc hit upon a solution. He said to the pilot, "We'll drop the empty. That should tell us all we need to know."

The pilot was too wise to argue. He took one final tug at the quart and passed the bottle to Doc. Doc opened the side vent in his window and told the pilot to take the plane down to twenty or thirty feet above the treetops, along the edge of the beach.

"If the soil is deep enough, the bottle should bounce," Doc
said, "I'll throw it in under the trees and we'll see what happens." A moment later they came to a small open space, and
Dunlop let it go. The bottle spiraled to the ground, hit, rose
several feet in the air again, and fell back to rest on the black
soil—intact. Doc and his pilot returned to civilization, he filed a
favorable recommendation, and on the strength of that report
the United Fruit Company invested tens of millions of dollars.
Of course, Doc's judgment, like his test, had been flawless.
Golfito proved to be one of the biggest and one of the best
decisions the company ever made.

That was not the last bottle of Dewar's White label to be
dropped at Golfito. Back in Boston, Joseph P. Kennedy, father
of the future president, had the Dewar's franchise in America
and was friendly with several Fruit Company directors. With
repeal, Dewar's White Label became the company's official
whisky. It's still my favorite—doubtless because I was raised
on it.

Following the short tenure of Thomas Cabot, Samuel Zemurray found himself in the position of having to succeed his
own successor. He came back as president in 1950, but only
long enough to pick a more durable candidate for the office. His
choice was Kenneth Redmond.

Redmond had started his long career with United Fruit as a
cashier in Fort Wayne, Indiana, following a stint as lieutenant
in the army during World War I. Cashier was the entry level
for a job in the sales department in those days, and Redmond
had gone on to a long, successful record as a salesman, then as
a branch sales manager, then to a position in the headquarters
sales organization in New York.

In New York, Redmond had received his final sales training
under a man named John Werner, a former longshoreman who,
despite his natty clothes and silver-tipped cane, always looked
as though he would be more comfortable with a hook in his
hand; he also retained the longshoreman's fondness for hard
drink, hard talk and hard living. Werner looked a lot like Babe

Ruth. He lived in an uptown hotel, but his office on West Street was actually a suite of rooms including a bed and shower; the company was his religion and he practiced it with a zealot's drive. Redmond doubtless was influenced by this attitude, although it would be inaccurate to suggest that Werner was his only model; in those days, just about everyone lived his job almost around the clock, and Redmond carried that quality with him to the presidency.

Until the early fifties, the company work week included half a day Saturdays, although most large companies had gone to a five-day schedule long before. That half day never ended at noon. There were always extra assignments to finish off, week's-end paper work to get out of the way, or a few long drinks late Saturday afternoon with the same men you worked with all week. I can recall the excitement of those times, particularly strong for me because I was the youngest member—or perhaps a better word at the beginning would be mascot—of a very exclusive club. The men's club feeling ran throughout the company and was to last for years, almost as long as United Fruit itself.

Redmond's selection as president meant, for the next few years, that the Boston money managers were not to play the dominant role in the direction of the company. Tom Cabot had provided a valuable lesson.

I was fast acquiring information about United Fruit that was to be an important part of my education. In the year that I began my career at $32.50 a week I learned, for example, that the company had liquid assets—really money in the bank—of over fifty million dollars. It had 66,000 shareholders. It admitted to earning a 12 percent return on its invested capital—although the real rate of return was much higher. It earned $4.32 a share and paid $4.00 in dividends. The stock was selling for $65. The company carried thirty million stems of bananas to the United States and Canada, and five million to Europe. It produced 1,200,000 bags of sugar. It owned or controlled three million acres of land. Only 139,000 of those acres were actually planted in bananas; the rest were euphemistically carried on the books as "reserves," although one of the most important reasons they were held was to guarantee that they would not become farm-land for our competition—whoever that competition might prove to be. The company carried another 102,000 acres under cultivation in sugar. United Fruit accounted for more than one-third of the world's international commerce in bananas; in the United States and Canada, that percentage rose to well over half the market. That year, the per capita consumption of bananas in the United States was seventeen pounds.

There is another set of numbers from the year 1952 that tells a lot about the company as it then operated. That year, United Fruit owned approximately three hundred company stores—for selling clothing, groceries, hardware, virtually all the necessities of life. These stores were located, of course, in the tropical divisions. In 1952 they sold nineteen million dollars' worth of goods to the company's employees, returning a gross profit of almost three million. On the face of it, the company was making even more of a profit from its own employees than it earned from an equal volume in banana markets which were somewhat more competitive. But these numbers hardly tell the whole story. In reality, the profit was far higher, but then the company began to write off overhead expenses and made other charges against those earnings—even though the expenses originated outside the company stores. The net figure on the three hundred stores for 1952—after all charges—showed an operating loss of around fifty thousand dollars. In this way, the company store could take with one hand and still maintain the appearance of giving with the other.

This same kind of bookkeeping convenience pertained equally to the company's passenger operations. Although this was a particularly profitable activity if properly accounted, the management found a complex series of ways to portray its passenger operation in red ink. For example, all of the costs of the ships' stewards' department were charged to the expense of carrying passengers, even though at least one-third of the people on each passenger ship were members of the crew and would have to eat the same amount whether the ship hauled human beings or lumber or bananas. Similarly, the entire purser's operation was considered as a passenger cost, even though the ships required a purser to clear each port regardless of what the ship carried.

United Fruit is neither unique in this respect, nor is the sleight of hand confined to overhead items. *Most* multinational companies use every tax and bookkeeping gimmick they can get away with to minimize their obligation to the nations in which they operate. The shell game is practiced on a global scale today with far more ingenuity—although with certainly not one shred more enthusiasm—than United Fruit Company demonstrated during those simpler days, starting with its very beginnings.

A look at the prices for sugar in 1952 reveals some of the discrepancies between what a country contributed and what it received. That year sugar cost the company $4.51 for every hundred pounds, and it sold in the world market for $7.15, creating a profit spread of $2.65. The company's investment in Cuba amounted to fifty-six million dollars by 1952, up only two million dollars over the figures for 1932. Exclusive of depreciation and other bookkeeping conveniences, this implied an average annual increase in the total Cuban investment of only one hundred thousand dollars a year, or just about enough to float the Cuban manager's yacht.

Although Fidel Castro never had access to those figures—and even today, numbers like these are carefully protected from the eyes of outsiders—it has always been nearly impossible to gloss over the chasm between what companies like United Fruit put into an indigenous system and what they take out. It is this stuff that revolutions are made of. And it is the stuff of what most multinational companies still refer to as "public relations." Castro, particularly, would be aware of the gulf; his father, Angel Castro, was an employee of United Fruit. Hardly a year passes, even now, that an occasional old-time Fruit Company employee or retiree doesn't wonder aloud how a couple of quiet, polite kids like Fidel and Raoul could have gone wrong.

A close Castro protégé, "Che" Guevara, applied for a job as a doctor in the Fruit Company's Guatemala division at about the time of the CIA-sponsored invasion of that country in the early 1950s. Company officials were unaware of his politics, and turned him down for other reasons. Similarly, we had turned down the application, in the 1920s, of a young man named Charles Lindbergh. Both went on to other things.

In those days, as now, there was much to criticize in the way the company operated. But our legitimate critics often were lost in the general din. And less legitimate observers could be enormously inventive in what they were willing to say about the company. One particular story is worth repeating.

During the late thirties, the story goes, the Nazis sent a spy named Ramun to Central America. They dropped him off with a burro-back full of photographic equipment, radio gear and invisible inks, then they pretty much forgot about him. All through the war, Ramun sent messages and espionage information back to the Fatherland. But by 1945 he found himself out of work.

Somehow Ramun got together with Herbert Hoover, Jr., and the two men then got some money from Herbert's uncle, John Edgar Hoover. The two men decided to go into the vegetable oil business in San José. Ramun sold all his spy gear for his share in the investment, and they opened shop. The new company was called Numar, which was Ramun's name backwards.

The only part of the story that is true is that Herbert Hoover, Jr., did put some money into a company called Numar, which later became a United Fruit subsidiary. But Numar is an acronym and stands for New Margarine. And it always did.

There was another clue to the company's future, back in 1952, that becomes more apparent through hindsight. When I started working for United Fruit, the jet age had already begun, and the world was almost within reaching distance of outer space. And yet whenever a company executive wanted to visit the tropics, he almost invariably chose to travel by a method that had already become a symbol of the unhurried, retarded pace of another era: he went by banana boat. Every business trip became a long vacation. Important decisions and critical acts were often deferred until it was too late; action and decisiveness were sacrificed to the very system those qualities had helped to create half a century earlier. Even in traveling between Boston, where the company had its headquarters, and New York City, the president and chairman would usually take the slow-moving Owl of the New York, New Haven and Hartford railroad, rather than cut their time to less than a quarter by flying. Time never seemed to be a problem.

In fact, time was to prove our greatest enemy.

Chapter 4

GUATEMALA

On January 1, 1953, just six months to the day since I began working for the company, I was given a job in Publicity and Advertising.

My new boss was a man named Ed Whitman. When I had first approached him, late in the fall of 1952, there had been no openings in his department. But the company that year earned a seventy-million-dollar profit before taxes, and I knew that if I persisted, a man in Whitman's position would not have to wait for a job to open up; he could simply create one. Which is what he did.

At that point, my education began in earnest. I enrolled as a night student at NYU School of Commerce. A college degree held no particular attraction in its own right—in fact, it probably would have been a liability if I had joined the ranks of United Fruit's management in those days because most of the top executives—including its president—were not college graduates. But there were a lot of things I didn't know about that I wanted to learn, things that would help me to understand my job better. So I took courses in accounting and advertising and journalism and economics and whatever else I thought would be useful. My real major was United Fruit Company.

The first assignment I became involved with in my new

position was related to the expropriation of our lands in Guatemala. The Department had only one task: to get out the word
that a Communist beachhead had been established in our
hemisphere. Our efforts would contribute eventually to the
overthrow of the Guatemalan government.

The Company operated two divisions in Guatemala, one on
the East Coast and one on the Pacific. Together, these two
divisions accounted for the lion's share of the company's tropical land holdings. Guatemala was chosen as the site for the
company's earliest development activities at the turn of the
century because a good portion of the country contained prime
banana land and also because at the time we entered Central
America, Guatemala's government was the region's weakest,
most corrupt and most pliable. In short, the country offered an
"ideal investment climate," and United Fruit's profits there
flourished for fifty years. Then something went wrong: a man
named Jacob Arbenz became President.

One of Arbenz's chief priorities, on being elected, was a program of agrarian reform. It was the age of land reform in most
of the nonindustrial nations of the world. A couple of years
before I joined United Fruit, a new law was passed in Guatemala giving the government the right to expropriate all un-
cultivated land. Although the law did not directly affect United
Fruit at the beginning, its obvious purpose was to break up large
land holdings, and the company properties more than met that
definition.

The company responded quietly at first, but on a number of
fronts. Responsible for putting the best face on corporate strategy was Edward L. Bernays, the "father of public relations,"
the biggest name in his field, and the nephew of Sigmund
Freud. In the 1920s Bernays wrote of his profession (the book
was entitled *Propaganda*): "The conscious and intelligent manipulation of the organized habits and opinions of the masses
is an important element in democratic society. Those who
manipulate this unseen mechanism of society constitute an
invisible government which is the true ruling power of our
country. . . . it is the intelligent minorities which need to make
use of propaganda continuously and systematically. In the active

proselytizing of minorities in whom selfish interests and public
interests coincide lie the progress and development of America."

Bernays was well known as an influential liberal, although
he had been retained by United Fruit for many years and had
handled a number of delicate assignments. He had close ties
to the press establishment, particularly *The New York Times,*
and he brought the Guatemalan situation to the attention of
Times publisher Sulzburger as early as 1951. The *Times* agreed
to have one of their leading editors look into the matter closely,
and Sulzburger himself made an inspection tour at the company's invitation. It was on that trip, while Sulzburger was in
Guatemala, that the first "Communist riot" took place in the
capital. Even from the perspective of two decades later, the
timing seems extraordinary. Bernays deserves credit for a first-
class public relations coup.

Ironically, although *The New York Times* was to play a
major role in the events that followed, the management of
United Fruit regarded the newspaper with a suspicion that
often crossed the border into outright hostility. The influence
of Senator Joseph McCarthy was near its height in America at
the time of the Guatemalan episode, and there were few institutions in the world more naturally disposed to the senator's
viewpoint than was United Fruit. The company needed Bernays
and it needed the opinion of the American public if it was to
accomplish its objectives in the tropics. But the fact that Bernays
was a Jew of foreign descent and a liberal besides, coupled
with the Fruit Company's (and McCarthy's) certainty that
the entire foreign news and editorial staffs of *The New York
Times* were under the influence, if not in the direct employ, of
the Kremlin, made several of the other top consultants to the
company very uneasy. Even today, there are some who believe
that Bernays's real sympathies lay with Jacob Arbenz. But in
his book, *The Biography of an Idea,* Bernays covers the Guatemala assignment in detail: he leaves no doubt that his real loyalties lay exclusively with the task at hand.

The core of Bernays's strategy was the selection of the most
influential communications media in America—the *Times,* sev-

eral other newspapers, two or three major newsmagazines, the wire services and the electronic networks—followed by a high-level saturation campaign to expose those media's reporters to the company's version of the facts. That campaign included guided press tours of the tropics, with as many as ten newsmen in a single junket. Typically, such a safari would fly first to Bogota, Colombia, and then on up to Panama, Costa Rica, Honduras and Guatemala, all under the company's careful guidance and, of course, at company expense.

These trips were billed as "fact-finding" tours, and there was very little selling done, once the journalists had agreed to go. The trips were ostensibly to gather information, but what the press would hear and see was carefully staged and regulated by the host. The plan represented a serious attempt to compromise objectivity. Moreover, it was a compromise that was implicit in the invitation—only underscored by Bernays's and the company's repeated claims to the contrary. It is difficult to make a convincing case for manipulation of the press when the victims proved so eager for the experience. The real victim, of course, was the legal, if leftist, government of Guatemala. But in the long run, the Company's participation in that government's overthrow would continue to haunt it—and would eventually cost United Fruit far more than it gained.

Appropriately, it was Herbert L. Matthews, a *New York Times* reporter, who some years later was to bring the role of the media into focus during this period. He said that the press, by the uncritical acceptance of stories that were often false or misleading, helped create the climate of opinion in the United States that would tolerate the events that followed. That acceptance, of course, was the company's prime objective. It was Matthews's unwillingness to believe what he was told, later in that decade, that brought him to the Sierra Maestra of Cuba; his series of articles gave *Times* readers, and the world, their first close look at a young revolutionary named Fidel Castro who until then had been described by Batista simply as a bandit who hid in the hills, emerging only to steal, destroy, terrorize. Castro did steal—often his victim was United Fruit, from whose

Cuban plantations he took trucks, gasoline, food and other supplies. He even kidnapped some of our employees.

As part of the Company's campaign to woo the press, at Bernays's suggestion, we took a series of ads in the *New Leader,* a widely read liberal publication. The company paid a thousand dollars a page which was several times higher than the going rate. These ads first took the form of public service space for Red Cross and Savings Bonds, then were signed institutional ads. The editor of the *New Leader,* Sol Levitas, was a friend of Bernays and the former mayor of Vladivostok.

In the late forties and early fifties the Company published four full-fledged newspapers given away free to division workers in Honduras, Costa Rica, Guatemala and Panama. The combined circulation approached or equaled the employee population which was around eighty-thousand. In many cases the only news the workers got was what they read in company newspapers. The papers were not successful. Many of the employees were unable to read, and for those who could, the papers did not give any hard or useful news, instead concentrating on superficial items such as births, weddings and parties, conveying the false impression that life on a banana plantation was a happy holiday. The papers made no attempt to discuss the real problems and issues which were of fundamental importance to the worker and the Company; they were discontinued in the late fifties.

Another factor in the downfall of the papers was the tremendous increase in the availability of inexpensive transistor radios; by 1965 fully nine out of ten tropical employees worked with small transistor radios in their shirt pockets with either the music blasting or with an earplug in their ears all day.

The Company also supported for many years a publication named *Latin American Report,* published by William Gaudet. It has recently come to light that Gaudet was a possible agent of the CIA, who used the publication as a credible cover for his numerous covert missions in Latin America. Gaudet operated out of the International Trade Mart in New Orleans, the same location as Lee Harvey Oswald's Fair Play for Cuba Committee. When Oswald visited the American Embassy in

Mexico City shortly before he assassinated John F. Kennedy, the signature appearing immediately next to Oswald's own on the Embassy visitors' register is that of William Gaudet. As of this writing, the coincidence has not been explained.

In 1953, the Arbenz government began legal proceedings to expropriate 178,000 acres of United Fruit Company land. United Fruit asked for sixteen million dollars, but Arbenz offered to reimburse the company through a twenty-five-year bond issue valued at $525,000, or less than four dollars an acre. The value of the government bonds was so low because it was based on the value the company had placed on its property for tax purposes. By then the company was ready for him.

At about the same time that Arbenz made his move, United Fruit financed and distributed several hundred copies of a book entitled *Report on Guatemala*. Its opening lines set the high tone which the book manages to preserve throughout:

> A Moscow-directed Communist conspiracy in Central America is one of the Soviet Union's most successful operations of infiltration outside of the Iron Curtain countries.

It goes on to point out that:

> Any Guatemalan who loves his country so much that he wishes to protest publicly against its being under the yoke of the Kremlin—now or ever—must face the startling fact that he is held to be subversive. It may be considered the official government viewpoint.

The author of the *Report on Guatemala*, a journalist for hire, was so proud of his contribution to literature that he insisted on a pseudonym, and then later requested that even the pseudonym be deleted from the title sheet. So the final product was a 235-page opus which was such a total distortion it couldn't even be copyrighted—because no one was willing to admit any share of responsibility for its authorship or publication.

That didn't stop us from giving it the widest possible circu-

lation: the company got it into the hands of every member of
Congress who would accept it (and in the days of Senator Joe
McCarthy, that was a lot of Congressmen), and we sent it to
every "major opinion-molder" in the United States, based on
Edward Bernays's famous list. Ed Whitman, the head of our
department, made a lot of speeches and used to say, "Whenever you read 'United Fruit' in Communist propaganda, you
may readily substitute 'United States.'" It was in that same
era that Eisenhower's Secretary of Defense, Charles Wilson,
made his famous statement, "Whatever is good for General
Motors is good for America."

At that time, United Fruit enjoyed a relationship with the
government of the United States which was very similar to
the position presently occupied by ITT, only United Fruit was
better connected in Washington and more skillful at the game.
Companies like United Fruit and ITT and Standard Oil became political instruments and carried out political relations by
other means, usually in secret, whereby the government got
what it wanted through the use of the company and the company got what it wanted as well.

The following memorandum by my boss, Ed Whitman, then
the company's director of public relations, gives some insight into
that relationship.

Pier 3, North River,
New York 6, N.Y.
November 4th, 1954

MEMORANDUM FOR FILE:

On Monday, November 1st I passed Thomas Corcoran on the street in Washington and nodded to him
in passing. Shortly thereafter, he 'phoned me at our
Washington office and asked if he could come over
there for a talk.

Here are some of the matters discussed by T. C.,
on which I made notes immediately after he left:

1. He said that it was not wise for him to be seen
talking to me in public places or conferring too often,
even in private, but that he welcomes this chance to

discuss a few matters. He said that Mr. [T. J.] Coolidge had urged him to see me and get my views on a safari that T. C. had in mind. He thinks it would be wise for him to get together a group, not to exceed 12 persons, to board one of our freighters at Mobile for a Caribbean trip. He did not suggest a specific itinerary but had in mind a couple of weeks absence from the country, and he favored the idea of a vessel because the group would be a captive audience and we could talk freely, show films, etc., without interruption. The principal person he would like to have on this trip would be Bishop Sheil, whom [sic] he believes would play a part of profound influence on his Catholic brethren in the Tropics in connection with the long range strategy of the Catholic Church in combatting communism. T. C. says that we need not be concerned that this would make an enemy of Senator McCarthy. He says that he can control and has controlled McCarthy (he states that he did so in connection with the recent Nicaraguan situation), and that he does this through Senator Dirksen. Also, he had in mind inviting Senator Sparkman of Alabama, as well as Senator Cooper of Kentucky. The former he assumed would be Chairman of the Small Business Committee. He also had in mind inviting a man whose name I did not catch, but whom T. C. regards as the "Mayor of Washington." He also thought that Whitman should go on this safari.

I did not commit myself to him. But at this juncture I question the advisability of our Company being overtly associated in any "junket" in which Mr. Corcoran and Bishop Sheil are involved—the first because I doubt the wisdom of embracing T. C. under the present conditions in Washington and I doubt whether Senator McCarthy would forgive the Company for any endorsement of the Bishop who so effectively castigated him last summer. It seems to me that the Church might probably rebuke a company for participating in affairs of the Church, and that if it is the desire of the Catholic Hierarchy to crystallize its anticommunist program in Tropical America, then it should be a responsibility of the Church to designate the individual to undertake this—not the Company.

2. T. C. implied that it was only a question of time

before some anti-communist international type labor organization would take over in Honduras and elsewhere. He thinks it may well be ORIT, and he thinks this despite the possibility of Carias taking power. In fact he believes that if Carias does take power, he will be liquidated. Moreover, T. C. does not believe that the executive of a tropical republic will regard the infiltration of an international labor movement as being prejudicial to the sovereign rights of a country. On that account, he believes that our best bet is to graciously go along with what he regards as inevitable, but that at the same time the Company should seek adroit means of pitting the power-loving labor leaders one against the other, thus preventing any one of them from becoming too powerful. Also, he thinks that we should learn a lot more about the internal affairs of ORIT (Inter American Regional Organization of Workers). To accomplish this, he believes that we would be smart if we were to retain Bill Robinson to handle our public relations labor affairs in Washington. (Robinson was formerly connected with the *New York Herald Tribune,* but more recently took over the affairs of Steve Hannigan Associates and already has some very powerful corporation accounts. He is one of President Eisenhower's very personal friends and advisors. Whitman has served with him on a political committee and regards him highly in terms of his integrity and ability.)

T. C. believes that if an international labor organization is accredited in Honduras, for example, the Company should overtly start experimental banana lifts via airplane. He recognizes that this is in no way a practicable operation but he feels that it would exercise a control of a labor organization that might otherwise get out of hand. The mere fact that labor would know that we were utilizing an artery other than rail and ship would cause them to go slow on strikes. The implication would be clear that eventually, if we were harassed, we might sidestep all the labor functions starting with loading cars in the farms right on through all the railroad, stevedoring, etc., operations and that this would be a blow to the expansion of job opportunities.

3. T. C. says that he has so persistently expressed himself to Mr. Baggett on the conduct of the anti-trust

These men started it all. *Top:* Andrew W. Preston, the merchant; Minor C. Keith, the railroad builder. *Right:* Captain Lorenzo Dow Baker of Wellfleet, Mass., whose schooner the *Telegraph* brought the first cargo of bananas to the United States.

The United Fruit empire, "El Pulpo," started here on Boston's Long Wharf in April 1871.

The history of the United Fruit Company demonstrates the dramatic change from sail to steam ships. The *Jesse H. Freeman,* commissioned in 1883, was equipped with an auxiliary coal-burning steam engine but relied mainly on her sails. (*From* The Twilight of Ships *by Robert Carse, 1965*)

In 1885 the wooden-hulled *Lorenzo Dow Baker* was built in Bath, Maine. Because propulsion came mainly from the coal-fed steam engine, the sails became relatively unimportant. (*From* The Twilight of Ships *by Robert Carse, 1965*)

Admiral Dewey, built in Philadelphia in 1898, and one of four similar admiral ships, carried 35,000 bunches of bananas. Her speed of better than 14 knots was almost twice that of the *Jesse H. Freeman.* (*From* The Twilight of Ships *by Robert Carse, 1965*)

From the beginning of the banana trade until 1960, bananas on their stems were shipped from the tropics in the holds of ships.

Banana generals and banana brass. The man in the middle with the epaulets is soldier-of-fortune General Lee Christmas, who was always available with a ready-made revolution if the company needed one. Next to Christmas in the white hat is Crawford Ellis, a United Fruit executive who later became president of the company. (*U.S. Public Health Service and Warren Bennett*)

Soldier-of-fortune Guy "Machine Gun" Molony *(second from right with cigar)* "negotiated" for Central America banana lands.

Banana cowboys—tough hombres.

Banana cowboys.

Honduras—in the early days banana workers lived in manaca shacks like these.

U.S. President Herbert Hoover and the current dictator of Honduras visiting a United Fruit banana plantation. (*Wide World Photos*)

Left to right: Senator Robert M. LaFollette, Jr., Samuel Zemurray, and aides Joseph W. Montgomery, and Davis Cloward at a dance in Honduras, 1949.

"Sam the Banana Man" Zemurray. (*Eliot Elisofon, Time-Life Picture Agency*)

Twenty years ago the United Fruit board looked like this. During the turbulent '50s, the company was confronted with such events as the Guatemala expropriation, the antitrust suit, banana diseases, and "blowdowns." *Seated, counterclockwise: T. Jefferson Coolidge,* chairman of the board, was U.S. Undersecretary of the Treasury from 1934 to 1936, and a great-grandson of Thomas Jefferson; *Emery N. Leonard,* secretary and treasurer; *W. Cameron Forbes,* partner, J. M. Forbes and Co.; *Crawford H. Ellis,* president, Pan-American Life Insurance Co.; *Channing H. Cox,* director, Old Colony Trust Co.; *John A. Werner,* president, Fruit Dispatch Co.; *Robert Lehman,* partner, Lehman Brothers; *Edward L. Bigelow,* chairman of the board, Second Bank–State Street Trust Co.; *Joseph W. Montgomery,* vice-president; *William H. Claflin,* trustee; *Charles H. Stockton,* lawyer, Choate, Hall, and Stewart; *Thomas M. Bancroft,* president, Mt. Vernon–Woodberry Mills, Inc.; *John K. Olyphant, Jr.,* vice-chairman and trustee, The Hanover Bank; *George P. Gardner, Jr.,* partner, Paine, Webber, Jackson and Curtis, elected chairman of United Fruit's board of directors in 1958; *John J. McCloy,* chairman of the board, The Chase Manhattan Bank; *H. Harris Robson,* vice-president; *Kenneth H. Redmond,* president of United Fruit. *Standing, left to right: Sam G. Baggett,* vice-president and general counsel; *Arthur A. Pellan,* member of executive committee; *Hartley Rowe,* vice-president; *John E. Toulmin,* senior vice-president, The First National Bank of Boston; *Alexander C. Forbes,* president and treasurer, Cabot, Cabot & Forbes, Inc. Absent: *Samuel Zemurray,* member of executive committee, and *General Walter B. Smith,* vice-chairman of the board, American Machine and Foundry Company. (*John Lewis Stage—Brackman Associates*)

United Fruit's general manager of tropical divisions, Andy Holcombe (*second from the right*), entertaining the President of Panama at the company's Almirante, Panama, division. *From bottom, left to right:* R. Arias E., second vice-president; president José A. Remón; Colonel Bolivar Ballarino, chief of National Guard; Andy Holcombe, manager and public relations man, Esteban Lopez. Remón was machinegunned to death at the Panamanian racetrack shortly after this picture was taken.

Colonel Carlos Castillo Armas, who, with the help of the CIA and United Fruit, overthrew Jacob Arbenz of Guatemala in the mid-'50s, chats with William L. Taillon, general manager of the company's division in the '50s.

suit that the latter will scarcely speak to him any more. T. C. implied that he could have settled the suit during the Truman administration, but that other advisers recommended to the Company that they wait it out until the Republican administration took office, the inference being that then they could readily quash the claim. (T. C. said he could have settled the IRCA (International Railways of Central America) dispute for a mere five thousand dollars, but that here again he was overruled.) The inference was that he could have settled the anti-trust suit although he did not specifically so state.

T. C. says that our Company is making a mistake in compromising any tropical aspect of the fruit. "Give them Meloripe, make some concessions domestically," he says, "but do not make any compromises whatever with respect to the jurisdictional matters involving your operations in the tropics." To do so is to defeat a clean cut settlement of the suit—and it will surely come up again and again in the years ahead to plague the Company.

T. C. says that any Company policy of expedience or compromise is an error. For instance, he says that we demand from the Guatemalan Government the return of all our expropriated property without any ifs, ands or buts. Thereafter, if we choose to sell areas to the Government for a nominal figure, that is a virtue and in no way prejudicial to the establishment of a precedent that other countries might use to harass us in future years. In general, T. C. thinks that our endeavors to arrive at a minimum consent arrangement with the Justice Department is all wrong. He believes we should fight and fight hard for the basic principles involved.

To that end he says that our friends, Herter and Saltonstall, should be stirred to action in behalf of our New England Company—strong action! He went on to say that there was a third New Englander, who he did not name, who should be avoided, because despite protestations of friendship, he is really not a friend of our Company. (Could he mean Cutler? Could he mean Martin? He did not mention a name.)

T. C. is actively pursuing and recommending that the Company pursue the line of coddling the Liberals. He says that the Company need not be concerned with

the Right Wing, but that it is the ever more powerful
Liberals that we must learn to play ball with. This
point of view is accepted, he says, by Messrs. Montgomery and Zemurray. These are the key figures
through whom he principally operates insofar as the
Company is concerned.

E. S. Whitman

cc: Mr. K. H. Redmond
esw:rc

Redmond was then United Fruit's president and Mr. Coolidge was Thomas Jefferson Coolidge of Boston, then the company's chairman of the board.

Thomas G. Corcoran, referred to as "T. C." in Whitman's
memorandum, had been appointed a company consultant by
Samuel Zemurray back in the 1930s, and he held the position
for the next thirty years. A former protégé of FDR, "Tommy
the Cork" was a dapper, energetic political go-between once
described by *Fortune* as "a purveyor of concentrated influence."
I remember being told at the time I met him, in the middle
fifties, that he had achieved the highest grade average in the
history of the Harvard Law School; I was sitting across the
room from him, and I wondered how it could be that this
ordinary man could also be a political and legal genius, could
rise to great stature, could be close to presidents and could
broker power for so long, largely on the strength of what he
whispered. I have thought of Corcoran countless times since—
whenever I saw a picture of a political advisor whispering con-
fidences into the ear of a powerful man.

Corcoran is still alive, living in Washington and still influential. Even as recently as seven years ago, I came across
his name in connection with people like Abe Fortas, who exerted an influence on the decisions of LBJ, in a story in *The
New York Times*. It was about that same time that Jack Fox
took Corcoran off the Fruit Company payroll. Whatever it was
that Corcoran had done for us in the past, Fox no longer regarded him as a corporate asset. It was a tough decision, especially when Corcoran began to react loudly with sounds of

great pain. But Fox stuck with it and "T.C." hasn't been heard from since by United Fruit.

The fact that United Fruit was a Boston company meant that we were especially friendly with national figures who represented what we used to call "our part of the world." *The Congressional Record* is loaded, for example, with comments and stories favorable to United Fruit which Representative John McCormack and other members of the House and Senate placed there on our behalf. There was a series of articles in the *Christian Science Monitor* by-lined by such company notables as President Kenneth Redmond, Vice-President Almyr Bump and Research Director Jesse Hobson—but in fact authored by Public Relations Director Ed Whitman—which McCormack managed to read into the record.

Spruille Braden, former ambassador to Chile, descendant of the Braden Chilean copper mining family, and once Under Secretary of State for Latin American Affairs, came to United Fruit in the early 1950s as a paid consultant, on termination of his official government responsibilities. His assignment at that time consisted mainly of speechmaking on the company's behalf and generally representing us in his capacity as a well-known, professional anti-Communist. He was also good at behind-the-scenes politicking for United Fruit in Washington, where he had lots of friends. I recall one of his speeches entitled, "Sounding the Alarm," which the company reprinted and distributed to the Bernays list of opinion-molders. We sent out hundreds of thousands of pieces of mail to that list: I doubt if there are that many opinion-molders in America, but we got all there were. Braden was based in New York but he had very close ties to Washington power. He reported directly to Kenneth Redmond, then United Fruit president.

Years later in his biography, *Diplomats and Demagogues,* Spruille Braden recalled that the then president of Nicaragua, Tacho Somoza ". . . was really the man who financed and equipped Colonel Castillo Armas so that he was able to overthrow the Communist regime of Arbenz in Guatemala.

"Castillo Armas, even with Somoza's help, was having a tough time of it until a group of Latin-American ambassadors called on the then Under-Secretary of State General Bedell Smith to point out the dangers of the situation. They stated that if Arbenz and the Communists won out the malignancy would spread throughout Central America, and it was important that the U.S.A. give its assistance through Tacho. Bedell Smith was persuaded and arms were sent to Somoza. The Communists were driven out of Guatemala, at least for the time being."

Another personality in our employ was former Senator Robert LaFollette from Wisconsin, who became ill and committed suicide while the Guatemalan campaign by United Fruit was at its height.

Former Massachusetts Governor Christian Herter, later Secretary of State under Eisenhower, was another close company friend.

John Foster Dulles, back in the early days when his law firm of Sullivan and Cromwell represented United Fruit, was reputed to have been the author of the actual concessions which the firm negotiated on our behalf from the governments in whose countries we operated. I was told this by Sam G. Baggett, long-time United Fruit general counsel and the man who should have known.

Another powerhouse in Washington during the Eisenhower years was General Robert Cutler, who headed up the National Security Council during part of that administration and served in private life as chairman of the old Colony Trust Company of Boston. He is the Bobby Cutler referred to in Whitman's memorandum about Tom Corcoran.

John J. McCloy, former high commissioner of West Germany and past president of the World Bank became a director of the company. (McCloy had earlier turned down a loan to Guatemala during the Arbenz era as a bad risk.)

Washington connections in later years were to include Robert C. Hill, former Ambassador to Mexico, Costa Rica and Salvador, who became a paid consultant to the company and also a director. Hill's name was mentioned seriously as a contender in the 1964 presidential election, and he came very close to being the Republican nominee instead of Barry Goldwater. Hill served with United Fruit for about the first eight years of the 1960s, until then-President Nixon appointed him ambassador to Spain; he later became ambassador to Argentina.

Charles Meyer also arrived on the United Fruit board in the late fifties. He was brought in by George Gardner, a long-time friend. Harvard educated, a Bostonian, and a former executive with Sears Roebuck, Meyer was named by Nixon as Assistant Secretary of State for Latin American Affairs, where he served for four years before resigning in 1973. Meyer was one of the witnesses called by the Senate Foreign Relations Committee investigating the conduct of American multinationals abroad: ITT had approached him—among others—with their million-dollar proposition for the overthrow of Allende's government in Chile. Meyer swore that the United States scrupulously followed a policy of nonintervention in Chile.

John McClintock was hired by the company in the mid-fifties to handle United Fruit's tropical public relations. He fell immediately into the trap of attempting to do it by remote control (ignoring Zemurray's "you're there, I'm here" philosophy) and at times his bureaucratic style appeared to be accomplishing exactly the opposite effects to what the company expected. McClintock's background had been in government, and so were his family ties: his brother had been ambassador to Cambodia, and was reputedly the model for the ambassador in *The Ugly American*. United Fruit's public relations operation in the tropics had never been much to begin with but by the time John McClintock was through with it—after about seven years—it was in complete disarray. In 1960, the company disbanded the tropical PR function completely.

Another good friend of United Fruit was Senator Alexander Wiley, Republican from Wisconsin, who was on the Senate Foreign Relations Committee during the Guatemalan episode. I saw him at Pier Three twice in 1953, visiting with the company's president and chairman. Wiley was a leading critic of the Arbenz regime, denouncing the "Communists in Guatemala" numerous times in speeches, articles and on the Senate floor.

There is no doubt that Communists played some part in the unrest in Guatemala. But our willingness to exaggerate their

importance and to create incidents—coupled with the willingness of the American press to amplify our cries of wolf throughout the United States—led not only to the collapse of the Arbenz
regime, but created such a subsequent environment in the
United States that, when a real Communist threat actually did
appear three or four years later in Cuba, the American public
and some members of the press were unwilling to believe the
truth. All of us saw ourselves as highly romantic defenders of
America against the Communist subversion of Latin America;
in fact, I now believe that very attitude to be responsible in
many ways for the deterioration of this country's relationship
with Cuba—including the invasion of the Bay of Pigs (in which
United Fruit also played a part) and the famous missile crisis.

In his book, *The Cuban Story*, Herbert Matthews said this
about the company's role in the Guatemalan Revolution of
1954: "A hostile and ill-informed American press helped to
create an emotional public opinion. This in turn worked on the
Congress and ultimately on the State Department. . . . Other
factors were, of course, at work in Guatemala, but the American
attitude would, by itself, have had the effect of strengthening
the Guatemalan Reds and making a United States reaction inevitable."

Another illustration of how close the company was to the
government in those days is provided by a small, private junket
which the company financed for three members of the White
House staff, shortly after Arbenz had been deposed. The trip
included one of Eisenhower's speechwriters, a presidential secretary and a White House department head. None of their names
has survived the test of history. But like their counterparts they
were close to the seat of power. United Fruit not only treated
them all to a pleasant vacation cruise, but was thoughtful
enough to bury the expenses of that trip in company accounts.
(Whitman's wife, Anne, not included in the junket, was also a
member of the White House staff, serving as President Eisenhower's personal secretary.)

A conditioned press responded to Arbenz's seizure of the
Fruit Company acreage with predictable wrath, and the Department of State, at the urging of United Fruit's powerful

friends in government, issued a tough aide-mémoire to Arbenz in which it reasserted the United States position with respect to private property. That same ultimatum called for the immediate return of the land to company ownership. Two tropical expeditions were arranged for the press almost within hours of the expropriation, each including eleven reporters. They included representatives of *Time-Life*, several large metropolitan dailies, *Newsweek* and the wire services. An avalanche of publicity favoring United Fruit followed the trips. We also distributed a confidential Guatemala Newsletter each week to a list of 250 American journalists reporting on economic and political events. These Newsletters were so successful that we later broadened them to include Honduras, Costa Rica and Panama which meant that for about eight years (1953–1960) a great deal of the news of Central America which appeared in the North American press was supplied, edited and sometimes made by United Fruit's public relations department in New York.

In the June 20, 1973, issue of the *New Republic*, journalist Tad Szulc, an old Latin-American hand, wrote about how U.S. corporations have cooperated in various degrees with the CIA and foreign opposition groups to stage revolutions and coups d'état. He then went into the United Fruit–CIA operation in Guatemala and said, "The company's Boston headquarters, as I still vividly recall, was at the time an excellent source for newsmen in following almost on an hourly basis the progress of the invasion."

I can't really say whether the company was the prime mover in what followed, or simply the prime beneficiary. In any event, the Central Intelligence Agency mounted a secret invasion of Guatemala, and United Fruit was involved at every level. I was told that the CIA even shipped down the weapons by Fruit Company boats. (In May of 1954, *The New York Times* reported on another shipment to Guatemala, saying that the arms included "submachine guns, hand grenades, automatic pistols, and forty rifles bearing hammer and sickle markings." It was a familiar CIA technique—one I was to use later myself.) I was also told by two of our tropical executives that the man who had been picked to lead the revolution, Colonel Carlos Castillo

Armas, was provided food and housing on Fruit Company property just across the Guatemalan border in Honduras and that the invading troops were assembled from, on or near the location of our Honduran division. Arbenz was overthrown within a matter of days.

The incident even produced some reasonably believable atrocity pictures. I don't know where they came from, but somehow we got hold of some photographs of several bodies—some had been castrated—about to be buried in a mass grave. The photos got the widest possible circulation and Arbenz got all the credit. For all I know, they could just as easily have been the victims of either side—or of an earthquake. The point is, they were widely accepted for what they were purported to be—victims of communism.

Armas was not the CIA's or the Fruit Company's first choice; General Ydigoras Fuentes was. Ydigoras Fuentes wrote in his book, *My War with Communism*, that "a United Fruit Company executive and two CIA agents" came to him for help during the Arbenz administration. Ydigoras Fuentes said that their terms, which he claims to have rejected, were that he would be the leader of the revolution if he would "favor the company, crush the unions, and establish a strong-arm government." As it turned out, Ydigoras Fuentes was to have his turn at the presidency anyway—as Castillo Armas' successor. It is likely that one of the two CIA agents to approach Ydigoras Fuentes was E. Howard Hunt, Jr., later to achieve fame for his role in Watergate and the Ellsberg psychiatrist caper. Hunt's own attorney identified him as "one of the principal figures in the overthrow of the Guatemalan government."

Further light on Hunt's activities in Guatemala was shed by Douglas Hallett, a young man who worked on Charles Colson's staff in the Nixon White House from June, 1971, to September, 1972, and who shared an office with Hunt. Writing in *The New York Times Magazine* of October 20, 1974, Hallett said:

> Although he kept his door locked, and locked it behind
> him when he was in his office, I thought Howard was
> a nice enough, if somewhat foppish, sort, until one
> day when he told me about his great regret in life.

When he was a C.I.A. agent presiding over the 1954
overthrow of President Arbenz of Guatemala, he had
held a group of prisoners on the airstrip just as he
was about to leave the country. He decided to show
mercy and freed them. A few years later, he learned
that one of the prisoners he had let go was Che
Guevara, the Cuban revolutionary; he said that had
been enough to convince him never to allow himself
to become compassionate again.

What was the real result of all this effort?

For Guatemala, the new regime of Colonel Castillo Armas
was no improvement over the deposed administration of Jacob
Arbenz. It was illegal to begin with; it was weak; it wasn't very
smart; and it lent itself to the same kinds of manipulation and
corruption that had made Guatemala such fertile soil for banana
imperialism at the turn of the century. Colonel Armas himself
was assassinated within a couple of years, and even today—two
decades since United Fruit Company and the Central Intelligence Agency conspired to make this hemisphere "safe" for
their peculiar version of democracy—Guatemala remains one of
the most unstable governments in Central America, as well as
one of the most dangerous countries to live in or to visit.

For the United Fruit Company, the part it played in this effort
to divert the course of history was to prove far more costly than
anything envisioned by Arbenz. In the first three years following the Castillo Armas revolution-invasion which the company supported, United Fruit took Tommy the Cork's advice
and turned back more than two hundred thousand acres of its
Guatemalan holdings, some for distribution to local farmers, and
all for no recompense whatever. Even at that, *Fortune* could say
of United Fruit in 1959 that "in Guatemala, Costa Rica and
Honduras, it is still the largest single private landowner, largest
single business, and largest corporate employer." That same issue
of *Fortune* noted that the United Fruit Company Board of
Directors now included "General Eisenhower's old comrade-in-
arms, General Walter Bedell Smith." *Fortune* failed to add that
General Smith, the man who had been Eisenhower's commanding officer at the outbreak of World War II, had more recently

served under Eisenhower as Director of the Central Intelligence Agency. The appointment of Bedell Smith anticipated by more than a decade ITT's election to its board of ex-CIA Director McCone in the midst of a similar Latin-American adventure.

For the government of the United States, the company's and the country's complicity in the Guatemalan affair was soon to prove an embarrassment. In order to focus attention elsewhere, and to cloud the surface appearance of the administration's true and close relationship with United Fruit, the Department of Justice, just a few weeks after the overthrow of the Arbenz government, initiated an action against the company for alleged violations of the antitrust laws. (Topic 3 in Ed Whitman's memo: the antitrust suit which Tom Corcoran allegedly felt could have been nipped in the bud for "a few thousand dollars.") It was meant as a public slap on the wrist but it would lead to consequences which few, if any, of the participants wanted or even suspected at the time.

Eddie Bernays moved quickly into the strategy of the new battle. A series of "strange coincidence" editorials began to appear in newspapers throughout the country, all questioning why the same government that had received so much help in fighting the "Red Menace" in Guatemala would suddenly act against its patriotic friend, United Fruit. The year 1954 was near the peak of the McCarthy era, and it was easy to sell the nation the idea that communist infiltration in Washington was so widespread, particularly in the Department of Justice, that the antitrust suit was a way for the Kremlin to strike back. We did everything we could to encourage the impression, including the production of a film entitled, *Why the Kremlin Hates Bananas.*

Twenty years later, as a direct result of the company's involvement in the overthrow of the government of Jacob Arbenz, United Fruit's seventy-year tenure in the Republic of Guatemala would finally come to an end.

Chapter 5

CAMELOT

THOMAS JEFFERSON COOLIDGE, who spent his last years with the company as Chairman of the Board, died in 1958, ten years before the raid by Eli Black. Several years after his passing, I had the occasion to visit his family home at Manchester-by-the-Sea on the North Shore of Massachusetts. I was following directions given by the family: pass one pond and then a second pond and at the second pond make a right turn and follow a winding private road for about a mile. There is a circular driveway leading up to a rambling, white brick house. When I arrived, I learned that the center entrance had been especially designed to house five original Gilbert Stuart paintings, including the portrait of Thomas Jefferson. One passes through the entrance to a hall where there are many artifacts and rare sculptures and treasures of every description. In one room, on a small table, is a collection of gold crowns—the kind that once sat on the heads of royalty. There are many art objects and treasures from the China trade, all amassed by several generations of Coolidges. One whole room houses the gold dinner plates of Thomas Jefferson. The famous cane belonging to Thomas Jefferson, which he bequeathed to James Madison, lies casually on a table in another room. Mrs. Coolidge's bedroom offered a fantastic view of the grounds and the sea beyond. In the bathroom off the China

room, on the wall, is the illuminated scroll presented to Mr.
Coolidge by the directors of the company when he retired. Later,
as I was walking across the grounds, I was attracted by a five-
foot-high Phoenician-style urn which was planted on the lawn
between the house and the rocks of the ocean's edge, undoubtedly a relic from the China trade. On my way to look at the urn,
I noticed a stone marker recessed in the ground which said
simply, "Pony," and underneath that, "Eighteen years faithful
service 1888."

On Coolidge's retirement in 1958, he was succeeded by one
of the four men who were to greet Black in the Algonquin Club
a decade later, George Peabody Gardner, Jr. In 1958, Gardner
was barely forty and twice blessed as the scion of two of Boston's
wealthiest and most powerful families, which meant by extension that he was also related to an unusually large number of
the Bostonians "who really mattered," including the late Thomas
Jefferson Coolidge, his immediate predecessor.

George was certainly wealthy enough to get by without having
to work—and for some years he treated gainful employment in
much the way less favored men act toward a hobby. He spent
time digging in the ruins in Mexico. He did some mountain
climbing. He was an account executive with BBD&O. He
worked on a Boston newspaper. He married a Russian ballerina.
Then he acquired a partnership in Paine, Webber, Jackson and
Curtis, one of the most powerful investment banking firms in
the world, and George's lifetime career took shape. He retained
his Paine, Webber partnership (an unusual thing to do and
something for which he was widely criticized) when he took
up his assignment at United Fruit, but he established an office
at the Fruit Company and divided his time between Fruit Company and Paine, Webber. The following year, partly with the
impetus provided by a highly unfavorable article on the company's management in *Fortune*, Gardner began to clean house.
Redmond left a few months short of retirement, in the company
of such old-timers as lawyer Sam Baggett and agricultural Vice-
President Almyr Bump. Al Bump had made a name for himself
within the company a short time earlier as the hero of the
Guatemala episode—he was there through most of the Arbenz

regime and had advanced the company's interests with great success in a difficult environment. As a reward he was brought to Boston and promoted, and a few years later he became the scapegoat for the 30 percent decline in banana production. *Fortune* magazine asked Al what he thought might be the solution to the production problem, and he answered, "Grow more bananas." He was an easy target.

Even with all the housecleaning, though, Gardner never became involved in the company's operations. Not surprisingly, as his next move he brought in a new president: Thomas Egbert Sunderland.

Sunderland had been vice-president and general counsel with Standard Oil of Indiana and had made a national reputation there as an antitrust lawyer, having won the famous "Detroit case" which was a landmark victory for the domestic oil industry. During World War II he had been responsible for a lot of the planning and coordination of America's bombing program in Europe. After the war he married Mary Allyn, the heiress to the National Cash Register fortune. I found him to be a cold man who seldom smiled. There was something of a sadness about Tom Sunderland but he was also smart and tough-minded, two qualities which at that point the company badly needed.

In 1958, the year before Sunderland's arrival, the company had signed a Consent Decree with the Department of Justice in connection with the antitrust suit. A Consent Decree means that neither side admits anything but they both agree to certain future conditions. One of those conditions was that the company would refrain from jobbing its bananas (selling directly to retailers), which had previously been a successful and profitable activity. There were other limitations, as well, but the most significant aspect of the decree was the company's agreement to establish, within ten years of the date of signing, a competitor of at least one-third its size. At that time, the biggest competitor was Standard Fruit Company, and Standard was about one-third of United Fruit's size. The government wanted three major elements in the banana business, and this guaranteed it.

Sunderland faced some formidable problems. The Consent Decree had been signed by men who were near the end of their careers with the company, and who had neither the energy nor the inclination to carry the fight any further. He found that the company's headquarters in Boston were headquarters in name only, that the real base of operations was New York City. The company was facing competition from government-subsidized banana production in Ecuador, which had blossomed almost overnight into a real threat. Standard Fruit had started packaging bananas in boxes, and the banana trade loved it; United Fruit had done nothing to meet the major new marketing challenge. The plantations were ravaged by disease which had lowered production, as Al Bump had noted, by about one-third. The fleet was old and in need of refurbishing or replacement. And Sunderland discovered that as president, he had twenty-two officers reporting to him directly, even though most of them were not even in Boston.

Sunderland's first major moves were toward cost reduction. He dispensed with all the overhead activities he felt marginal or superfluous, cutting back personnel. Aside from the changes Gardner had made at the top, it had been twenty-five years since the company had a major personnel cutback and it had grown very fat. Next, he moved to Boston all those people in the company who were still reporting to his office. The Public Relations Department was the first to be reduced in size: in fact it was virtually eliminated. Our number declined from twenty-eight men to five. Ed Whitman and I were the only two to survive from the New York office. John McClintock, who had been in charge of tropical public relations, as I mentioned, from out of the Boston office, was among the casualties. His former assistant, Gale Wallace, survived; Wallace was a former Latin-American editor for the UPI. In the spring of 1960, Whitman and I dutifully closed up shop at Pier Three and headed for Boston. It was a move that came at an ideal time in my family life; my wife Joan and I had two little girls by 1960, and we weren't looking forward to raising them in New York City.

The move was not quite as happy for Ed Whitman. Sunderland and Whitman appeared to be at loggerheads almost from the beginning. One of Sunderland's first decisions, on reviewing what Public Relations had been doing up to his arrival, wa to take the film *Why the Kremlin Hates Bananas* out of circulation and destroy the prints. It was only a 12½ minute film, and he didn't even sit through to the end. The movie had been Whit's pride and joy, and he believed in it. Sunderland then made it clear that he would be looking to public relations for services quite different from those it had provided in the past. For one thing, he expected us to take an important role in the production of the Company's annual reports, which until then had been handled almost exclusively and unimaginatively by the secretary's office. Within nine months of the move to Boston, Whitman decided to retire; the job of director of public relations was to remain vacant for the next four years.

With Whit gone, there was no one to interpret to the rest of the PR staff what Sunderland wanted and how he expected us to get it done. I knew that unless I found out for myself, and fast, there was a good chance that we all would soon be following our former colleagues. So I went to Sunderland and asked. He told me that he wanted someone to write the shareholder letters, produce the annual report, and come up with occasional creative ideas on how the company could advance its position and sell its products. These sound like perfectly logical things for a public relations department to be concerned with, but they were truly novel for the public relations department of United Fruit. Until that time, most of our energies had been directed to various forms of combat with ideologies, with other bureaucracies, with history. We had been practicing public relations up to that point as a highly elaborate art form; Sunderland made it clear that we were to begin operating as a business. In the following year I took responsibility for such mundane functions as the annual meeting arrangements, and I found Sunderland calling on me with increasing frequency.

One of the things I learned about from Sunderland was personal publicity and that it was an appetite that grew with what it fed on. We fell into it gradually. It was logical that we started to peg our stories and releases to him until eventually his personality dominated the company's public relations. At first he appeared to be pleased by the stories we were able to generate, but soon I sensed that the pleasure was giving

way to impatience for more, and then to mild dissatisfaction
with whatever we produced, no matter how flattering the stories
may have been. Tom Sunderland is certainly not alone in this
respect: personal publicity is like dope in the effect it has on
some people. But it is not much fun for the public relations
man who has to keep the habit supplied. Sunderland increased
my salary by about 50 percent in the following two years and
in general he gave every indication that he was satisfied with
the job I was doing. But in the area of personal publicity, the
more he got the more he wanted.

One good illustration was a story which appeared in *Time*.
The story was built around United Fruit, and I had worked
hard to see that the editors were supplied with as much information on Sunderland as they could possibly use. Sunderland himself was an unusually good interview, probably because of his legal background: he knew how to answer the
tough questions and he always supplied the additional dimensions to a situation which good reporters were quick to snap up.
On top of that, the story he had to tell was genuinely news-
worthy: Tom Sunderland was an unusually energetic and effective president, and his decisions and policies were paying
off in some obvious ways—in increased production, higher
profits, rising stock prices. It was important to the company
that the story be told, and it was important to me personally
that *Time* treat us favorably. Even under the best of conditions,
there are plenty of things that can go wrong with an article in
Time. *Time* had never been friendly toward United Fruit. I'd
seen the thick file on the company and they could have been
sitting on additional information we didn't know anything
about: that the Food and Drug Administration thought bananas
were a health hazard, or that there was going to be a boycott
of our products because of something one of our division managers had done in the tropics. The amount of space allocated
to United Fruit could change drastically with the development
of a national or international news story which made our article
obsolete or redundant. We could be squeezed into a half column
or dropped completely. It was a nervous few weeks. But the
story finally appeared, and it was a beauty. There was a photo-

graph of George Gardner on one side of the spread, and a picture of Tom Sunderland, and a shot of one of our banana divisions. Every fact was favorable if not entirely accurate. Even more important, the tone of the piece was just exactly right—optimistic, free from the bias or innuendo with which an editor can color a story if he has prejudged the subject. I read my advance copy with growing excitement, then took it in to Sunderland and laid it on his desk.

When he finished reading, he leaned back in his chair and looked thoughtfully at the ceiling—and stayed that way for about a minute. Finally I said, "Well, how do you like it?"

Sunderland picked up a yellow lead pencil and began to absently tap it against his big, even white teeth. The most I could get out of him was something like, "Um-m-m." He seemed to have no reaction at all.

"I think it's pretty good," I said. I was beginning to feel very let down.

"Not bad," Sunderland answered. "Not bad."

I waited a moment longer before I got up and started for the door. He was still tapping his teeth, but he stopped as I reached the far side of his office. "Tom," he asked, "before you go—tell me what it takes for a man to get his picture on the cover of *Time*."

I have the feeling to this day that he remembers me as the guy who let him down, who didn't do everything he might have to win him that cover.

One of my most memorable experiences with a Sunderland annual meeting turned into a full curriculum in financial public relations. It started off with Ed Toland, our Treasurer and Secretary, telling me that he had sent out a letter with the annual reports inviting any interested shareholders to take a company bus from New York City to the site of the meeting in Flemington, New Jersey. United Fruit, like many other large American companies, had chosen Flemington for the site of its incorporation because of the town's favorable tax and business laws in an earlier era. It's a pretty town, almost inaccessible to public transportation (making it nearly ideal for annual meetings), and had achieved some fame as the site of the Hauptmann kidnap trial following the death of Charles Lindbergh's son. The town boasted a glassworks, and its bucolic setting made Toland's offer an attractive day in the country with a free lunch supplied by the company. There were more than sixty-thousand shareholders at that time, and the gesture soon took on the dimensions of a monumental blunder. The meeting place specified in the report could not possibly accommodate all the people who responded to the invitation, and we were bound by law to hold the meeting where we had stated. I was dispatched to Flemington to see what could be done.

It turned out that the only place in town capable of handling the number of people who had said they would attend was the high school gymnasium. The reply cards that had been returned from Toland's invitation showed we had to hire nine buses to make the ninety-mile trip from Grand Central Station. Our lawyers advised us we could hold the meeting anywhere we wanted, just as long as we officially convened it at the hotel first, as advertised. That meant we would have to start one place, hold the actual meeting in another, and eat in a third. It was turning into a circus.

Flemington, New Jersey, is not the easiest place in the world to reach from Boston. It meant a plane ride to Newark, the rental of a car, then a two-hour drive from the airport. And every time I would return to Boston with my report to Sunderland, he managed to think of one more detail for me to check on, and back I would go. After five trips in almost as many days, my original indifference to Flemington had been turned into a real hatred, and I never wanted to see the town again. On returning from that fifth trip, I laid out the full plans for Sunderland, convinced at last that they were foolproof. He studied the schedule, which even included a full blueprint of the auditorium floor plan, and asked, "Where's the men's room?"

I was ready for that one. "Right here," I said, pointing to the appropriate portion of the blueprint. "You may remember, Mr. Sunderland, that you brought up this question last time we spoke, and you asked me to be sure that the signs saying 'boys' and 'girls' were replaced with ones saying 'Men' and 'Women' for the meeting." It wasn't like Sunderland to forget that kind of detail, and I felt pretty good about the way things were covered.

Sunderland nodded patiently. "Of course I remember. That men's room is at the back of the auditorium. But where's the one for the people on the stage? You don't expect me to have to walk the entire length of the auditorium, do you, with people knowing exactly where I'm headed, right in the middle of the meeting? Is there another exit? Or better yet, is there another men's room closer to the stage?"

I looked desperately back to the blueprint, realizing that it didn't show the answer to his question. I felt that awful sensation in my stomach which had started to come over me at times like that. It meant only one thing: another trip to Flemington.

I returned with the missing portion of the blueprint the following day, plus an extremely lucid paragraph detailing exact directions to the men's room from the stage. I presented all this to Sunderland who merely nodded that same, patient nod and told me to mark it with arrows on the day of the meeting. I gritted my teeth and tried to convince myself it was all some kind of test.

But it wasn't. Tom Sunderland was a brilliant man, one of the most capable executives the company ever had, and he led United Fruit through several very difficult years. In the course of that leadership, he made some of the toughest decisions any company president ever faced, and he never flinched. His only real failing was that he didn't know how to get along with other people and build a team.

Unless you consider the size of the banana industry, some of Sunderland's decisions may sound less than heoric. For example, he decided United Fruit should market its bananas in boxes. Amplify this by as many as 35 million stems a year, and the true dimensions begin to suggest themselves. We went through about forty box designs before coming up with one that did everything we expected of it. Everything imaginable had to be considered. Where do you put the holes? How much ventilation is required, and how much is too much? How high can you stack them on top of each other before the bottom one collapses? How high should the lids be? Where does the writing

go and what does it say and in what language does it say it? It
wasn't simply a matter of sticking them in a cardboard box.
Sunderland's decision also meant that we went into the pulp and
linerboard business—because when you use one hundred million
boxes a year, there is just no cheaper way to do it than to make
them yourself. And his decision meant that he had to overcome
the inertia, the apathy and even the opposition of the majority
of executives in the company. Even though Standard Fruit had
already demonstrated that boxes were a much more manageable
way of handling bananas, and even though the trade responded
so favorably to Standard's innovation that we were losing a lot
of business, all the old-timers at United Fruit were saying that
boxing was a flash in the pan, that we were still number one,
and if we just waited them out Standard wouldn't be able to
keep it up and everything would return to normal. "Normal"
was another word for the past.

Sunderland also made the decision to convert the company's
production to another banana variety, which amounted to heresy.
For years the company suffered from a historic blight in the
tropics and where bananas grew at all they were disastrously
lighter in weight than before the disease hit. The weight loss
was a result of a management decision, made in the previous
administration to spray blighted crops with an oil. This time,
the spray had not been tested properly, and it stunted the
bananas' growth. The Gros Michel or "Big Mike" was the
strain we were growing in all our divisions, and the old-timers
swore by all they held sacred that there was just no way to
replace it, that anything else would be thrown out of the markets, that nothing would grow on our plantations except the
"Big Mike." But Sunderland overrode them. He ordered that
the company's entire plantings—over one hundred thousand
acres—be replaced by the new Valery, a variety which had its
origins in Viet Nam. The Valery was not only disease resistant,
but it was a lower growing variety than the Gros Michel, which
meant that it was less susceptible to another major hazard, blowdown from the heavy winds of tropical storms.

And Sunderland went out and hired Jack Fox to become
Executive Vice-President.

Fox had begun his business career in the Worcester, Massachusetts, territory as a salesman for IBM back in the thirties, was a close friend of Tom Watson, Jr., who at that time covered Providence, and Fox also knew George Gardner. There was a lot of Boston money—including Coolidge money—in Fox's previous company (Minute Maid Orange Juice Company), and in fact Fox had earlier approached the Fruit Company with the proposition that it might want to acquire Minute Maid while he was its president. He wound up selling the company to Coca-Cola, but Gardner remembered him and introduced him to Sunderland who came to the conclusion that even if United Fruit had not wanted his company, we would benefit from the acquisition of Fox himself. Fox had taken a top job with Coca-Cola just a couple of weeks earlier, but he saw Sunderland's invitation as a call to adventure and he accepted quickly. Sunderland gave him responsibility for all the company's activities related to bananas.

Fox lost no time in turning to the function that interested him most and where he recognized the company's greatest weakness: marketing. He called a meeting one day and announced that in the next six to eight weeks we were going to start branding the bananas. He cited the fact that Chiquita was the property of United Fruit, but that so far it had been used as an umbrella for the entire banana industry. Unless we could directly identify our product in the marketplace, Chiquita would go on serving our competition just as much as, if not more than, she served us which meant that she was actually costing us business. There was a sign of impatience around the room from the old-timers because the company had been trying for years to figure out a way to brand bananas and now this "Orange Juice Man" was going to do it after only six weeks. But Fox continued; he said he did not yet know exactly what form the brand might take, but the possibilities included everything from a rubber stamp imprint to a new process called electrostatic printing, where a negative charge was deposited on the bananas' surfaces, then the bananas were passed through a "developer" and the brand emerged. He even said the label might be a piece of gummed paper. But whatever it was, the brand would be

placed on every third banana. Some of the more secure old-
timers laughed out loud. One of them—a Southerner—did a
quick calculation and almost collapsed in hysteria. "Shee-it,
man," he said to Fox, "Do you realize what that would amount
to in a year? *One billion* stickers! You've got to be out of your
mind!"

Fox was still new at that point, and he was something of an
oddity in the banana business. His suits were of light colors
and sometimes loud patterns that were a definite departure from
the banker's blues and grays favored by the other executives,
and he always had a rich suntan. He looked like a man who
had gone out for athletics in college and had stayed in shape.
He liked people, he knew how to work with them and get things
done. He smiled easily. He had the philosophy that a job should
be fun for everyone involved, and the more they enjoyed what
they were doing, the better they did it. At first, almost everyone
agreed that Jack Fox was one hell of a guy—but when it came
to bananas, he had a lot to learn. In the meeting that day, Fox
stopped and asked the old-timer to repeat the number of labels
he had just calculated.

"One billion!" the man said. There was more laughter.

I was watching Fox closely, and I knew that the size of the
number had caught him momentarily off balance. Fox is a strong
believer in ideas first, numbers second; he takes the view that
ideas are how things get started and that numbers usually are
the way they get stopped. He recovered his balance magnifi-
cently. He nodded his head in confirmation and said, "That's
just what I make it. One billion." Everyone stopped laughing.

We next got in touch with a couple of possible suppliers.
The first to arrive was a little old man who had been selling
the company pressure-sensitive printed mailing labels for years
and who expected that this order would be just another day's
work. We described the problem, and he nodded. When we
were through with our side of the presentation, he asked if we
had any idea how many labels we would need in the initial
print run. Clearly he expected us to say something in the neighborhood of fifty or one hundred thousand. By that time we
had calculated the requirement more precisely, and we told

him 2½ billion; he rolled his eyes, the color drained from his face, and he quietly fell over backward in a faint. When he regained consciousness, he said, "It's nothing, I always do that when I get excited."

The biggest problem was finding a simple, inexpensive method to attach the labels. We called in machinery and equipment designers and theoreticians from all over the country and spent weeks reviewing systems. They all failed in two important ways: they were too complex to operate without a college degree, and they priced out at somewhere under ten dollars per label per banana. The answer finally came from a different source altogether: a young laborer in the company's division in Honduras. His device has no moving parts, and is power-fed by the operator's thumb and forefinger. It's a masterpiece of simplicity. As a result of that invention, the Fruit Company became the largest single user of pressure-sensitive materials in the world.

Fox's concept proved to be the most important marketing innovation in the fresh produce industry's history, and for a long time it gave the company the competitive advantage it needed to recover its declining share of the market and restore its earning power. Eventually, of course, competition was forced to respond in kind, but by then Fox had placed United Fruit solidly back in the front of the race.

Another Fox innovation, absolutely unique in the produce industry, was the introduction of a rigorous system of quality control for the production of bananas. He told management that if we were going to put our name on the product, even though it was not made by a machine, we had to take some responsibility for how good that product really was. It upgraded the quality of bananas in markets throughout the world, and customers began to pay a premium price for quality fruit.

Sunderland and Fox came to realize that the company still lacked an indispensable ingredient for continued success: they knew a real management team had to be built, and they faced the fact that neither of them had been able to do it. So they decided to look for a man they hoped could make that happen. They hired Herbert Cummings Cornuelle. With Cornuelle's arrival, the group that would meet Eli Black five years later was now complete.

Herb was in his mid-forties, a former president of the Dole Pineapple Company, and physically and intellectually one of the most impressive figures the company had seen since the days of Zemurray. He was about six feet four, slim, wore blue suits and blue broadcloth button-down shirts which contrasted with his long, carefully kept, silvery white hair. His personality was Pacific American—good-natured, open, refreshing, soft-spoken with the suggestion of Sweet Lelanie and Bali Hai. Previous to assuming the presidency of Dole, he had been that company's Director of Public Relations (a slightly sore point with him in later years; he didn't feel the title implied much substance.) Cornuelle was an instant success at United Fruit. He was like the kind of racing car that gives the impression of great engineering even when sitting in the garage, and people throughout the company began to feel that at last we were really going to travel in style. Sunderland and Fox had made most of the hard decisions already, and they had paid for them: Fox was admired enormously by the staff people who worked with him, but the operations people, especially in the tropics, resented his new ways of doing the old jobs . . . it was inevitable. With those problems already out of the way by the time Cornuelle arrived it was equally inevitable that Cornuelle would be popular.

Before he had gone to work for Dole, back in the early fifties, Cornuelle had run a charitable trust, the William Volker Fund. He had written a book about Volker titled *Mister Anonymous*. He was a Phi Beta Kappa from Occidental College, the son of a minister, and the brother of author Richard Cornuelle who at the time was the literary darling of the radical Right.

Cornuelle came to United Fruit on April 15, 1963, a time when another charismatic personality, John F. Kennedy, was near the height of his popularity. We were all very conscious of Herb's magnetism and of his resemblance to Kennedy, in style if not in substance. In many ways, both men were a part of the same phenomenon, the *Hud* syndrome, where America was coming to look like her heroes. Cornuelle, like Kennedy, spent a good deal of his creativity on the elevation of hopes and on coinage of aphorisms that rang like gold when uttered, but which often left his listeners slightly puzzled and uncertain of what they had really heard.

Almost overnight, Cornuelle managed to do for the company what Fox and Sunderland together, because of their commitment to the solutions of operating problems, had been unable to accomplish in the previous four years: he got all the top executives of United Fruit working together toward the same goals. At that time, it was the most important job in the company. He became executive vice-president when Fox became president and Sunderland moved up to chairman. Then he was elected President and Fox, still chief executive, became chairman.

But the management team Herb Cornuelle put together seemed somehow lacking in one important qualification: innovation. It seemed to me that the executives spent most of their time tracking the company's course, following where it was carried by its own momentum, rather than setting a direction. It remained for Jack Fox and Herb Cornuelle to decide where the company should go.

It was not an easy job. The decade of acquisitions was already behind us, starting in the fifties and finally running dry in the middle sixties. The company had so many problems of its own during that period that it was unable to devote the energy and money required to take advantage of this relatively new business phenomenon. By the time United Fruit had solved those basic problems in its banana and sugar production and had generated enough cash to make acquisitions or diversification feasible, the gold rush was over. The alternative route of debt financing was so alien to the way most of the company's directors had always done business that it was never seriously considered. So by the mid-sixties we began to acquire the leftovers and the rejects.

One of the companies we bought was in Victor, New York, about forty miles from Rochester. J. Hungerford Smith was a small manufacturer of syrups and fruit toppings for desserts. It would probably have proved thoroughly resistible even to a company as hungry as United Fruit, however, if it were not for the fact that J. Hungerford Smith owned A&W Root Beer Drive-Ins of America; with twenty-five hundred stores and drive-ins in the chain, A&W was both the largest and the oldest operation of its kind in the country. Unfortunately, it was also the most unprofitable. We swallowed it whole and got a case of indigestion that lasted several years. And we picked up a lot of little companies in other parts of the country, such as a freeze-dry shrimp processing firm, a catfish farm in Honduras, and whatever else we could dig out of the heap. But we never managed to tie into anything really substantial or worthwhile. The company—and the price of its stock—seemed stuck in the doldrums.

There were some near misses—Canada Dry, Booth Fisheries, the Gorton Company, Pepperidge Farms—but we always managed to stumble short of the altar. Booth Fisheries, for example, was then the second largest fish company in America. It would have been a great acquisition, but the Fruit Company Board spent so much time quibbling over price that we lost it. Nate Cummings of Consolidated Foods moved in and practically picked Booth off our hook. With one company, Winchell Donut, we even went right up to the actual signing. Jack Fox and I had flown out to the West Coast and he was an hour away from putting his name on the papers when he discovered that there was a serious discrepancy between what we thought of Winchell and what a closer look told us the company actually was—a big enough difference that it would have turned a reasonable acquisition into something very different. Fortunately, we were able to back off in time.

All during this period, the pressure was building. Research papers on United Fruit by analysts were appearing in investment houses all over the country, saying we looked good on the surface but pointing out that we had all our eggs in one basket. These reports cited the instability of the governments in the countries where we operated, and some suggested that we were a sitting duck for the next Latin revolution, as witnessed by our experience with Castro in Cuba where the company lost $58 million. There was a cloud over the company which continued

to be reflected in the price of the stock. At one point in the early
sixties, the low was $15 a share. Through the efforts of Sunder-
land himself, then Fox and Cornuelle, the price gradually rose
into the thirties and then the low forties. But that rise was due
principally to improved earnings from our banana operations,
and the cloud remained. United Fruit, once the bluest of the
blue chips, was now regarded as a risky investment.

Just before Christmas in 1967, Jack Fox told me that the
big break the company needed was right around the corner.
He said that he had just completed arrangements for the acquisition of the largest single block of shares in the Del Monte
Company, and that sometime during 1968 we could look forward to taking over the entire company. He told me he knew
the Del Monte management, that they were great guys, had
good golf scores, and were doing a good job running their business—but not as good a job as we would be able to do, once we
made our move. It was an exciting moment.

At first, things went just as Jack had said they would. Within
a few days we bought the block of stock and became the largest
single shareholder. There were rumors in the press and financial
circles of our intention to acquire the entire Del Monte operation. But the management of Del Monte was to slip our noose.
They were thoroughly familiar with the Consent Decree we
had signed with the Department of Justice, and they knew
we could not increase our share of the banana market while
we were under a legal obligation to cut back—so they simply
went out and bought another banana company. It was a little
operation in Florida called West Indies Fruit Company. We
learned that golf wasn't the only thing they were good at: it
stopped us cold. We were able to sell the Del Monte stock
without losing any money on the overall transaction, but we
had lost something more important: we had lost the look of a
winner.

If our Camelot had a Round Table, it was the enormous slab
in the United Fruit Company board room. That table had been
ordered by Tom Sunderland, rendered from some of the most
magnificent trees in the Western Hemisphere, and transported

to Boston. It had arrived in flawless condition, one enormous monolith shaped like a gigantic surfboard, capable of seating two or three dozen people in comfort. In fact, it was so big it couldn't fit through the door or up the elevator. Carefully, slowly, in exactly the right weather to avoid damaging rain or winds, the table had been winched up the outside of the building to the tenth floor. It was an occasion equal to the erection of the first stone statue on Easter Island or the first Mayan stela in the jungles of Guatemala. Once the slab reached the outside of the Board Room, the pulley stopped, blueprints were checked, measurements were made—and the table was quickly lowered again to the ground. It was too big to fit through the window. They wound up cutting it into two pieces. During the Del Monte episode, we had all sat around that table, each of us privately assured we were invincible. That table was a good symbol of the past; cut up, it was a better symbol of what was to come.

Edward Dale Toland, Jr., was our Treasurer and people used to refer to him as the man who had everything. He had a family background that qualified him for the Social Register, had attended a couple of Ivy League schools, had a war record, was a good tennis player, owned two cars and an airplane, had a great sense of humor, was articulate, had a cultivated radio announcer's voice, and was handsome. Men liked him and women found him attractive. Ed was closely involved in several of the company's abortive acquisition attempts, and their failure hit him especially hard. He became convinced that United Fruit had lost all of its original momentum, or at least enough to assure further deterioration in the years ahead. The more he thought about it, the more it depressed him. He finally went out and got another job. Ed and I were close friends, and his decision was a sad one for all of us. His new job was with American Maize Company in New York City, which meant, of course, that he would be leaving the Boston area. President Kennedy had died a few years earlier, but Ed Toland's farewell party marked the real end of the Fruit Company's version of Camelot.

As I walked over to the Sheraton Boston Hotel that noon-time, I thought back to the time, just a few weeks earlier, when our bid to take over an especially appealing company seemed likely to succeed and the spirit of optimism was at its height.

That day, at Ed's luncheon at the hotel, Jack Fox looked over at Toland and said, "We hate to see you go, Eddie." Jack meant it, and Toland knew he meant it; both were clearly moved. Ed was then expected to say a few words, but he was choked up and the words wouldn't come. His reaction was to cover his feelings with an odd, forced gesture. He reached into the breast pocket of his jacket and took out a dozen or more cigars. He had never smoked one in all the years I knew him; probably he had bought them downstairs as we came in, just for this occasion. He said something like, "I just can't say any-thing, but here—I bought you all a present." And he started throwing the cigars around the table, almost at random. It was obvious that he was embarrassed, and his present awkwardness only served to make matters worse. Tears appeared in his eyes. Jack began to laugh and eased him through beautifully, but we all imagined we knew what was happening in Ed Toland's mind, and it made his leaving worse.

At about five o'clock that afternoon, he came by my office. We talked for a while, and he finally got up to go. "You're a great bunch of guys," he said. "These have been the best years of my life." He was forty-nine. He had been with the company for ten years. "I hate leaving. I hope you never go through this yourself, Tom. You should stay with the company for the whole trip. It's too tough when you decide to get off." I put my arms around Ed, something I can't recall doing to any other man; I felt an enormous sorrow at his leaving. It was my turn to be at a loss for words and my turn to wipe away the tears.

That was on Friday afternoon. On Saturday, Ed drove down to New York. He picked up a ticket for speeding in Con-necticut. On Sunday night he checked into the Yale Club in New York City. Monday he reported for his new job, worked all day, and went back to his club that evening. He rode the elevator to his room on the twenty-first floor, took a shower, put on his pajamas, opened his checkbook and wrote out a check for

fifteen dollars, payment for the speeding ticket. He put the
check in an envelope, addressed it and put on a stamp. He wrote
a couple of other letters, one to his wife, and one to his son and
daughter. He put them in envelopes too. He opened his Bible.
After a moment more he got up and carefully put on the clothes
he had taken off a few minutes earlier. He put them on over
his pajamas. Then he pinned a note to his jacket, saying who
he was and where he was staying, opened the window and
jumped.

A little while later, I got a call from a reporter on the *New
York Post*, who said, "One of your executives took a dive out
of the Yale Club this evening. Name's Edward Toland, know
him?"

Will Lauer, another officer of the company and an old friend
of both Ed's and mine, was in New York that day and we made
arrangements for him to identify the body. Lauer walked into
the morgue and as the attendant pulled out the marble slab,
the first thing Will saw was the shoes. "No," he said immediately, "this can't be Ed Toland." Ed had always been an
impeccable dresser. But the shoes were old and battered, as
though they belonged on a derelict. They were brown, and the
laces were black.

The attendant from the Coroner's office realized where Will
was looking. "I'm sorry, Mr. Lauer," he said, "that happens all
the time. The shoes are the first things to be stolen. They were
gone when we got the body. You'll have to look up here." There
was very little remaining of the head; Will saw what was left
of Ed's remarkably white and perfect teeth. Even then, it was a
moment before he could be certain it was Ed Toland.

There were three stories on the Fruit Company in *The New
York Times* that day. One was the claim by a San Francisco
reporter that banana skins were being smoked in Haight Ash-
bury and that they produced a state of euphoria. The second
detailed the failure of another attempt by the company to diversify. The third was Ed Toland's death. It was the worst day
of my life.

I think many of us learned some important things from Ed's

death. We were to apply what we learned in different ways. For Jack Fox, especially, the tragedy meant an irreplaceable personal loss and he made a great effort to understand it. He spoke with clinical and industrial psychiatrists, particularly at the Menninger Clinic (which has made a specialty of executive psychology) in the hope that if a similar situation should ever arise again, he might be able to recognize the symptoms in other people in time to do something to avert it.

Chapter 6

PROPOSITIONS

EVERYBODY MAKES jokes about bananas. Some of the best jokes have been made by people who didn't know they were being funny. Just a couple of years ago, for example, I heard that a women's prison in the Southwest still has a regulation against bananas within its walls, and I followed it up and found the story was true. The prison authority who verified it was very anxious for me to understand that the prison had no axe to grind with bananas *per se*; in fact, she said, the inmates are allowed banana puree—just not, well, you know, just not *whole* bananas.

I said I understood.

And I did. It's a problem that has been with the banana right from the beginning. In fact, some of the earliest references to the banana call it by the name *plantain Musa paradisiaca*, which many scholars cite as evidence that it was the banana, and not the apple, in Adam and Eve's Garden of Eden. For some, reason, people have looked at the innocent fruit as a sexual object ever since.

Back in 1956 I was invited to a meeting to deal with precisely that phenomenon. The unlikely site of the meeting was Pier Seven, which was headquarters of the Fruit Dispatch Company, United's marketing operation. Our guest was a Viennese psychologist whose name I have mercifully forgotten but who had a short time earlier approached Russell G. "Pat" Partridge, our director of advertising and sales promotion. First, a word about Partridge.

Pat was a graduate of the Harvard Law School, circa 1910, who had been with the Fruit Company from the end of World War I. He was one of the most creative men in the company and a true zany. He was also the genius who gave the world Chiquita Banana—plus banana neckties and cuff links. He lived his whole life around his work, and he loved every minute of it. He was probably the world's greatest advertisement for bananas: he died just a couple of years ago, nearly ninety.

Pat opened the meeting on Pier Seven that morning by telling us that he had been approached by the Viennese psychologist and that he was enormously impressed by what he had heard. The meeting was to give the man an opportunity to make a formal presentation of his theories. Pat told us that the general theme of that presentation would be built around how the marketing operation could turn a profit from an apparent adversity— or, more specifically, how they could cash in on the banana's, ah, shape.

Enter Viennese psychologist, complete with full spade beard, looking like the half-quart version of Sigmund Freud. He had on a misshapen black homburg that was about three sizes too big, and an overcoat that almost touched the floor. One of the men next to me whispered, "I'll bet he stole the hat and coat from the same guy at the Automat." It was in the middle fifties, as I said—not the best years for little men with beards and exotic styles of dress. The man on my other side whispered back, "They're not stolen. He and Toulouse-Lautrec have the same tailor." It was not a promising beginning.

But for the next fifteen minutes, he held us spellbound. He had a heavy, and at times impenetrable, accent. His vocabulary consisted at least 20 percent of words unknown to any other person in the room. I caught a word or two here and there that I could understand, such as "libido" and "phallic symbol" and "sublimation," but they were all run together in a way that I couldn't begin to decipher. And I suspected that his accent had

really very little to do with my confusion—that if his speech had
been delivered instead by Laurence Olivier, I would have been
equally at sea. It was a virtuoso performance. We were all convinced that what we were listening to was terribly important to
us personally and the company and the whole banana industry,
and each of us was impatient with himself that he could not
grasp more than one complete sentence in ten.

Things became much, much clearer as soon as the warm-up
ended and we got a look at the graphics the psychologist had
brought along with him.

The first display was a photograph, intended to illustrate a
recipe. On the plate was a pineapple ring. Inside the ring a
peeled banana had been stood on end; the banana had been
sliced near the base so that it would remain upright. In the tip
of the banana, a maraschino cherry had been attached by means
of a toothpick. At the banana's base, lying on the pineapple ring,
were two Kadota figs, side by side. The entire production had
been encircled with whipped cream and garnished with shredded
coconut. For the benefit of anyone who didn't get the idea right
off, he then tipped the picture on its edge.

There were two more exhibits, but we never got to see them.
There was a vice-president at the meeting who had given every
indication through the earlier part of the presentation that he
not only understood all that was being said, but that he strongly
supported that kind of innovative thinking. Looking back on it,
I wonder if he even knew what the little man was talking about
when he mentioned phallic symbolism. He knew what was
meant when he saw that picture, all right, and he arose from
the table, his lower lip trembling with outrage and his huge fists
banging the table. Pat Partridge prudently folded up the show
at that point and pushed the bewildered psychologist from the
room. It probably saved his life.

Just a few years later, however, the company's advertising
agency was to take a large page from the Viennese scholar's notebook, without our knowing about it until after the fact. We got
a call one day from *Life* magazine's advertising department,
wanting to explain why they had been obliged to turn down

one of the Fruit Company's insertions. The company was spending two or three million dollars a year in the media in those days, and whoever was in charge of approving concept and copy within United Fruit was either asleep at the switch or thinking about something else when the agency had presented this particular layout.

The illustration showed a nice yellow banana, almost full size. The art director had drawn a red circle around the circumference of the banana with a marking pen, and another line with arrows at both ends along the banana's length. Then he had written the numbers beside the lines, indicating the banana's length and thickness: 1¼" across by 8" long. It was an eye-catching idea, and sufficiently ambiguous that several of the leading ladies' magazines in America had accepted the ad without comment rather than risk being called dirty-minded. *Life* viewed it with a more skeptical eye—and then they read the text:

What Does a Banana Have to Be a Chiquita?

It's sort of like passing the physical to become a Marine.

The banana's got to be the right height, the right weight, the right everything. Right off, it has to be a good 8" along the outer curve. And at least 1¼" across the middle. It has to be plump. The peel has to fit tightly. The banana has to be sleek and firm.

It has to be good enough to get through a 15-point inspection. Not once, but three separate times.

Occasionally, though, a banana comes along that's got everything going for it—except maybe it's a smidgen under minimum length.

We should pull it, we know. But our inspectors have hearts too.

Which is why you may sometimes find a Chiquita Brand banana that isn't quite 8" long.

Come to think of it, though, you sometimes find Marines named Shorty, too.

Right after Pat Partridge came up with the idea of Chiquita Banana, the agency people came up with a jingle that was to make history. It became so popular across the country, back in the forties, that it could be found on just about every jukebox in the United States and it even appeared on the hit parade. In the final lines of the song Chiquita tells where bananas come from and warns people not to put them in the refrigerator.

The only reason that a refrigerator is mentioned in the jingle is that it rhymes with equator, and the company was anxious to remind people that the banana was an exotic fruit from a far-away part of the world. Refrigeration can change a banana's external appearance, but so can sitting it on the window ledge in the kitchen. As the shopping habits of the American public slowly changed over the years, that one line in the jingle was to cost the banana industry millions and millions of dollars.

The trouble with a good jingle is that its message sticks for a long time after the ad campaign has ended. The company's market research indicated as far back as the 1950s that the appearance of the deep-freeze and larger refrigerators was allowing the American consumer to shop less often, but to buy more each trip. We stopped telling people to keep bananas out of the refrigerator. The only way we were going to bridge the gap between shopping trips was if the buyer bought more bananas every time she was in the stores, and the only way she was going to stop the extra fruit from drawing fruit flies was by putting it in the refrigerator.

The problem was, we knew bananas were an impulse item, which meant they didn't appear on most buyers' shopping lists. It was this same factor that provided the core of what the Viennese psychologist had in mind back on Pier Seven: the housewife reaches out, when she sees a banana, and grabs it almost by reflex. And we were never able to find a successful way to educate that impulse so the shopper bought more each time she reached. The result is that people still buy bananas pretty much the same way they bought them back in the forties, enough for a day or two or maybe even three; but the rest of the week they do without.

It's too bad. Refrigerated bananas taste altogether different—a lot like ice cream. The peel turns black, but the pulp is perfect.

While bananas can be refrigerated, they cannot be frozen: the cellular structure changes and the result is an unattractive slime. Freeze drying works all right, though, and for a time the Fruit Company supplied Kellogg with the fruit ingredient of its cornflake and banana breakfast food. We would start with a banana puree which we molded into a banana shape and then cut in slices and freeze dried. They looked like wooden nickels, dry, in the package of cornflakes. The concept was fine, but it turned out that the banana slices took about as long to rehydrate, once the consumer added milk, as it took for the flakes to turn soggy. Scratch one breakfast food.

Not all of the propositions that came to United Fruit were directly related to bananas, and not all of them were even funny. Shortly after the Guatemala affair, a man who identified himself as "Mister Brown" walked into Ed Whitman's office on Pier Three and offered to sell the company a complete revolution in any country of its choosing.

Mr. Brown was a mulatto and spoke in a cultivated voice that made it difficult to be certain of his nationality. Probably he was an American but he could have been a West Indian. He was well dressed in a tweed business suit, and his manner was low-key, gracious, almost diffident. He had the style one might expect from a recent graduate of the Harvard Business School who had gone into selling cemetery lots.

He told Whitman that he realized the Fruit Company had extensive interests to protect in Latin America and that there might be occasions when it would be more efficient or discreet not to involve our own Department of State. He said he represented some interests who were in a position to put together any kind of package the event called for, including not only tanks, rifles, machine guns, cannons, gunboats, landing craft, airplanes and that kind of thing, but they could supply the manpower as well. He used the word "mercenaries" once or twice, but he favored the term "personnel." He was a very classy kind of guy.

Whitman had been around long enough to realize that Mr. Brown meant every word he said. He also suspected that the very utterance of such an offer was in itself a crime, and that Mr. Brown's presence in our offices was enough to involve the company, willingly or not, as an accessory. So he asked him a few rather hurried questions, then told Brown he would have to give the matter some further thought and discuss it with the rest of the company's management. Mr. Brown even went so far as to suggest some price ranges—what the company might expect for an investment of, say, one million dollars, compared to what they could buy for three times that amount—and then he got up to go. He told Whitman he would be in touch.

As soon as he was alone, Whitman called the Boston office and described Brown's offer. He was told to get in touch with the FBI. Probably because the offer involved the possible sale of illegal weapons, the FBI alerted the Treasury Department as well and together they sat down with Whitman and developed their strategy for a trap.

Mr. Brown called a few days later, and Whitman invited him to come in for another talk. This time, there was an FBI agent sitting at one of the nearby desks and a T-man at the desk right next to him, both looking about as innocent as Frank Lovejoy in *I Was a Communist for the FBI*.

I was sitting at my usual desk when Brown walked in; he took in the whole room with one sweeping glance and it was clear that he was counting the house—and he knew there were at least two people on hand today who hadn't been there on his last time through. Brown never turned a hair. He walked over to Whitman's desk, sat down as though he had all the time in the world, chatted affably about topics no more incriminating than the weather or the stock market, then thanked Whitman, stood up, shook his hand and turned to go. The room had been wired in advance of his coming, and the FBI got as much out of the tapes of the conversation as if they had recorded Elsa Miranda singing the Chiquita jingle.

As soon as he left the room, I walked to the window on the West Street side to watch him come out of the building. The FBI and Treasury agents had left their desks and were watching as well. When Brown emerged from the entrance beneath our window, an FBI agent on the other side of the street began to follow him. Within half a block, a second agent picked him up and the first agent left him. A block or so farther on, the switch was repeated with still a third agent.

About twenty minutes later, one of the FBI men came back and told us what had happened. Brown had gotten onto the subway at the Wall Street station, and he and his follower rode as far as Fourteenth Street. Brown got off at Fourteenth, and the agent did too, assuming that Brown was about to switch to the express. Just as the doors were closing behind them, however, Brown stepped back onto the train, exactly like in the movies, smiled and waved good-bye to the agent on the platform. We never heard from him again.

There was no way to know for sure at that point, but the FBI and the company both thought that Mr. Brown had approached us on behalf of Colonel Herbert Fauntleroy Julian, better known as the Black Eagle of Harlem.

Julian is a well-known arms merchant and soldier of fortune who had made his first big mark on his profession during the Ethiopian War. He so impressed the late Emperor Haile Selassie that he was given the contract to create the Ethiopian Air Force, supplying the planes and training the pilots. A packaged revolution sounded just like one of the items on Colonel Julian's menu, and he had sold similar services to buyers of all ideologies and political persuasions throughout the world in the years since Ethiopia. He also had a finely developed sense of PR: in 1940, for example, he challenged the German ace Hermann Göring to an aerial duel.

On April 1, 1958, a couple of years after the incident involving Mr. Brown on Pier Three, I received a telephone call from a man who said he was Colonel Julian himself. He had asked the switchboard how he could be connected with the President of United Fruit, and the operator suggested he take it up with someone in Public Relations. The caller asked me my name and introduced himself. He had the same cultivated voice I remembered from Mr. Brown, but older and with a stronger West Indian accent. He asked if I could help him by getting an important message to the president.

He then explained that he represented some people who had a large amount of money in Cuba. He told me that Castro had placed a ceiling on what people could spend in that country, and that Cuba was in the process of converting from one kind of currency to another. I knew about the situation: the Batista regime had printed enormous quantities of paper money during their last few months in power, and much of it had been hoarded or expatriated by profiteers. Castro's plan was to switch from green currency to money printed in bright pink; the profiteers' money would become worthless, and hoarders still in Cuba would not be able to convert to the new paper without explaining how they happened to have so much hidden away. Nor could they make any large purchases.

My caller said that the people he represented wanted to sell their green currency to United Fruit Company, and we in turn would be able to distribute it through our weekly company payrolls on the island. I asked him how much money was involved. He said the amount was a hundred and twenty million Cuban pesos, which at that time was traded at par with the American dollar. I took a deep breath. He added that there would naturally be a substantial discount on the transaction: his people were willing to sell at a fraction of the money's face value.

I told him I would get back to him, and then called Boston. At first, I was told the company had no interest and then that management wanted to think it over. But a little while later I was called back and told to turn down the offer.

Probably the element that made up management's mind was the risk. If it became known that United Fruit was involved in a plot to undermine the Cuban economy, who knew what consequence might follow? It was even conceivable that Castro would expropriate the company's land holdings and throw us off the island. Farfetched, but possible.

Besides, the Cuban economy had already been turned into a house of cards under Fulgencio Batista, and all that remained was for it to collapse. History does not always make the fine distinctions between causes and their effects, and when Castro uncovered the real state of the country's finances, many economists in the United States were quick to say that Castro himself was responsible. But United Fruit knew that Batista and his cronies had stolen the guts out of the country, and doubtless realized that it would be too risky to involve United Fruit Company as an accomplice to the final act, despite the opportunity for profit.

I got my final call early the following morning. Before I had the chance to give him the company's answer, he told me that the thought had crossed his mind, after we had spoken the afternoon before, that perhaps I had not taken his message seriously because it was April Fools' Day. I told him that had not been the case, but the company had decided to turn him down. He thanked me very graciously and that was that.

I have often wondered since whether his friends were able to unload their money, or if they were stuck for a hundred and twenty million dollars.

In the early days of the Kennedy Administration, the CIA approached Fruit Company management and told them that the United States was sponsoring a counterrevolutionary movement with the objective of unseating Fidel Castro and bringing "democracy" back to Cuba. The project was masterminded by an old hand at such things, E. Howard Hunt. We were told of the CIA's plans in detail, including the training of mercenaries in Guatemala and Nicaragua by U.S. personnel. The plan would culminate in a large-scale invasion of Cuba by air and sea. That's where we came in. We dealt directly with Robert Kennedy. The main company contact was J. Arthur Marquette, a crusty New Orleans seafaring man who had worked his way up from the ships to become vice-president in charge of steamships and all Terminal Operations. Marquette told me how much he disliked Kennedy—everything from his arrogant and demanding attitude to his "dirty long hair." But he was the Attorney General and he and the CIA wanted us to supply two of our freighters to convey men, munitions and material during that invasion. The arrangements were made and it was all very cloak-and-dagger: our own board of directors didn't know about it, and certainly only a handful of us within the company were party to the secret. Once the counterrevolution ended—on the beaches of the Bay of Pigs—the logs of those two ships were sent to Washington. Some time later the logs were returned to the company encased in sealing wax. As far as I know, they are still in company vaults, the official record of our participation in that fiasco permanently safe from public view.

Some of the most interesting propositions that came to United Fruit were ones the company itself solicited. By the mid-sixties, when Sunderland and then Fox and Cornuelle had brought the company to a turn-around point, management decided to take a realistic look at some of the social problems which had been building and worsening from the time of Zemurray and which had been largely ignored. Most of those problems were located in the tropics but their effects were being felt in the United States and Europe.

Fox and Cornuelle went to IBEC, the Rockefeller-backed International Basic Economy Corporation, and asked them what they thought we ought to be doing in the area of housing and community development. IBEC had a lot of experience in South America, the Caribbean and particularly in Puerto Rico, where they had undertaken assignments ranging from the design of substantial programs in workers' housing for large corporations to the funding and development of whole townsites. The Fruit Company engaged IBEC to study our tropical operations. The IBEC team of housing experts visited every one of the Company's tropical divisions.

They met resistance right from the beginning from tropical division management. At one point, the resistance took the form of a direct protest to IBEC from one of the Central American governments: the protest stated that the country resented IBEC's presumption in looking at local housing and recommending how the citizens of that country should be living. We learned later that one of our own division managers had been behind the incident. It was far from being an uncommon experience: if the tropical managers didn't like something, very often they would sabotage it.

A high-ranking executive in one of the Costa Rican divisions was responsible for a similar situation as a means of deferring his transfer to another part of the company. United Fruit had recently acquired two companies in Costa Rica, and the move had proved mildly unpopular locally. So the executive deliberately stirred up the situation until it became a public issue and a small national crisis, hoping that it would convince the home office how valuable he was to the company right where he was, dealing effectively with an emergency of his own making. It was not a new technique.

Despite such setbacks and other resistance, IBEC was able to complete the study and report to Boston on its findings. One aspect of their job was to provide the first real inventory of its housing the company had ever seen, not only by number but by type, with a breakdown of the total human population the company was sheltering. It was pretty shocking.

In their preliminary report, they stated that the company had created, and was perpetuating, a "culture of poverty." It was requested by the company management that that particular phrase be struck from the final report. The Fruit Company's Boston management did not resist the concept, but they knew that the wording would make it far more difficult, and perhaps impossible, to sell the changes suggested in the report in the tropics. IBEC concurred and the phrase was dropped—but I never forgot it.

There was another phrase from that report which was not delated and which I will not soon forget. IBEC said that many, or even most, of the people they spoke with expressed a "desire for freedom." The report went on to explain that the desire was not just an abstract longing but was an attitude based on the fact that they were not free at all, that they were completely at the company's mercy for everything they needed simply to stay alive.

The report made specific recommendations as to the amount of money the Fruit Company should spend over the next few years if this situation were to be properly redressed. As I recall, it was in the neighborhood of thirty million dollars. It also recommended the types of houses the company should build, pointing out that bedrooms, for example, should open off halls so that people were not required to pass through one bedroom to get into another, and that there should be closets instead of hooks on the walls. It outlined various types of financing which could be made available to the workers for buying these houses from the company. None of the recommendations was ever implemented.

The suggestions were practical enough. In fact, a couple of labor unions came up with similar plans later which would permit some of the company's dockworkers to own their own homes. But the company itself was beset by new ills shortly after the IBEC report was completed, and the initiative the study might have provided was completely lost.

Even if there had been no problems at home, however, I have some strong doubts that the IBEC study would have ever led to any real changes in the way the company did business in the tropics. The division managers paid lip service to the concepts, but then each of them made a plea for special circumstances in his own jurisdiction, explaining why such revolutionary changes would never work. It was the same old story of entrenchment and the status quo. Why should we change when everything is going so well?

I remember a conversation I had a few years ago with the wife of a manager of one of our tropical divisions who had been promoted and moved up to Boston. She told me how sorry she was to leave the tropics, and she pointed out that the promotion and salary increase had actually worked a hardship on the way her family was now able to live. She enumerated the privileges a tropical manager's family enjoyed, from free rent of the best house in town, unlimited entertainment expenses, servants, transportation to any place in the world covered by the Fruit Company fleet, a twin-engine, radar-equipped airplane at their continuous disposal, a yacht, usually a beach house or other vacation retreat, to their own semiprivate medical staff and hospital. She said she had added it all up, and for her husband to support that same scale of living in the suburbs of Boston, he would have to have an income of a quarter of a million dollars a year—after taxes. She was right.

She might have added that there were intangible benefits as well, the most obvious one being that as the manager's wife she had the highest social status in her sphere, about the same as the First Lady in a small republic. I've known of cases where the wives had even more real control of the way the company operated in the divisions than their husband did. That kind of control-by-default can be unpleasant, even dangerous, to everyone involved: it can be arbitrary, petty and often vicious. Promotions and reprisals can be based on factors having nothing to do with how well a man performs his assigned job, but instead, for example, on how well he or his wife gets along with the wife of the manager.

Another area where Fox and Cornuelle felt the company was weak was its relationship with its various publics in Latin America, and they commissioned the Cambridge-based research firm of Abt Associates to study that situation at around the same time IBEC was looking into housing.

Fox and Cornuelle knew the company had to do more than offer window dressing, that if its public relations policies were to be successful they would have to involve matters of real substance. They had held this conviction for some time, but until the company had ironed out the enormous problems of profitability, they had not been able to act on it.

Abt Associates was retained to travel throughout Central America, not just in the Fruit Company divisions but in the capital cities and in the schools and universities, speaking with Latin Americans in all walks of life, trying to get a profile of their opinions about the company and some suggestions for its future role. They spoke with students and educators and laborers and clergymen and government officials and leaders of unions and publishers and reporters—and a picture began to take shape. Will Lauer and I were the company's project leaders in the study, and we met extensively with team members before and after their trips, giving them as accurate a picture as possible of how the company operated both at home and abroad. Will was the Fruit Company's vice-president of personnel and labor relations and he was particularly good at bringing to light many of the hidden issues reflected in the attitudes the Abt team encountered in the field. Similarly, I tried to give them a view of the company as it really was, without the traditional patina of public relations.

Jack Fox was, in my opinion, the first chief executive since Zemurray, who looked at good public relations as being based in good deeds. Back in the early fifties, when Zemurray saw which way the company was going after his retirement, he sold his interest in United Fruit down to the last share. And once Fox was to lose control over the company's moral direction nearly twenty years later, he too would divest himself of the onus of implied responsibility for its future.

The Abt team ran into the same reception in the tropics as had been met by IBEC. If anything, the division management kept them even more distant because of the ethically sensitive questions they asked. In addition, by this time, 1967, beards were in up North, but in the divisions it was still the Eisenhower fifties.

The division managers had an explanation for their attitude toward beards: since Castro's rise to power, beards were politically provocative through all of Latin America. Division managers upheld the proper decorum of the company, they believed, "even when the home office was so damned stupid as to send down a bunch of long-haired billygoats to pry and ask everybody a whole bunch of garbage about the way the division managers were doing their jobs."

But the Abt people persisted, and they produced an impressive report. A meeting was arranged at the Harvard Faculty Club: Fox and Cornuelle where there, and Will Lauer and I and a few other headquarters people—plus all of the division managers, who had been brought up from the tropics.

Clark Abt ran the show and made it clear from the start that they had found some very ugly things.

The Abt study revealed the Fruit Company's involvement in volatile societies that threatened to overwhelm us unless we could change with the times. Where once the company had shaped the social history of its tropical realm, it now lagged decades behind, denying the existence of injustices which lay at the heart of how we did business.

The format Abt elected for his presentation was a series of "decision trees," with alternative assumptions about what might happen to the company, what paths it might choose to follow in the future, and where those events and choices might lead us. A decision tree involves multiple possibilities, and Abt had organized them on the basis of what was optimum, what was likely with a little good luck, what was likely with a little bad luck, and what we could look forward to if things really turned sour.

The first thing I saw when the decision trees were displayed was that there was almost no way for the company to improve its present situation, and that the best we could look forward to in almost every area was a retention of the status quo.

Clark Abt made his presentation at night. The following day was spent in discussing it. He knew that what he had said was unlikely to be acceptable to the division managers, and he made no attempt to sugar-coat his findings. The next day it became clear that he had opened old wounds; the managers were hostile, they denied that there was any conflict in their divisions or between the divisions and the worlds they lived in; they made excuses, they rationalized as "a special case" everything that they couldn't deny outright, and in general they acted out the very attitudes which Abt had set down in the report. If I found any fault in his performance, it was only that his criticism was not as harshly presented as the facts justified and that his recommendations for change not made to seem as desperately urgent as indeed they were.

Abt may have felt, as I did, that though division managers were at the heart of the problem, the solution would have to come from higher up. I was by then so familiar with the division manager mentality and the tactics they used in protecting their territorial imperatives, I was sure they would negate the purposes of the meeting. But Cornuelle and Fox insisted that they be invited: it was the straightforward way to do things.

One division manager in particular serves as an epitome of what the Abt group encountered. He was in his early forties, had a pocked, lined face, and indoors or out his eyes were hidden behind sunglasses. He had spent almost his entire working life in the tropics, and his character and appearance had taken on the colors of his environment. He operated in a world of tough men, men who became police chiefs and generals in armies and heads of Central American states and who stayed in power because they never relented, never weakened, never let go of the old ways.

Once, when Abt suggested that the local workers should be given more choice, more freedom, more responsibility for their own futures, this particular manager leaned way back in his chair, his legs crossed at the ankles and stretched out assertively in front of himself, his face a combination of amusement, bewilderment and contempt. "Sheet-it, man," he said. "Supposing Leroy don't *want* to carry the ball? He don't *want* to—what're you going to do?"

Leroy, of course, was his name for any man who wasn't white.

Several of us had felt that the company's days in Latin America were numbered. But if intelligent action on the Abt report might have given us a reprieve, a thrust at the heart of United Fruit diverted the company from the task of reform. So the Abt and IBEC studies—and all of the fledgling commitments they represented—were pushed aside. Eli Black had begun his raid on United Fruit.

Chapter 7

THE LAST TANGO

IN MARCH OF 1934, the month I was born, a beautiful, young Armenian-American girl named Alice Tunjian went to work for United Fruit Company as a stenographer. I joined the company eighteen years later, and, after a decade more, Alice Tunjian became my secretary. A couple of years later, after spending some thirty years on the job, she retired.

Alice was still relatively young, and in a short time she discovered that retirement did not yet agree with her. So she went to work for a brokerage firm in New York City. She had brains and beauty, good skills, was a conscientious worker, and she became the secretary to a senior partner with Donaldson, Lufkin and Jenrette. In the late summer of 1968, Alice learned that her new employers were about to engineer an historic takeover. The target was United Fruit, the company for which she had worked most of her life and from which she was collecting her pension. The man who would put the plan into effect was named Eli M. Black.

For the next several weeks, despite the enormous temptation to call me, to warn her old friends of what was about to happen to them, Alice chose to remain loyal to her present employers. She never said a word.

Donaldson, Lufkin and Jenrette had been interested in the

101

Fruit Company's stock for some time, but we had always regarded them as friendly toward our management. United Fruit stock had gone from $17 a share in 1965 to $60 by mid-1968. But by the end of the summer it had settled down to around $50, and William Donaldson saw that our acquisition and diversification efforts appeared to be stuck. He talked with Fox and Cornuelle from time to time, but so did a lot of other brokers and analysts. What made Donaldson different from the others was not what he said to us, but the plan he had for profiting from the Fruit Company's embarrassment of riches. It was widely believed at that time that United Fruit had around a hundred million dollars in cash. Earlier in the year, it did, but United Fruit had then gone on a spending spree, investing heavily in such activities as floriculture and lettuce. Even though the amount of cash proved to be exaggerated, Donaldson's maneuvers would earn his firm a fee of well over a million dollars in the next several weeks.

After the raid in the spring of 1969, Donaldson was interviewed by Chris Welles for an article in *Investment Banking* on the Black takeover. He said that his view of the company a year earlier was that "the fundamentals were beginning to deteriorate, and disillusionment was setting in." It was an interesting conclusion, in view of the fact that the Fox-Cornuelle team had raised earnings almost sixteen times over their level just three years earlier. But in a way Donaldson was right: it was the era of the conglomerate, the time of the Lings,* Bludhorns,† and Blacks, and even though United Fruit had taken some spectacular strides toward profitability, it had managed only stumbling baby steps in the direction of diversification and acquisition. Even more important, the Fruit Company directors and management understood almost nothing of the game of debt leverage, which Donaldson knew was Eli Black's specialty.

---

* James J. Ling who founded Ling-Temco-Vought, Inc., was perhaps the greatest player of the merger game of the sixties. LTV ran into serious financial trouble but no other company had grown so fast or so much in a decade.

† Charles Bludhorn, another well-known conglomerate builder whose Gulf and Western Company also had a meteoric rise in the sixties.

Perhaps Donaldson recognized that the company was a victim of its own traditions. Despite efforts by Cornuelle and Fox to change the United Fruit product mix, the company was still guided in its management policies, especially its financial policies, by a business ethic that was fast becoming an anachronism. It was based on the principle that a company never spends money it doesn't have, that it never gambles on future profits with future earnings. It was the same New England morality that judges a man's character by his worth—because personal wealth is a reflection of shrewdness and thrift, and shrewdness and thrift are habits of character. Nothing could be more fundamental. It was the logic of Calvinism, and it was dangerously dated to anyone familiar with the new techniques of corporate giant-making. It was even out of step with the way the federal government operated the national economy.

Donaldson teamed up with Eli Black because of his remarkable skein of financial successes. Black was forty-eight years old, had taken his early training in the brokerage business and then had gained control of American Seal Cap, a small company that manufactured the liners for bottle caps. In a short time Black had used that unglamorous base as the fulcrum for a spectacular debt lever. He built American Seal Cap's sales to forty million dollars a year and then used it to pry loose control of John Morrell & Company. That one acquisition gave Black's company a sales volume of nearly a billion dollars a year. By swallowing John Morrell, a company twenty times its size, Black's newly dubbed AMK Corporation became one of the fastest growing conglomerates in America.

Donaldson went to Black and told him he had access to three large institutional shareholders of United Fruit who together held about 10 percent of the Fruit Company's stock, and he could deliver that stock to Black. Legend has it that Black contemplated this offer for three days and three nights before calling Donaldson back and accepting.

Black had been around the course enough times to know that he need not complete the entire race to place in the big money. Both he and Donaldson anticipated that Black's entry would create new interest—even some excitement—in the mar-

kets for the Fruit Company's stock. The price would rise and
Black could ride it for a while before committing to take his
profits or to go all the way.

If he did have the skill and the luck and the endurance to
stay with United Fruit to the finish line, he was certain of a
payoff there as well. "Whatever our eventual intentions, we felt
the move had to make sense as an investment," Black told a reporter the following spring. "The stock was selling at thirteen
times earnings, with a balance sheet that made us feel very
comfortable, and there was reasonable possibility for profit. If
something did work out, there was several million dollars there
to be put to work. Who wouldn't lend United Fruit two hundred million dollars? If you consider AMK's historical twelve or
thirteen percent return on capital after taxes, we could get maybe
nine or ten percent on that two hundred million dollars plus the
one hundred million in cash that's already there. That's twenty-
seven million of additional income." *

In order to get the three institutions holding the Fruit Company stock to agree to give it up, the offer was made to make
them partners, in effect, in the gain that would follow Black's
purchase. The plan was simple: if Black made a tender offer †
to the other shareholders of United Fruit stock, the shares he
had purchased from the three institutions could be renegotiated
by the original owners at the higher price. While Donaldson
was sewing it up with the institutions, Black was talking with
Samuel Zemurray's old nemesis, the Morgan Guaranty Bank,
working out the terms of a thirty-five-million-dollar short-term
loan with which to buy the stock. Morgan agreed to let him have
the use of the money, but with one important stipulation: the
takeover, if it was to happen, must be a friendly one, and the
entire note was subject to immediate recall if United Fruit decided to put up a fight. Clearly, Morgan did not want Black
gambling with their money. Besides in the days since Zemurray's
first encounter, Morgan Guaranty had become a long-time sup-

* Chris Welles, "The Battle for United Fruit," *Investment Banking
and Corporate Financing*, Spring, 1969.

† An offer by an individual or company to buy the stock of another
individual or company.

porter of United Fruit. So was Donaldson, Lufkin and Jenrette.

The trade was made the next day, September 24, at $56, which was 5½ points higher than the previous closing price, a premium of 10 percent to the institutions who agreed to sell their large block holdings. The 733,000 shares had a total value of forty-one million dollars.

That same day, Black picked up another 7100 shares on the open market at the same price.

These transactions raised a number of questions which have never been fully answered. The rules of the New York Stock Exchange require that all investors be provided access to the same information at the same time. But the three institutional sellers of United Fruit stock certainly knew before anyone else that Black was contemplating a run on the company, a fact implicit in their agreement with Donaldson that the 733,000 shares would revert back to them for renegotiation when and if a tender offer was made.

Conceivably, Gustave Levy might have provided some insights to this paradox. Levy was chairman of the New York Stock Exchange and a Senior Partner in the investment firm of Goldman, Sachs & Company. A reporter pointed out that a number of other institutions felt they had been slighted in the transactions which took place on September 23 and 24, to which Levy conceded, "It would have been better to trade that block off the floor." The reporter called this "a somewhat novel suggestion for a NYSE official"; he also observed that Levy was a personal friend of Eli Black, that Levy's firm of Goldman, Sachs & Company was the chief investment banker for Black's AMK Corporation. In fact, approximately half of the 733,000 shares traded to "unnamed clients" in the transaction of September 24 were handled by Levy's own company.

Another rule of the New York Stock Exchange states that all members of the Exchange must be treated alike. But in his first and second moves in the marketplace, Eli Black offered to renegotiate the price of the stock after the fact, a guarantee to the institutional sellers which he did not repeat to others whose stock he also acquired.

Over the next year, this issue was to arise again and again, brought up by former Fruit Company shareholders and even the Federal Trade Commission. But each time the questions were swept away without being fully answered. There has never been a formal inquiry.

Black's technique with United Fruit's management was essentially the approach he had taken in his successful raid on John Morrell. On the evening of the twenty-fourth as he sat with Fox, Cornuelle, Gardner and Folsom at the Algonquin Club, he limited his remarks to two topics: the company's virtues—and his own. He assured them that he thought they were thoroughly capable, that he had bought into the company purely because it made good investment sense. No mention was made of his agreement with the three institutional sellers regarding a possible tender offer. On the contrary, he stated flatly that a takeover was not his intention. A year later, Black himself was to recall that conversation. "I said we respected their ability, their autonomy and their integrity." Black also told them that his own integrity was his most important single possession. "I am a man of my word," he said repeatedly, "and my word is my bond."

Regardless of how Black chose to represent it or how the Fruit Company management chose to receive it, the rest of the financial world quickly recognized AMK's transaction of September 24 as the classical opening move in the game of takeover. As Black and Donaldson had anticipated, other players soon started trying to deal themselves in.

The first of the new arrivals was Zapata Offshore Drilling Company. Fox and Cornuelle had met with Zapata management about a year before, but in those days the Fruit Company had considered acquiring Zapata. Now the roles were reversed.

There were lots of things wrong with Zapata, in our opinion, but their attentions were first received as a form of reassurance that the Fruit Company was still an attractive proposition, despite the stroke it had suffered just the day before. This kind of reassurance is seldom very substantial, and it collapsed almost at the first meeting. Zapata stock had risen to the point where the management of United Fruit no longer felt it was a good investment, which is one reason we had broken off negotiations a year earlier. Fox still remembered their management as being "an attractive bunch of guys," and Robert Gow, a Zapata vice-president, was the son of Ralph Gow, an old and respected member of the Fruit Company's board.

Robert Gow and Zapata president, Doyle Mize, called on Fox and Cornuelle. They explained that Black's objectives were clear to them, and that they had no intention of letting him take over United Fruit because they wanted to take it over themselves. They let Fox and Cornuelle know it would be in their best interest not to oppose them. In marked contrast to the polite, almost diffident style of Eli Black, Gow and Mize wasted no time on amenities. They said they intended to re-shuffle the company's management and make some major changes in the board. Without realizing it, they did as much to advance the case for AMK as if Eli Black had stage-managed the entire confrontation. By the time the meeting was over, Fox had reconsidered his earlier judgment: Gow and Mize were no longer an attractive bunch of guys.

One of the reasons Fox no longer found Zapata attractive was that when Fox had tried to explain some of the complexities in managing a company of United Fruit's size, particularly in view of the unusual history and the special relationship between the company in Boston and its tropical constituents, socially, politically and economically, the Zapata executive impatiently waved all this aside. "Bullshit," he said to Fox. "There's nothing special to running this company. What's the big deal? So you have to have dinner with the President of Honduras once a year."

During the next few days Zapata put together a rather per-plexing package of paper which our analysts finally decided was worth about eighty dollars for every share of United Fruit stock, or about 50 percent more per share than Eli Black had paid in his opening move.

At that point, Black's investment of forty-one million was potentially worth nearly sixty million. He just sat quietly on the sidelines, never interfering with the way United Fruit's man-agment conducted itself, never harassing Fox or giving him un-welcome advice. By the same token, he was always fully accessible if Fox should call him, always gracious, low-keyed, still the stalwart admirer who said he believed in United Fruit and knew its management would always do whatever was right.

At first, Fox said the company was thinking over the proposed Zapata offer: it took a while to untangle it.

But that hesitancy was the feint of a moment only, and soon we issued a news release saying United Fruit would vigorously oppose Zapata's attempt to take over the company.

By then the scent was out, and United Fruit began receiving offers and propositions from all sides, through telephone calls, letters and personal visits. I remember that on one day Jack Fox received a total of twenty-six telephone calls, each with a different proposal. It was impossible to weigh every one of the offers as thoughtfully as if they had been spaced further apart, but there were some that could safely be rejected out of hand or after the most cursory glance.

Fox and Cornuelle were able to see an additional message in the sheer volume of this activity that was not as apparent when the proposals were viewed singly. There was no question that the Fruit Company was under attack, that their own management successes in restoring profits and liquidity had made them mortally vulnerable. As the attack gathered momentum, they decided they would never be able to turn from a defensive to an aggressive stance, that they simply didn't have the time. They decided that a forced marriage was inevitable, and the best they could hope for was a mate of their own choosing.

Herb Cornuelle thought first of Dillingham Corporation in Honolulu, a real estate company with interests in construction and mining. During his years with Dole, Herb had gotten to know Dillingham management and to like them. The Dillinghams were among Hawaii's first families, and descendants of the founder still ran the company. Cornuelle discussed the idea with Fox, put out some initial feelers, and then he, Fox and Tom Warner, the financial vice-president, left for Honolulu. They took elaborate precautions that Black, who was watching carefully from the sidelines, would neither discover their mission nor even notice their absence. The entire trip was made over a weekend, with all three men flying from Boston to Honolulu, meeting with Dillingham management and returning home between Friday evening and Monday morning. It was the equal to a trip halfway around the world. Yankees had ventured to the Hawaiian Islands for profit in the past, and at first it looked as though Cornuelle, Warner and Fox had been successful. One week after Donaldson approached the institutional investors and Eli Black went to Morgan Guaranty for his short term loan, and six days after Black had first introduced himself to John Fox by telephone, Dillingham announced a cash and securities package worth over seven hundred million dollars in exchange for United Fruit Company's stock. Ten days later, they raised the ante to seven hundred seventy-one million.

But then Dillingham began hearing from its stockholders, and what they heard was not good for United Fruit. What did Dillingham know about bananas? More to the point, what did they need to know? Everything was going very nicely as it was. It soon became clear that Dillingham's shareholders had no interest in complicating their lives, that they were not willing to have dinner with the president of Honduras even once a year. The final offer fell apart in two weeks: Dillingham said there were "legal and tax reasons" against the consolidation, and they pulled out of the sweepstakes.

The next dance was with a partner much closer to home. Textron Corporation, one of the country's oldest and most solidly based conglomerates, was only forty miles to the south, in Providence, Rhode Island. Chastened by our adventure in the South Seas, we started making eyes at the boys next door. Again, romance bloomed overnight.

Textron looked good for a number of reasons. They had as much experience as anyone in the business of debt leverage, but they always had employed it with admirable restraint. They had a good record of growth, but they made sure that integration remained a higher priority than mere acquisition for its own sake. Unlike most conglomerates, they had stayed relatively clear of the kind of complicated paper transactions which the brokers called Chinese money, and had engineered their growth without the sacrifice of enormous calls against their future earnings.

Equally to the point, we knew Textron management, and they, like Dillingham, were "our kind of people."

Two days after Dillingham backed out, Jack Fox got together with G. William Miller, Textron's president. On October 27, a Sunday, Miller and Textron's Chairman Rupert Thompson took a bus from Providence to Boston. The representatives of the Fruit Company were Fox, Cornuelle, Warner, Gardner and I. We met in the board room on the twenty-eighth floor; on a clear day, from that room it is possible to see as far away as Providence.

Thompson and Miller talked philosophy during the first part of the meeting, and said a lot of things we already knew but were glad to hear anyway. They told us they felt our corporate styles were nicely matched, that they thought there was a good fit with the personalities and backgrounds of our officers and directors and those of Textron. The talk was not of acquisition, but merger.

Fox, Cornuelle, and Gardner were ecstatic. They were across the table from men they could understand, that they could talk with, that they could trust. Textron was an old-line New England company built by two old-line New England businessmen—Royal Little and Rupert Thompson—and Bill Miller was even older-line American being part American Indian. Everyone in the room had good manners. They all appreciated the same kinds of jokes and had even served on many of the same boards of directors. That Sunday afternoon we drafted a press release saying that the wedding was on, and there was a good deal of relief and chuckling at the expense of poor Eli Black, who was going to be left standing at the altar. Everybody felt terrific, and even the references to Black were moderately generous and lacking in rancor.

The release went out the next day. On that same Monday morning, a Mission Impossible type task force of Textron specialists descended on the company: accountants, lawyers, analysts from the Textron Secretary's office and bookkeepers. They were like a well-rehearsed company of Chinese ballet dancers and they went through United Fruit Company from top to bottom, all in perfect, unified precision. Our own personnel were astonished. For Fruit Company people to have accomplished the same task would have required weeks of work; it took Textron five days. Everything was laid out according to the proper form: blanks were filled in and the forms went down to Providence where they were marinated in some larger system and then evaluated. Textron had been through it all many times before.

The release we issued jointly was a minor classic in its genre, filled with the metaphors of aspiration so dear to the readers of the fine print in annual reports, an atlas of major landmarks and new horizons and freshly blazed trails. It also said that Textron was going to pay two shares of their own stock for every share of ours. At the going price for Textron, that offer was equal to $86 for each share of United Fruit. If the merger went through at those rates, Black's forty-one-million-dollar investment would be worth over twenty-two million more than he had paid for it.

Eli Black watched all this activity with his usual poise and continued to assure Jack Fox of his admiration.

In the days that followed the joint Textron—United Fruit release, however, ground swells began to be felt in Providence. Some of the larger Textron shareholders let Thompson and Miller know they were not pleased with the prospective merger, for the same reasons that balked the Dillingham union: bananas and the customary business of the intended appeared to many stockholders like a poor mix. Lack of investor confidence in the merger lowered the market price of Textron stock. It dropped one point. Then another. It was a clear, time-honored signal.

Miller and Thompson wasted no time at all in translating the message. Textron was run by the same rules and incentives that governed United Fruit and just about every other publicly owned company. The price of their stock was more than a source of pride or a measurement of their success as managers, it was the basis by which each of the officers and directors of the company could determine a part—and often the most substantial part—of his own personal net worth. If the pending merger had caused the stock to go down instead of up, then the management had made an error in judgment and they would pay for it. Miller and Thompson deserved a lot of credit for getting the Textron stock to $43 and they were determined to do whatever had to be done to keep it there.

In the middle of the Textron negotiation, I received a telephone call from the *Wall Street Journal*. The reporter wanted me to confirm a rumor that International Harwood had entered the race with a bid of 415 million dollars' worth of its debentures for the stock of United Fruit. I said I didn't know, and in fact had never heard of International Harwood; I promised to check it out and call him back. The reporter added that International Harwood had made an offer for the acquisition of Textron, with a larger package of debentures valued at 850 million dollars. The combined offers totaled over one and a quarter billion dollars.

I went to Fox with this news, and he reacted exactly as I had. We started looking through the voluminous file of correspondence and notes in which we had attempted to keep track of all the offers made to United Fruit, and an hour later we turned up a page of International Harwood's letterhead.

The letter set forth the same figures that had been quoted to me earlier by the reporter from the *Journal*. But as I looked at it, I could easily see why it had been passed over. The letter appeared to have been written on a toy typewriter, with each character either higher or lower than the ones around it. In some places it seemed that the ribbon was running out of ink or had missed the stroke completely, so that the character was etched instead of printed. It was not the kind of letter one would be inclined to take seriously.

I saw that the address was in Elmhurst, New York, and I recognized the street. "This isn't exactly the high rent district," I said to Fox. "Warwick W. Harwood [the name at the bottom of the letter] must be the richest kid on the block." Besides, the neighborhood was not a business area, but was comprised of low and middle income apartment houses. Jack asked me to look into it, which I did.

The report I got back from New York a few hours later was pure Alice in Wonderland. Warwick W. Harwood was not only the president and chief executive of Harwood International, but he appeared to be the rest of the company as well. Headquarters were in his rented apartment, and the company's assets consisted mainly of unpublished manuscripts by Warwick W. Harwood which the author had modestly valued at two million dollars. He had a BS in psychology, according to the report, and he had a bank account of slightly more than a thousand dollars. Jack and I discussed him briefly, then I called back the *Journal* and gave the reporter the lowdown. The story appeared the next day, and that was the last we heard of Harwood International. United Fruit—once a blue chip—had become fair game for anyone with a letterhead and a typewriter.

Meanwhile, despite the lavish attentions of Harwood and Textron, Zapata pursued the Fruit Company with undiminished ardor. They met no opposition from Eli Black. On the contrary, Zapata management was later to accuse Black of having called them repeatedly during this period quoting the selling price of his 10 percent block of United Fruit stock at steadily increased value. Zapata gave serious thought to these offers, even when Black's asking price reached $125 a share. The consideration that kept them from accepting, they claimed, was the possibility that the New York Stock Exchange would not prove so lenient in their rulings with Zapata as they had earlier proven with Black, and because of restrictions against trading on "insider" information, Zapata might be forced to pay the same high price to all the other United Fruit shareholders. All of these negotiations were unknown to our management at the time, although, of course, we were fully aware of Zapata's continued interest. When asked by a reporter about the alleged offer to sell at $125 a share to Zapata, Black dismissed the claim as nonsense. He said that he had received offers from numerous sources, but that he had no intention of selling. He also said: "Buying our block was like starting a race nine lengths ahead. It gave us the aura of a winner right from the start," an odd choice of metaphor from a man who claimed to have bought the stock as a long-term investment.

The aura of a winner is something Zapata lacked. Zapata had approximately $55 million in the bank, but they did not have Black's powerful coterie of friends on the Street. They did not have Black's credit with Morgan or elsewhere, and, even more importantly, they did not have Black's style. And their actions were based less on planning than on counterpunching reactions to other people's initiatives.

One of the accusations leveled at Black during this period—
and not only by Zapata—was that AMK was breaking another
Stock Exchange rule by "warehousing" Fruit Company stock.
Warehousing is a form of collecting: it was suggested that Black
or his associates were going from one broker to another, telling
each privately to reject the Zapata tender offer—and any other
tender offer—because AMK would make a substantially higher
one later on.

The rumors reached Bill Miller at Textron. Miller later
claimed he had discovered Black secretly lining up shares representing 20 percent of the Fruit Company's outstanding stock.
A merger between Textron and United Fruit would require a
two-thirds majority vote by the shareholders of each company,
and Miller believed that warehousing would make a fair stockholders' referendum impossible.

Not only is warehousing against the rules of the Stock
Exchange, it is against the law. Black denied that he had ware-
housed Fruit Company stock.

But by mid-November when Black met privately with Jack
Fox, another side of Black's character had begun to emerge. He
told Fox that his interest in the Fruit Company was changing—
that he sought a more active role. He told Fox of friends of
AMK who controlled or owned large blocks of the Fruit Company's shares. One weekend, Black invited Fox to visit him at
his home in Westport, Connecticut. Black was as pleasant,
gracious and soft-spoken as ever. But during the course of the
visit, he accepted a couple of telephone calls in Fox's presence.
He made certain Fox knew the calls were from those friends,
and that the subject of each call was United Fruit. Jack described the meeting to us the following Monday morning. It was
unsettling to all of us.

While common sense dictated the public denials, Black did
acknowledge to a reporter that AMK had "a lot of friends, and
Goldman, Sachs has a lot of friends, and we all had the hope
and expectation that something further would develop."

By the beginning of December, we all knew that Black's
take-over strategy was building to the point of more dramatic
confrontation. We had been working steadily for almost two

and a half months, none of us had taken a day off, and management was exhausted. For the first time since I had met him, Jack Fox looked haggard. He had lost his tan, the strain showed in his eyes, and by noontime every day he had grown a five-o'clock shadow. The hard pace was beginning to take its toll. It was at this point that Black began to exert the first overt signs of pressure and move in for the kill.

He told Fox that Zapata was about to launch a new offer, and that it was time for Fox to make a choice. Textron was still in the picture, at least in theory, but Black and Fox both knew that the field would reduce to Zapata or AMK.

Since the Thanksgiving holidays, Textron's change of heart had been obvious, but unstated. When that courtship had been at its height, the management of both companies had decided they would need a new name once they were married, plus a new corporate image. Textron hired the firm of Lippincott and Margulies to consider the design problem, and United Fruit hired old friends in Cambridge, Abt Associates. Abt, in turn, hired experts in linguistics, semantics, communications, and technology, of whom Cambridge has many. It was a blue-ribbon panel—Harvard and MIT professors, a Pulitzer Prize winning biographer—and if we needed further assurances of its quality, we were told of the difficulty Abt encountered in getting some of its own staff members to accept employment, even of such narrow scope, for a company with the sullied reputation of United Fruit.

The Abt team developed an impressive list of prefixes and suffixes, and fed it into a computer. The product was a printout of about ten thousand names. They then applied to this list a set of more or less subjective criteria, and eliminated many of the names—like ICOPOOPS. Problems of regional pronunciation were discussed at some length, including a diverting excursion into the problems the Japanese have with the word "baseball." They edited and whittled and discussed and tested further, and the final product was fourteen possible names that were not known to have any other meanings; that were not smutty or suggestive or hard to pronounce in any language, and that were not known to be in use by any other company. Those

names were CENTRAD, MERION, EXECON, METRO-
MEGA, CAPITEX, METREX, PANOMEGA, CORPORAD,
PANTERRA, EKOMEGA, TERREUS, EXINOR, CENTAR
and EXANTOR. Over the Thanksgiving holidays, United Fruit
took this handful of names down to Providence, and there we
met with Textron and the people from Lippincott and Margulies.

The Abt people who came with us went over about as well
in Providence as they had fared earlier in the tropics. They
brought along a monograph of about twenty pages describing
how they had come up with the fourteen names, and it was a
scholarly, plodding piece filled with obscure references, medieval
symbols and labored explanations. The L & M team was in
sharp contrast: they dressed and looked as though they were
from the business world rather than the academe, and their
defense of their product—somewhere around six names—rested
almost entirely on their firm's worldwide reputation. The contrast was not wasted on the management of Textron; I knew as
I watched the meeting drag on that the Textron management
had lost all appetite for the merger, and that everything they
looked at from then on would just take the form of a new excuse to call it off.

When Eli Black posed his choice to Jack Fox in early December, Fox finally faced the inevitable and called Textron to ask
if they were still in the race. Miller said that they no longer
were. He said that they had made the decision several days
earlier; for some reason he had just not quite gotten around to
letting United Fruit know about it until Fox called. It was
really discouraging the way "our kind of people" kept treat-
ing us.

Fox and Cornuelle then took the decision to United Fruit's
officers and directors. There was a lot of questioning, a lot of
doubt and some opposition. But one by one they began to cave
in. I should also add that there was a lot of one other element:
apathy. Many of the directors and some of the company's officers
just were not interested in what happened. They didn't have a
large financial stake in the company's future, or they were too
old to care, or they had other fish to fry, especially if they were
interested in politics. The issues all had finally come to one final

question, and that was simply who had the greater endurance. There was just one holdout, and that was Vic Folsom, the Fruit Company's general counsel, and the fourth member of the team that had first met Black that night three months earlier; he kept up the fight to the very last. The record shows him as the only director who did not approve the company's acceptance to the offer of acquisition by AMK.

The last tango was coming to an end for United Fruit. Almost all its suitors had either retired to the sidelines or had been outclassed or escorted from the floor by force. The prospect of being abducted into a marriage with Zapata had by this time become truly repugnant, due more to our distaste for Zapata's management style than to any attractive alternative represented by AMK. On December 5, AMK announced a new tender offer—some twenty-five-year convertible subordinated debentures, fractional shares of AMK stock, and a ten-year warrant to purchase one and a half shares of AMK common stock. I sat down with Fox and we wrote a letter to the shareholders and a release to the press, supporting AMK's package. Its value was about ninety dollars a share.

Zapata countered with a new package, which they had been putting together over the past few weeks in anticipation of the AMK escalation. The new Zapata offering contained a fatal flaw: it was so complex that most financial analysts could not understand it, and many others felt it lacked the value placed on it by Zapata. The package was built around a new security which Zapata called a "two-dollar noncumulative preference stock."

On December 16, Zapata took its offer to the Securities and Exchange Commission for registration as required by law. AMK still had to assemble the final elements of its own last offer, and Zapata was confident that they had beaten Black to the draw. But then a series of events took place which the Zapata forces— and a good number of other people—were to find almost incredible.

Over the course of the next sixteen working days (which were interrupted by Christmas and New Year's), while AMK

labored to put together a tender offer that the shareholders of
United Fruit would be unable to refuse, Zapata found itself
enmeshed in explaining to the Securities and Exchange Commission the intricacies of its tender offer. Slowly, and to the
growing amazement, then anger, then outright rage of Zapata's
management, the advantage of their early entry began to dis-
appear. There was plenty to explain in the Zapata package, but
everyone involved—the Zapata management, Black and his
friends, and the SEC—all recognized that in a race to the finish
line, timing could be everything. Fifteen days after the SEC
had received Zapata's offer, AMK finally completed their package and delivered it for registration. The following day, Zapata
managed to clear the last SEC hurdle and at last emerged from
their long ordeal. But the process that had taken Zapata more
than three weeks took AMK a mere twenty-four hours. The two
offerings reached the public in a photo finish.

It was variously suggested that Black, Levy and the SEC each
bore responsibility for the delay in Zapata's release, and each
in turn denied it. Levy said, "I don't have any influence down
at the SEC. I wish I did." Zapata suspected that the campaign
had been lost, and so there was no point in carrying those suggestions any further.

When the final battle lines were drawn, the weakness of
Zapata's position was fully apparent. Now that the Fruit Company was officially on Black's side, the AMK camp consisted of
Hornblower Weeks and Paine Webber (the latter represented
by United Fruit's onetime Chairman, and still a director,
George Gardner) as well as by Black's original supporters at
Goldman, Sachs and Lazard Frères. Zapata faced all this power
with only Lehman Brothers to back them up, and considering
that Robert Lehman had served on the Fruit Company Board
for over twenty years, there was some doubt on our part about
how much loyalty Zapata could really expect from their single
ally.

Robert Lehman's name had come up about a year earlier in
a conversation, during a flight to London with Ben Sonnenberg,
the publicist. Several months before I had ever heard of E. M.
Black of AMK, Sonnenberg predicted that the United Fruit

Company would be taken over by a corporate raider. He said United Fruit didn't know where the action was anymore, and that we had no connections with the "Jewish investment bankers of New York." I cited Lehman, and Sonnenberg waved the name aside as though to say I was being absurd. He said Lehman was an old man, and that we shouldn't look for anything from him. Sonnenberg also expressed the opinion that I should get out, and several months later he put me in touch with a job opening in another company.

Even out of registration, Zapata's prospectus remained impenetrable to most of its readers. And when the proxy solicitation began in earnest, it became obvious that Zapata had failed to cultivate the necessary acquaintances among the arbitrageurs * who now fully controlled the Fruit Company's stock. On the other side, Black's familiarity with the arbitrageurs, with how they operate and how they think, was to emerge as another one of AMK's formidable strengths.

I remember sitting down with Jack Fox one night, when we were trying to write a letter to our shareholders. The arbitrageurs had bought out many of the holdings of individuals and families and foundations and institutions that had been with United Fruit for longer than lots of our employees; these old shareholders had seen the rise in our stock as an opportunity to make a profit— or they had seen it as a bubble. But when we were sitting together that night, we estimated that as much as half of the company's stock was in the control of institutions and individuals who had not owned a share of United Fruit six months earlier and who were riding with it for a familiar motive: profit. No matter what else we said to them in the letter, the new shareholders would be swayed by no other consideration—not what was best for the company, not what was best for the employees, not what was best for the consumers of our products, not what

---

* Arbitrageurs simultaneously purchase and sell the same securities, commodities or anything else. They make their profits from the slightly unequal price the seller is willing to sell for and the buyer is willing to pay. Usually, they also get a small fee for making the transaction. The spread between purchase and sale is usually small but since the volume in a given security can be large, arbitrageurs can make quite a bit of money.

was best for the governments of the countries where we operated. Half the people we were writing to were strangers.

By the time the two companies came out of registration, Zapata's Gow was already suffering strong misgivings about the real worth of the company he had been chasing so hard and so long. He wondered constantly whether Zapata was paying too much for United Fruit; but each pang of doubt was offset by an even sharper instinct for what Zapata would be able to do once they got their hands on the Fruit Company's reputed hundred million dollars. So in a last-ditch effort to make up for the lost advantage they had suffered at the hands of the SEC, and despite all of Gow's misgivings, Zapata made one final effort to sweeten the ante in their quest for shares. In mid-January Zapata announced a new offer. Black had promised to better anything Zapata could come up with, and so he did: he increased the debentures from $20 to $38, raising the value Wall Street experts placed on the total offering to just under a hundred dollars per share.

A couple of days later, in a move that lent additional substance to the rumors that he had been warehousing, Black announced that he had "assurances" of receiving 40 percent of the Fruit Company's stock. Zapata publicly discounted the claim as exaggerated, but the next few days proved that Black's estimate was nearly exact. During that same period, Zapata received a minuscule 31,000 shares. Black made one of his friendly, low-key telephone calls to Mize and determined that Zapata was ready to throw in the towel. As another Zapata executive stated the situation, the company "decided to get out with honor and a little cash." It was agreed that AMK would buy the 270,000 shares finally tendered to Zapata for $85 each, paying with a subordinated note in the principal amount of $17,600,000 at 6⅞ percent interest payable in ten equal annual installments. Zapata was also to receive $3.8 million in cash for their expenses. Zapata didn't get the big prize, but they came away with a great deal of money for three months' work.

How much did Eli Black wind up paying for United Fruit? Combining the convertible debentures, common stock and warrants in his final package, one reporter projected the cost for

100 percent of the company's outstanding shares at $540 million, or $200 million more than United Fruit was then worth. A year later, it was apparent that that projection had been too moderate. In acquiring 80 percent of the company, AMK actually gave up cash, bonds and stock worth $630 million. Of this amount, less than half, $286 million, was charged to the net assets of United Fruit. A book written a couple of years later explains what happened to the rest of that money. "[AMK] charged the remainder, *over a third of a billion dollars* (my italics), to the goodwill account. Now, AMK knew this was not right . . . $300 million for United Fruit's goodwill (and trademarks) is preposterous." *

In any transaction of that size, loyalty to the winner is bound to be profitable. In paying off his allies, no matter how late in the battle their allegiances had been pledged, Black's accounting was more direct and a lot easier to understand. Zapata, to whose persistence Black owed much of his own success, received the $3.8 million "expense" settlement mentioned above. Lazard Frères and Company, United Fruit Director Stanley Osborne's firm, received a quarter of a million dollars from United Fruit for acting as the company's advocate during the acquisition, then received an additional $384,802 from AMK for handling the exchange offer for United Fruit stock.

Goldman, Sachs received over a half million dollars with more to come in 1971 and 1972. And for George Gardner, the former Fruit Company Chairman, the transition meant a fee of over $565,000 to his firm of Paine Webber, plus retention of his seat on the board of the surviving company.

Tom Warner, the financial vice-president who had known E. M. Black from his days at Price, Waterhouse, eventually became an AMK Vice-President and received options on a tremendous number of shares in the new company's stock—at two dollars a share. I never could figure out why Warner was given those two-dollar options—none of the other former United Fruit executives got any. Warner said that it was just part of his total package of management incentives.

---

* Abraham J. Briloff, *Unaccountable Accounting* (New York: Harper & Row, Inc., 1972).

In the March 10, 1973, issue of *Business Week*, there was an article on Felix G. Rohatyn, described as "the archetype of the new generation of investment bankers that is taking over Wall Street." Rohatyn was with the firm of Lazard Frères, and it was he who represented that firm's interests in the two transactions with United Fruit and AMK in 1969 which netted Lazard $634,802. In commenting on Rohatyn's many successes in helping conglomerates, Lazard senior partner Andre Meyer said that merger and acquisition services are "the most spectacular and sometimes most profitable part of our business." Later in that same article, *Business Week* said, "Reflecting Meyer's concept of investment banking, the Lazard firm has for years operated on the well-founded theory that corporate boards provide excellent listening posts, as well as income generators for its partners." Obviously, they are not alone in the philosophy. Directors are privy to all sorts of advance information about the company itself, other companies of the men they sit with, companies they are going to acquire, etc.

Black's outside allies were not the only ones to benefit from his victory. Effective at the time of the merger, his own five-year contract called for an annual salary of one hundred and fifty thousand dollars and deferred compensation of another fifty thousand per year, bearing interest at the prime rate. Black's longtime associate Maury Kaplan had a contract which paid him one hundred forty-three thousand dollars; he also was entitled to deferred compensation of fifty thousand per year at the prime interest rate. Black and Kaplan also received a bonus from time to time.

A few years later, despite the lackluster earnings, the directors approved a raise for Eli Black to a base annual salary of $225,000, and for the year 1974—the last full year before his death—he received $273,000 including his deferred compensation and accrued interest.

Another old friend, Bob Gallop, started with the company at a base salary of around $115,000, plus deferral benefits, plus a periodic bonus, along with retirement benefits from the company for the rest of his life. He too worked himself up to the point where his latest employment contract called for him to receive $180,000 per year plus pension benefits of $50,000 per year. When Gallop resigned from active service with the company, his employment agreement was amended to provide for his employment as legal advisor at an annual salary of $144,000, but was otherwise unchanged. During the period January 1, 1971, through December 31, 1974, Gallop accrued deferred compensation of $266,667. He continues to be available in a consulting capacity and will be paid $72,000 annually during his lifetime prior to December 31, 1979. The payments at the rate of $50,000 per year provided for in his employment agreement will be paid commencing January 1, 1980, or the date of his death, if earlier. Not bad for a few years' work.

Another form of recompense, of course, is the stock option plan. In the time-honored tradition all of the inner circle were in for substantial amounts. If there were some way to go short on a stock option, they could have made millions.

During the time of the takeover, there were daily admonitions from the directors and managers to "think of the shareholders." This same injunction could easily be interpreted to mean, "Think of the price of the stock. Think of us."

But a public company has more numerous constituents than its shareholders. During the course of the struggle to gain control of United Fruit, I came to the conclusion that those other constituents were far more important to the company than one might infer from the voice assigned them. What about the employees? And what about the consumer? Then as now, bananas were eaten by more people, in greater quantities, in more places in the world, than any other fruit. Not one word was uttered on behalf of the millions of people who would be forced to pay more for what they ate. At its peak, United Fruit Company served as the sole economic support for a total population of almost half a million workers and their dependents. If this same number of people had been associated as a sovereign nation instead of a corporation, their rights to at least a minimal degree of self-determination would have found defenders around the world, and the raiders would be driven into another line of work. But not one word was spoken in their behalf. They were totally ignored.

Almost all of the officers of the company—myself included—held options on stock at a price averaging somewhere between $18 and $30 a share. If a man held 25,000 shares in that kind of option, the gain represented by Eli Black's assault on the company was already more than $1,250,000 when the stock hit $80. Several option holders told me they were certain the stock was going to go as high as $125 or even $150, a potential gain, in the case of the man with options on 25,000 shares, of over $2,500,000.

In the face of that kind of personal profit it is unworldly to expect a man to make a dispassionate, disinterested judgment on behalf of the other shareholders, the company itself, its employees or the consumers of its products.

Chapter 8

THE TROPICS

I TALKED TO Eli Black several times on the phone before I met him. The first face-to-face meeting came in midwinter, 1969; the raid had begun six months earlier, and although the actual merger was to drag through the courts for another year, Black was certain of his victory. We met for lunch in the Falstaff Room of the Sheraton Boston.

There were two other Fruit Company representatives at the luncheon: Dick Johnson, a vice-president of our Numar operation in the tropics, and Will Lauer. The purpose of the meeting was to discuss the naming of a new building in San José; Black had become closely involved with the day-by-day activities of the company, and I had learned through Fox and others that he was particularly interested in public relations.

As we sat down at the table, Black smiled and asked if we were hungry. I had come into the office early that morning and had missed breakfast, so I smiled back and told him I was starving. A moment later a busboy arrived with a plate of cheese and crackers. Before the plate touched the table, Black reached over and took it from the busboy's hand. At first I was certain he was going to pass it around the table, but instead he placed it in the middle of his own place setting, then clasped his hands in front of it. "Now," he said, still unsmiling, "what's on the agenda?"

For the next several minutes, Johnson and Lauer talked with Black about the building in San José. They told him that it was the largest office building in Costa Rica, although it would hardly be noteworthy by North American standards. I added a comment here and there, keeping my eye on the cheese and crackers. The only way I could get one, other than by asking for it, would be to reach across Black's arm; and Black was making it very clear by the way he positioned himself directly over my quarry that to violate his territory in that manner would be a serious breach of etiquette. I sat back for a few minutes longer, weighing the demands of my neglected stomach against the possible consequences to my career. Finally, when Black still showed no signs of action, I found a brief pause in the discussion and said, "How about some cheese and crackers?"

Black was looking at Lauer, and when I asked the question he never even glanced in my direction. It crossed my mind that the request had not registered, so I decided to rephrase it and try again.

"You're not planning on eating those crackers and cheese all by yourself, are you, Eli?"

Again, no answer. Lauer glanced over at me sympathetically for a brief moment, Johnson smoothed the dinner napkin on his lap and Black continued the conversation about Costa Rica as though the two questions had never been asked.

I leaned back in my chair. By that time I had given up all hope of the cheese and crackers, and I looked around the room for our waiter, to signal him that we were ready to place our luncheon order. But the waiter was nowhere in sight. I decided to forget about my stomach and leaned forward to rejoin the conversation.

Two or three minutes passed. Black made it clear that there was nothing the matter with his hearing when it related to the subject at hand; he nodded in agreement with all of my suggestions; he asked me questions and listened attentively to my answers; he made numerous comments. And then he unclasped

his hands and picked up the knife which lay along the edge of
the cheese and crackers.

Black turned back to Will Lauer and asked him some more
questions. As Lauer answered, I watched the knife dig down
into the bowl of cheese; the other hand reached out and selected
a Ritz cracker from the plate, and Black poised the cracker on his
fingertips as he carefully stroked a rounded, tantalizing mound
of cheese spread over its face.

The cracker remained balanced on the fingertips of Black's
left hand for at least the next five minutes. He asked Lauer
questions about the height of the building from the street and
its height above sea level. He asked about the color and materials
of the facade, about the use of each floor, about the size of the
lobby. And then he asked if Lauer could tell him how the Fruit
Company was regarded in Central America in general and Costa
Rica in particular. My eyes never left the cracker.

No reasonable person with Will Lauer's experience could
have answered in less than fifteen minutes, and there have been
learned tomes on the subject which barely scratched the surface
in three or four hundred pages. I leaned back again, this time
accepting my defeat.

It was then that Black reached across the table and placed the
cracker on my butter plate. He put the knife down where he
had found it, and he refolded his hands before him, keeping the
food within their embrace, for himself alone to dispense or to
keep. Black didn't say a word, but his expression made it clear
that he felt he had made his point.

Shortly after that meeting, I visited AMK corporate headquarters in New York City. And like my first glimpse of Black,
it was a revelation. The acquisition that was then in the process
of creating the seventieth largest public corporation in the
United States had been masterminded from a six-room suite of
offices on Park Avenue. That was it: six rooms, most of them
divided by partitions of frosted glass. There were a handful of
desks, and on almost every one was an adding machine and one—
Maury Kaplan's—had a computer terminal for instant stock

quotations. On the surface it was totally devoid of any sign of imagination, flair, or personal style. At first I thought there must be more to it, that I had stumbled into a corner of the actuarial department of some other company, or that a door would open to reveal long vistas of teakwood and brass, that I had taken the rear entrance into the corridors of power. But that was all there was. One desk without an adding machine belonged, I was told, to Eli M. Black; it was in the office at the corner of the building. I was also told that it was lunchtime, and the staff of AMK was occupied with preparing Mr. Black's meal.

As I looked around me, I wonder how it could have been possible for the handful of men in these rooms to have taken over two corporate giants—first the John Morrell Company, and then United Fruit. Sometime later, I read *The Godfather* and came to the passage where the Don tells his *consiglieri* that a dozen men with machine guns are no match for a single lawyer with a briefcase. And I wondered what the Godfather would have thought of Eli Black's operation.

I knew what Herb Cornuelle thought of it. He told me of his impressions after his first trip to see AMK's corporate headquarters, and he told me that Black would be a "benign influence." He said that AMK was just a handful of little men in a half dozen offices up on the twenty-third floor of a New York City skyscraper, and that they would not be able to run the United Fruit Company. He was right about that, but what he never considered was the possibility that they might try.

In the spring of 1969, Eli Black decided to make his first trip to the tropics. He described it to me as "an inspection tour," and he asked Will Lauer and me what he might expect to encounter. Again, we met for lunch and again Black cornered the crackers and cheese. Only this time he lost no time in distributing the rewards: he spread two crackers with the mound of topping and gave one to each of us; "I'm very much looking forward to this trip," he said. "Now, what will I find when I get there?"

One morning in 1952, while I was still in the passenger de-

partment, the assistant purser on one of our ships became ill
and had to be taken ashore to a hospital. My boss asked me how
I would like to take his place. It was early fall, and I remember
racing home to pack. The ship was set to sail at four that afternoon, and I barely made it back in time, running to the pier with
a suitcase borrowed from Mr. Collier, the postman who lived
next door to us.

The first stop was Havana, where we stayed just long enough
for two other members of the crew—the radio operator and the
Chief Steward—to take me downtown for an introduction to
Cuban nightlife. We walked single file among the tables of a
small, dimly lit, crowded, pungent-smelling café, and passed
through a doorway to a room in the rear.

The theatre was barely larger than its single piece of scenery—
a large bed with patched, rumpled, filthy gray sheets. The setting could have been from a wax museum, with generations of
dirt everywhere. The players arrived about five minutes after
we did; by that time we had been served rum drinks in Coke
bottles and four middle-aged Germans had taken the remaining
chairs around the bed. I won't pretend I didn't know what was
in store, but there is just no way that an eighteen-year-old boy
can look forward to an experience like that with any reasonable
idea of what he will actually feel when it happens.

The man was black, with a long knife scar on the outside
of his right forearm from the elbow to the wrist. There were
tightly wound black watch springs of hair across his shoulders,
and for the first ten seconds or so he was wearing a pair of red
and white candy-cane-stripe Bermuda shorts. The woman was
either Spanish, mulatto or both, about thirty years old, one
breast larger than the other. The man and woman both seemed
angry and wasted no time in preliminaries. Almost immediately
there was such a stench of perspiration and smoke in that small,
closed room that I thought I was going to choke. I took a quick
gulp of the warm rum in the Coke bottle, gagged, stood up,
pushed my way to the door, still gagging, shouldered my way
through the crowd at the bar, made it to the entrance by lowering
my head and clamping my hand to my mouth, finally got as far

as the sidewalk and vomited in the gutter. I walked back to the ship by myself, feeling scared and sick, and went to bed, not to return to Cuba again for almost six years.

The next stop was Kingston, Jamaica. Then Barrios, Guatemala. I remember thinking that I was really finding out what United Fruit was all about during that two-week voyage. I saw more color, more natural beauty, more strange places than I had experienced in my previous lifetime. People came and went; so did towns and islands and countries. But the time was still several years in the future before I was to really have an appreciation for the business of United Fruit, before I understood the true basis for its power and wealth. The tropical places we visited were always miles away—sometimes by road, sometimes by rail— from the private universe in which the company's bananas were actually grown. I didn't see inside that universe until I had been with the company for another five years.

"You say this will be an inspection tour," I said to Black. "Does that mean you intend to visit each of the company's tropical divisions?"

He passed me another cracker, "No, not at the moment," he said. "I intend to divide my time between Golfito and La Lima."

Will Lauer asked, "How much time altogether?"

"A week," Black answered. "Maybe ten days." He looked at us both thoughtfully for a moment, as though uncertain how to say what came next.

"I want to get to know our people."

We both nodded. "You've already met some of the tropical people here in Boston," I said.

Black unclasped his hands to wave the remark aside. "Not the managers. The *people*," he said. "The men and women in the fields. The ones who pick our bananas."

Lauer and I looked at each other and then at Eli.

Black added, "I plan to live on one of the farms."

I quickly answered. "You can't do that, Eli."

"Why not?" He smiled, and I suspected he had already covered the same ground with others in the company.

"For one thing, there are no facilities," Will Lauer said.

"The only guest accommodations are in division headquarters. Out on the farms they wouldn't know what to do with you."

He nodded. "I'd stay in a worker's home."

"The workers have no homes," I said, "not in the way you'd expect. They live under a tin roof with walls of cinderblock and screens. And even if you decided you could stand that for a whole week—what about the family you'd be displacing?"

"All right," he replied quickly, "I'd stay with the manager. I'd let them know I was coming, and they'd prepare a guest room."

Lauer and I looked at each other again. Black nudged my arm and I looked down to see another cheese-decked cracker on my plate.

"You're the last person I'd expect to object," he said to me. "After all, it would be great public relations."

"Eli," I said, "let me tell you some stories about the tropics."

In 1957, the company had decided I was ready for my first real indoctrination trip to the tropics. I had been with United Fruit exactly five years, and it looked as though I might be making the job a career. As an employee at my level, it was very difficult to get down to the tropics, and the trip was a compliment that was not lost on me. For a month, I would visit several locations, work on the farms and in the office of the division, getting first-hand experience in the business of growing bananas. There was no formal training program in those days, because the old company men didn't give much thought to how the next generation would be trained. But if you were lucky enough to be selected as a comer, the informal training was terrific. Similarly, there was no formal aid to education—but if your boss liked you, he would handle it out of the expense account, as Ed Whitman had taken care of some of mine. I left for Costa Rica on a company ship, and arrived seven days later at our plantation in Golfito.

Nobody was there to meet me when I arrived. I walked around for a couple of hours, and finally a pick-up truck appeared and the driver asked if my name was McMann. When I nodded, he jerked his thumb in the direction of the opposite door. I walked around in front of the truck; he gunned the engine, and I jumped, which gave him a big lift and gave me a hint of what was in store for me. He drove me in silence to a guest house where I was to stay, let me out with my suitcase and drove away. I went inside and looked around. Already I had begun to suspect that the managers of the tropical divisions resented visitors from the North, and what I saw convinced me further.

The house was a large room on stilts with a tin roof and absolutely nothing in the decor to distinguish it from the charity ward of a leprosy hospital. It smelled of mildew; the division gets about two hundred inches of rain each year—most of it in three months. Fruit Company houses have hundred-watt bulbs burning in the closets around the clock to keep mildew off clothes and shoes. I started putting away my things, feeling little of the elation with which the trip had begun. Suppertime came and went without anyone letting me know where I could eat, and without my being able to find anyone whom I could ask. By the time I got so hungry it hurt, it was very dark outside and I could no longer see the road, so I gave up the idea of exploring the plantation headquarters or looking for food. I turned out the lights and went to bed.

Up to that point in my life, my experiences with the tropics were limited to what I had seen in the movies. The trip I had made a few years earlier had taken me to that part of the world, but only to its edges. After my reception at Golfito, I was prepared for the worst.

The worst started within minutes of my turning out the lights.

For a short time, I lay quietly in the bed, listening to the sounds of the jungle and waiting for my eyes to grow accustomed to the dark. The tropics are so filled with every form of life—from millions of different insects, on up through the higher forms of scale and fur and feather—particularly scale—that I wondered if the noises would keep me awake.

A moment later, I knew I would have a far bigger problem than mere noise. Under the sheets, right in bed with me, something had started crawling across my legs.

It was before the time of James Bond, but I had no trouble

imagining the whole deadly spectrum of possibilities from snakes to centipedes, scorpions to poisonous mites. I managed to leap from the bed and cross the room to the light switch almost without setting foot on the floor. Then I cautiously approached the bed again and slowly drew back the covers.

Nothing.

I shook out the sheets, and still nothing. I looked carefully at the old, stained mattress and on the floor all around the room, and then back to the sheets again for a closer inspection. Whatever it was had evidently gotten away. I then proceeded to examine myself carefully in order to rule out that last possibility, and finally got back into bed.

Within a few minutes, I felt it again. This time it felt like hundreds of ants crawling across my body.

I got up again, repeated the ritual, and decided to spend the rest of the night in a chair with the lights on and my eyes wide open. Toward morning I actually dozed off a few minutes at a time, but the chair was the type usually found in kitchens, with a straight back and made of metal, and the night was so hot and humid anyway that those few nods didn't help much.

The first person I saw the next day was the housekeeper. She was a woman of about thirty-five, but at the time she looked much older. I had never met a woman who had spent her life in the tropics, which is one reason I misjudged her age by thirty years. The other reason is that I was only twenty-three myself, and even thirty-five seemed old. But her face was deeply lined, her hands were gnarled, and she was missing several teeth. She said good morning in Spanish and started to straighten up the room. I decided she was the person I should tell about my difficulties of the night before.

I went over and pointed to the bed. "Bugs," I said, trying to remember the Spanish word. She look at me dubiously.

Realizing I was not getting through, I pulled back the covers and pointed to the sheets. I made motions with my hands to indicate animal life, and I repeated the idea of insects several different ways. My two years of high school Spanish had completely deserted me at that point, and my English was obviously doing no good at all. She looked at me and her face grew darker by the moment. The more she looked that way the more frustrated I became. I hit the mattress several times and said, "Dammit, there are bedbugs in this bed!"

That was all it took. Her eyes opened wide, but only for a moment; then they became very narrow and she left the room, yelling words at me in Spanish which required no translation. I was sure I had offended her pride in her housekeeping.

Within a short time one of the division executives showed up at my door. He was one of the few Americans at Golfito—most of the supervisory personnel at that particular division were English or European. He introduced himself tersely and asked if I was ready to go. I said I was, but that I wanted to tell him about a little problem I had had the night before. He didn't want to hear about it, but he waited patiently for me to continue.

"Well," I said, "there are bugs or something in this mattress."

He looked at me with complete contempt. "Ain't no bugs in these here beds. This here's a clean place, Mistuh. If they's any bugs here, you brought them down on you."

"The hell I did," I said. "There are bugs in this bed and I didn't get any sleep last night because of it."

He almost smiled. "That a fact?"

I could see that I wasn't going to get much satisfaction, so I then told him about the conversation with the housekeeper. I asked if he would talk to her and explain what I had been trying to tell her. He said he would be back in a minute, and he went down the stairs. The guest house was built on stilts, and the woman lived in a little room beneath it, at ground level. A few minutes later, the man came back up to the room.

"C'mon, let's go."

"Did you tell her what I was saying?"

He laughed. "Yeh. Don't worry over it."

"Did she say why she got so mad?"

"She thought you was trying to fuck her."

He started back down the stairs and I followed him. I thought he would go over and tell the housekeeper what had happened, what I had really meant when I had slapped the mattress with my hand. But instead of going back under the house to the screened room where the woman lived, he turned toward the pickup truck. I could see the woman behind the screen, and she turned sullenly away when she saw me looking at her. "Hey!" I said. "You've got to tell her. I have to live here for the next ten days."

He started the engine and told me to get in. As we drove down the long, dusty road to the division's office, I asked him one last time if he would let the woman know that she had misunderstood me. He was tired of hearing about it, and he waved me quiet with his hand. "Don't worry about her." He looked at me a moment later, and he could tell it still bothered me. "Man," he said. "C'mon, she's just a Spic . . . she's nuthin'."

Several days later, I met an acquaintance from New York, an Englishman, and his French wife. They were on a TV network assignment trying to travel the length of the Pan-American highway from the United States to South America. They had already discovered that the trip was impossible: the road disappeared for long stretches, and in places it was washed out by flooding or was so narrow that a car could not pass. They had a Jeep for the trip and were planning on seeing their journey through to the end, no matter how they did it. They were the answer to my prayers.

My first stay at Golfito had not been happy for anyone. The supervisors weren't about to give up their prejudices toward visitors from the Boston or New York office, and I was treated as though I were Martin Bormann or the bearer of a particularly virulent strain of banana virus.

In every tropical division, there is a section known as the *pueblo civil*, the the civil town, most often right alongside the company town which usually is on United Fruit land. The difference between the two is day and night. The company town is painted and manicured with flowers and fences and lights on the corners. The civil town has a trench of open sewage down the main street, with poverty and sad sights everywhere. The civil town has grown up in most of these divisions solely because of the presence of the company town. There are only two thriving industries: the cantinas, or bars, and the whorehouses. Every face you see in the civil town looks back at you with hatred, and most of the time you know they are sizing you up as prey: for theft, for sex, for revenge. Beyond learning how the company operated, which is why I was there, Golfito offered very little in the way of diversion. I was anxious to get out.

My friends were at a point in their trip where they were forced to travel by rail. United Fruit maintained a stretch of tracks between Golfito and the adjacent Panama division at Puerto Armuelles, and they were offered the use of a motorcar and a flatbed on which to carry their Jeep into Panama. A motorcar is an ordinary Ford or GMC truck which has been equipped with steel wheels for travel over rails. We talked over the possibility that I might make the trip with them. I mentioned it to the Golfito Division management who couldn't have been more pleased. So we loaded our motorcar the next morning and left before dawn.

By midday, after traveling through endless miles of banana land, our driver announced that we had finally arrived at the border, a dot on the map called Puerto Gonzales. (Although the trip already seemed longer than anything any of us had ever done before, we were fortunate in not having encountered any banana trains; there is a tradition—or an iron law—from the time of Samuel Zemurray that says no person or no vehicle, under any circumstances, ever goes ahead of a banana train. In the years that followed that trip, that law was to account for a good many hours of my life.) We got out at Puerto Gonzales and went over to talk with the border guards.

Because we were leaving Costa Rica, the Costa Rican guards were not really concerned with us. So we started speaking with the guard for Panama. As soon as I saw him, it crossed my mind that he might be a problem. He was short, with an enormous stomach that hung out over the top of his gun belt. He had a couple of troops with him in a Jeep, and the Jeep itself sported a swivel-mounted .30-caliber machine gun. Both the troops were wearing bandoliers of ammunition. All three of them could have been character actors in the movies. The chief guard told me that the border was closed.

I asked him why. He said there was trouble in Panama City, and he had orders not to let anyone get through. I had known about the troubles for several days, and in fact I had been passing through the Canal Zone when the worst riots were taking place. Several students had tried to plant the Panamanian flag on the banks of the canal, and a number of them had died in the shooting that followed. The shooting came from the Panamanian Army, which was protecting the country's treaty with America. I tried to convince the border guard that the riots were over and that his orders no longer stood. He seemed to weaken, and after a moment more I was sure he had given in. I told the guard that my friend was an Englishman and that his wife, who impressed the guards on both sides very much indeed, was from France. And lastly I pointed at myself and said I was American. "That's the Big Three," I said, capping off an argument which I thought he would find irresistible. He nodded and smiled. "*Si*, the Big Three." But his English was only slightly better than my Spanish, and I was not certain he had understood everything I had said. I told the driver to get back in the motorcar, that we were going on through.

"Oh, no, *Señor!*" the driver said. "*Por favor!*" But the driver spoke no English at all, and I was adamant. So we all got back aboard and started across the border.

We actually went quite a distance. The guards were standing at the side of the track, but no move was made to stop us, and we must have been going about forty or forty-five miles an hour by the time we hit the switch. The motorcar jumped the track, and with all four of us holding on for our lives it dropped fifteen feet down the embankment into the jungle. The Jeep and the flatbed carriage followed, missing us by inches.

All four of us were near shock, but no one was injured. We climbed out of the wreckage and looked up the slope to the tracks. The two soldiers and the Panamanian border guard had pulled the Jeep even with the point of derailment, and they had us lined up precisely under the .30-caliber machine gun. The guard had lost all his former pleasantness.

I knew a little bit about what that particular kind of gun could do—in the Army Reserve a few years earlier, during summer camp, we had disposed of some excess ammuntion by using it to cut down trees whose trunks were roughly the same dimensions as my own. We climbed slowly up the embankment and walked back along the tracks, the Jeep following us with its machine gun trained on our backs.

We reached the border station, and the guard drew a ten-foot circle in the dirt with his heel. He managed to make it clear to us, despite the language handicap on both sides, that if any of us set foot outside that circle we would be shot. Then the guard and the two soldiers walked some distance away and began to talk quietly among themselves. It crossed my mind that they could be deciding whether to execute us. I asked the guard if we could speak with him again. The conference continued for a few minutes longer without the guard giving any indication that he had heard me. Finally they seemed to reach an agreement, and he walked back to the circle.

I told him we were sorry about the problem I had created. I said that crossing the border was now the furthest thought from our minds. We knew we had put him and his men to unnecessary hardship, and now all we wanted to do was pick up the mess we had made of things and be on our way home. But, of course, three men and a girl could not very well carry a motorcar up a fifteen-foot bank. He was much calmer now than he had been right after the incident. He watched a spot in space just a few inches above my forehead, his arms folded above his enormous belly. Now and then he nodded. I asked him if we could go back for help from the nearest Fruit Company farm, and he agreed that we could send our driver—on foot—but the rest of us would have to stay within the circle. At first, the driver winced at the prospect of taking such a long walk, but he must have compared that with the fate of the rest of us who were forced to stand for another several hours in the hot sun. When he rounded the bend of the track and disappeared from our view, he was actually jogging.

I never expected to see him again, but several hours later he returned with six men from the company farm at Laurel, five miles away. My friends had endured the day's events with unusually good humor, but by now it was midafternoon, the tropical sun had given us all bad burns, and we had been without food or water for the entire day. When our rescuers came into sight at last—and we saw that six men had been sent to do a job easily requiring two dozen—our elation soon gave way to disbelief, then terrible disappointment.

The Panamanian guard was equally let down, and he told us we could leave the circle at last and join in the effort to untangle the wreckage.

All we could manage to do was to straighten the fenders of the motorcar. This allowed the wheels to turn, but without more muscle or machinery there was no way to get the car back up onto the track. By five that afternoon, near dusk, we sent the driver back for additional men.

He returned at seven with twenty-four laborers. They swarmed down over the motorcar and within minutes, like an army of ants bearing away the body of a prey, they set it back up on the tracks. By then it was pitch dark, and there was no way to extricate the Jeep from the flatbed which had tumbled with it into the jungle. So we got into the motorcar with the blessing of the guard, who made no secret of his elation that our mutual ordeal was near its end. We put the engine in gear and drove all the way to Laurel—backwards.

It was in Laurel that I first met Harvey Johnson. Harvey was a Fruit Company overseer in charge of the farm there, and the only white man in the village. He was a rangy, handsome Californian, with a deliberate way of speaking and moving. It was Harvey who had sent the second team of rescuers, which is why they arrived so much faster than the first group; he had accurately assessed what was needed and had responded with an efficiency entirely in keeping with his character, as I was to appreciate more and more over the coming years. He was already a part of the company establishment, with just the right mixture of color and dependability in his makeup to guarantee a successful future. When we met, he was in his early thirties.

In the following years, I returned to the tropics many times. After a while, each trip began to have the effect on me of a journey into my own past.

The reason was that very little ever changed.

The company divisions are enclaves; much like army camps. Each has a Division Headquarters. There are commissaries. There are three classes of clubs: the so-called American clubs or first-class clubs are the equivalent of the army's officers' clubs; the second-class clubs are for Latin clerical and supervisory personnel, similar to noncoms in the military; and the third-class clubs are for the workers—the enlisted men.

The American Club is almost always situated on the golf course. Labor is cheap, so every division has a golf course, built on company land at company expense for company use—and they are among the best in the world. Over the years, the company had spent an enormous amount of money on golf—on the courses, on their maintenance, on professionals who are brought in for demonstrations, on tournaments.

The big attraction at the second-class clubs is bowling, and most of them feature several lanes, plus the same embellishments you would find in the United States such as Coke machines, jukeboxes and a heavily chromed bar. In the third-class clubs, the attractions are drinking and dancing. The third-class clubs offer the only real action in the company town—unless you want to cross over into the *pueblo civil.*

The best house in town is occupied by the most important person, the division manager. The next most important person, his assistant, lives in the next best house. And so on.

The company owns it all, lock, stock and barrel. It owns the clubs and offices, the sheds, the land, the banana plants, every piece of equipment, the golf course and tennis courts, the sewer lines and streetlights and fire hydrants, the railroad lines, the motorcars, the trains, the docks, the boats, the airplanes, the radio stations, every house from the division manager's right down to the lowest worker's, along with every stick of furniture and even the plates they eat from and the knives and forks on the tables. Even the water in the faucets and the electricity in the walls are supplied by the company.

Division managers usually live in a house on a hill. In some areas, where the land is flat, these hills have been created artificially. No houses that stand as high as the division manager's may be built on company land, just as some state capitals in this country prohibit anything to be built that will stand as high as the state house—and for the same symbolic reason.

If a person has been assistant superintendent of agriculture and gets a promotion, it means he has to move from the house of the assistant superintendent of agriculture into the house of the superintendent of agriculture. He has to leave one neighborhood and move up next to his new peers in another, even though he doesn't want to move and even though he and his wife and family may be resented because his promotion has caused disruption in everybody's lives.

There are lots of ways in which the Fruit Company could have gotten out of the housing business years ago. But the tropical management held on: the power it gives them over the lives of their subordinates is not easily taken away. The Division Headquarters also houses the world's most extensive network of privately owned schools and hospitals, all staffed by company personnel, all operated at company expense.

The schools are operated at the community level as well, in the company farms which make up the rest of the divisions.

They are generally one room for all grades, a tropical equivalent of the little red schoolhouse of rural America fifty years ago. The education is not very good by U.S. standards, but it's a long way ahead of any local alternatives.

The farm communities range in size from two or three hundred people to several hundred. There is usually one overseer, and like Harvey Johnson he is often American, although there are some Latin exceptions. The workers' housing is either old style or new style: old style means large, two-story wooden barracks exactly like those used on American military installations from the time of World War I; new style is a tin-roofed cement block structure on a slab, which the company calls "ranch" housing. And each farm has its own workers' club, similar in design and function to an American Legion Hall in the North American Midwest, where there are occasional parties, a bar and imported movies—mostly American cowboy and Indian pictures.

The roads everywhere are dirt. I never could understand why no grass is grown anywhere in the vicinity of a worker's house; all year round he lives in a world that alternates between the fine dust that seeps into his house, his clothing, his lungs and his food and the rainy season variation on the dust which is a viscous, ankle-deep wallow of brown mud.

Over everything is the pleasant odor of burning soft wood, which the women use for cooking.

Despite the difference between life in the Fruit Company divisions and life in the United States, there is no denying that United Fruit has greatly improved the physical quality of the workers' existence. It has given them a measure of education where before they had none. It has provided for their health, where before sickness often meant long incapacity or early death. Even the homes they live in are far above the standard for other agricultural workers in the countries where the company operates. But, of course, these advantages to the worker, just like everything else in the company, are purchased at a price. Often, it is a price of which the workers themselves are unaware.

A visitor to a Fruit Company division is either accepted as a guest or he is turned away. Despite their one-time low tolerance for visiting employees from the North, tropical management of United Fruit is famous for its hospitality. If they like you, you're a guest for almost as long as you care to stay, free. If they decide they don't like you, you can't even get on company property. They like John Wayne, for example, and he has often visited the company's Central American plantations, anchoring his yacht in a bay protected by United Fruit property, playing cards long into the night with company "banana cowboys" and living as the company's guest for days at a time. But one doesn't have to be big movie star to enjoy the same treatment.

That hospitality was one of the things I liked best about the tropics. I felt I was with a company that knew how to do things right. And it was a hospitality that went far beyond free drinks and free food and a free place to sleep: with the right introductions, a guest who expressed an interest in the Mayan ruins, for example, would immediately be loaned the use of a plane and pilot for almost as long as he liked, and he would even be given a guide to help him understand what he was looking at. Or if he wanted to go deep-sea fishing, he went deep-sea fishing on a company-owned yacht with a company-paid crew.

In many ways, the tropical divisions of United Fruit still operated as an extension of the personalities and imaginations of men like Minor C. Keith and Lorenzo Dow Baker, updated to reflect the development of modern conveniences, half a century after their deaths. To visit them was to submit your freedom, your self-sufficiency and your pleasures to the dispositions of a benevolent, all-powerful host. To be employed as a worker was to submit your life and your entire future. And once you had submitted, no country or ideology or system of government on earth had more power over you.

That was the price.

I used to think there was no catastrophe so big that the company couldn't protect everyone, including myself, under its umbrella. We had our own army of workers (at one time 90,000 of them), our own navy in the Great White Fleet, our own air force, our own police. We had enormous economic and political power. We owned more land than the half-dozen smallest countries in the world put together. We controlled natural resources that ranged from timber to mineral reserves and soil so rich that in some regions even thirty feet below the surface the loam was still black with fertility. We raised our own food—not only bananas—but were also one of the largest cattle farmers in Central America. And because we were so nearly self-contained, we were almost invincible. There are a lot of Americans living in the tropics today who still feel that way. Some of them would

like to see the company use its power to make life better for the
workers and better for the countries in which they operate.
Others would like to see things stay just the way they are forever. But whichever way they felt they knew that the real power
of the company was controlled not in the tropics but in the corporate headquarters in Boston, and the mandate from headquarters had been singular and clear: make money.

During my numerous trips to the tropics in the years that
followed the indoctrination tour, I got to meet most of the company's agricultural management personnel. I met a lot of the
laborers and their families as well. And I liked almost all of
them. Among the Americans, many of the managers came from
southern towns and farms, and they brought with them many
of the habits—including some of the courtliness and some of the
bigotry—that characterized the South of thirty or forty years ago.
They considered those beneath them to be in their benevolent
charge, and although that attitude may be abhorrent, there were
few instances of unfairness or abuse.

There are relatively few crimes of violence, and even the
famous Latin machismo has a quality of innocence and good-
naturedness that is slow to give or take offense. There was a
time when many of the company's supervisors and management
people would carry pistols everywhere they went, but it is a
practice that has all but disappeared. Except for theft, very little
of the local crime crosses boundaries of race or social caste.

The company once advertised in a New Orleans newspaper
for a first baseman for its Honduran baseball team. As an afterthought the ad said, "Some knowledge of accounting helpful."

One of the company's supervisors, who later rose to become
an Assistant Manager of one of the tropical divisions, was a
Texan named Remington Patterson Coon. His friends called
him Pat. A few years ago, Pat told me about a murder he had
witnessed back when he was a young man.

He had been sitting on the steps of the bachelor barracks, just relaxing, watching the world go by. "Down below me, also on the steps, was this here laborer, honing his machete. He was stroking that there knife like it was a woman. Had an edge you could shave by. You know these fellows are proud of their machete and take good care of it."

I told Pat I knew that.

"Coming down the street is this other man, also a laborer, and the fellow on the stoop looks up real sharp, like he seen a rat. The man just ambles on by, and the fellow with the machete sort of gets up at a crouch, sneaks along behind him, then raises that knife over his head with both hands and comes on down with everything he's got—right here."

Pat pointed to the crown of his own head, then drew a line right down the middle of his face with his index finger.

"Just like a pineapple. Split him down to the shoulders. Two profiles, one half face on either side."

"Jesus," I said. "And what happened then?"

Pat Coon thought it over. "I'll tell you what happened then," he said at last. "I puked, that's what."

"Well, now," Black said, "that brings up one other thing that has been on my mind—my personal safety."

I nodded.

"I recognize that I would make a great prize for someone to kidnap while I'm on this trip. But I've thought it out, and I don't see any real problem. All we need do is see that the house I stay in is surrounded by armed guards. I'll be perfectly safe."

An hour later, Will Lauer and I had convinced him that it made more sense—and was probably better public relations—if he planned to stay at division headquarters. He'd be a lot more comfortable, it would be fare less trouble, and he'd be much easier to protect.

The more I heard about the trip from Black, the more it took on the appearance of a Monopoly winner's satisfied gloating as his own man came to rest on a property he already owned. Black knew he was way ahead, so he wanted to stop for a while, to count all of his money and hotels, to make certain that Park Place and Boardwalk were really there.

But when he returned from the trip several days later, it was clear that something he had seen had disturbed him. He walked into Jack Fox's office and said he was terribly upset by the condition of the workers' housing and that we should be thinking of remedies. By this time, Fox knew Black well enough not to entertain any false hopes of reviving the IBEC study or calling back the people from Abt Asociates. What disturbed him, Black went on, was that the workers in the tropics were living wretchedly because they had absolutely no sense of pride in themselves or their homes, and that they were letting *our* housing fall into ruin. He suggested to Fox that a film be made showing these people how to take care of the company's property.

I spoke to Fox about it too.

"That's just the problem, Jack, it's the company's house and not theirs," I said. "Would you have pride if you lived in a quonset hut or a tin-roofed shack belonging to your employer, and nothing in it was owned by you?" Fox shared my views: I talked with him at some length, I even sent him a memo on the topic.

Jack was a realist and he told me I would be smart to let the subject drop. But Eli never dropped the housekeeping movie idea and in the next couple of years he made several attempts to get one off the ground.

Chapter 9

THE TAKEOVER

EARLY IN 1969, other AMK personnel began making occasional appearances in Boston. Each new face was guardedly scrutinized by the staff and management of United Fruit, all eager for a clue to what the new company would be like. Years earlier, when I was in high school, I had read an eyewitness account of the German invasion of Brussels in World War I. Belgium had fallen, and the population was waiting for the conquering army to appear in the capital. By midmorning, a solitary messenger was sighted at the outskirts, riding a motorcycle. That was all for several hours. Then two or three soldiers appeared on bicycles and they too entered the fallen city. Later in the afternoon, more bicyclists appeared, and then the first infantryman or two. In between each new arrival were long stretches of nothing; the population just held its breath and kept waiting. By nightfall, the invasion had built to the volume of a thin, erratic trickle. But the trickle kept up all through the night, and it kept growing. The next morning it continued, and all through the day and the following night and the day after, until at last the stream had turned into a torrent of tanks and trucks and heavy machinery and communications equipment and material and hundreds of thousands of German soldiers. All this had been preceded by that one soldier on a motorcycle.

For me, a vanguard of the advancing AMK army arrived in the person of Phil Fuchs, who appeared one afternoon in mid-1969 at the doorway to my office.

Phil was in his early thirties, about my height; one of his very first remarks was about his weight problem, some self-deprecating half-joke that I quickly forgot but which was to be repeated in kind in virtually every conversation I was to have with him during the next several months. The other subject Phil wasted no time in opening centered around his being the nephew of Eli M. Black, and the implication was that he was a power to be reckoned with. He asked me to treat this latter intelligence as a secret, because nobody else in the company—either in United Fruit or AMK—knew about their relationship. I could tell from the way he said it that he was covering familiar ground: he spoke as though his uncle were the only thing he had to negotiate. Over the next several weeks, half a dozen different people came to me with Phil's "secret."

With his credentials thus established, Phil spoke of a new order, and told me to face facts: that the old United Fruit management had "pissed away money" and that I had a soft job: "Whadda you do, come in at around ten o'clock in the morning? Go home around four? You guys are living the life of Reilly, and goddammit that's all about to change."

I looked at him for a long time. If this was the first of the new order, what could the rest of them be like?

One of the virtues of public relations is also one of its greatest weaknesses: just about everyone can do some of it. I recognized, on more sober reflection, that Phil's only real problem was that he desperately needed something to do—and at first glance, my job offered a solution.

I quickly sensed that he was even more of a problem to his uncle. So one day I went to Black with a solution that involved spinning off a small part of my responsibility. Black listened attentively, and when I finished he said, "Good. Very good." He spoke carefully, pronouncing most of the letters in a word; it was a variation on the New York City accent, but in Black it sometimes sounded curiously flat, G-O-O-D, with little inflection. And that is how Phil Fuchs became vice-president of the United

Fruit Company Foundation. Later, when the wonders of that assignment began to pall, I suggested that Phil also be made editor-in-chief of the house organ. That suggestion, too, was V-E-R-Y G-O-O-D, and it was done. Still later when I left the company, Phil became vice-president in charge of public relations. The life of Reilly was finally his in its entirety.

We kept waiting for an invading army behind Phil Fuchs, but in the course of that long, suspenseful year we finally came to the realization that Eli Black's troops were a small cadre, some powerful friends, and lots of mirrors. The United Fruit management stopped asking how Black had accomplished the takeover, because the answer had become apparent at last; now the question was how had we allowed it to happen. And the answer to that was there for anyone who cared to examine himself sufficiently to find it. Black finally completed his negotiations with the shareholders and with the SEC, the last papers were signed, and United Fruit was his.

In normal times, a public relations man has a variety of jobs to keep him busy. He writes speeches for other people to deliver, and he might even deliver a few himself. He writes booklets and articles and press releases and brochures and annual reports. He tries to interpret public opinion for the people he works for and he tries to influence it. He deals with the press, holding conferences with them to explain topics that are too important or too complex for a mere release, and he tries to see that the good and true stuff gets printed and that the bad stuff doesn't, true or not. He may be asked to get tickets (for shows and games), to fix tickets (parking, speeding, etc.), to even get drinks and girls; but if he's any good at his job he won't be asked twice. He spends a lot of time thinking of creative, useful things for his company or his client to do. And he spends a lot of time responding to events not of his own making.

In my years with United Fruit, some of my responsive duties included bailing out a homosexual executive who was arrested for cruising the men's room at the Greyhound Bus Station, dealing with the police and the newspapers when one Fruit Company employee smashed in the head of another employee with a hammer in a drunken brawl (it killed him), suicides, blackmail, hurricanes, floods, expropriations and the occasional revolution.

The famous skyjacker who jumped out of a 727 over the jungles of Central America was a former Fruit Company employee. They picked him up when he got a haircut in a little fishing village in Honduras—and tried to pay for it with hundred-dollar bill.

PR problems can turn up anywhere.

Those are the things regarded as the incidentals: waiting for the balloon to go up or for the phone to ring. And, of course, no PR man really does make his living doing those things— they're the necessary footnotes to the way he spends the other 95 percent of his professional life.

A friend of mine was approached by a beautiful girl on the streets of Panama City one morning a few years ago and she asked him if he would be interested in a "little party." He said no and told her he was on his way to an important meeting. She was used to being turned down at that time of day, but with an eye for future business she asked him if she could give him her card. My friend was too polite to say no again, so he took it. It said three things: the girl's first name on the top line, the words "Relaciones Publicas" on the second, and her telephone number on the third. When he got back to Boston, he gave the card to me. He thought I might be interested in my competition.

When one company takes over another, the PR man can find himself in a strange position. The Securities and Exchange Commission has stringent rules about what a company may say about itself while a tender offer is in registration. And when the tender offer is actually being made to the public, the company that is being acquired has little need for an independent voice; as a rule, the acquiring company does all the talking for both of them. So for roughly the first six months of 1969, I found myself with almost nothing to do.

It was a great time to think. At the turn of the year I was nearing my thirty-fifth birthday, which added an unwelcome dimension to my problems. Midpoint in my life, just when my career should have started gathering real momentum, I felt instead that the only company I had ever worked for was disintegrating under my feet.

I remember a conversation I had with Boston basketball star, Bill Russell, at about that time, when he told me how he hated to play in the All-Star games. He told me that the teams weren't really teams at all, that they were groups of the best players brought together once a year for a single purpose—to make money—and that they had no other commitments of any kind. When Russell played with his own team, the Boston Celtics, he was part of a real organization, and even though he was a superstar he knew that organization was bigger and more important than the best of its members. On a team, everyone worked together. In the All-Stars it was every man for himself. I realized that almost overnight the raid against United Fruit had turned the management of the company into a group of All-Stars.

And I had the time to take a long, hard look at my own job. Russell had impressed me greatly with the decision he had recently made to leave the Celtics, to follow his own course even when it meant turning his back on an enormous amount of money, prestige and security. We were close friends, and we talked every day for two months before he made up his mind. His decision to quit started me thinking for the first time about alternatives to what I had been doing most of my life. I looked around my office one morning and took inventory. The first thing I examined was my file of press releases for all occasions. There were a lot of potential threats to a company the size of United Fruit, and I had attempted to anticipate every one of them. If anything went wrong, I had a press release which could be issued immediately presenting our official position. The file included what we would say if systemic chemicals turned up in our competition's bananas; we didn't use systemic chemicals, which appeared in both fertilizers and insecticides. There was a statement for release if word got around that we were doing business with Russia and that we were trying to increase the volume; the headline on that one was *not* "Why the Kremlin Loves Bananas," but the thought crossed my mind. There were releases on bananas in the dieter's regimen (nutritious but not fattening), as a panacea for heart disease (high in potassium), and for just about every social, political or natural coningency we could imagine.

I thought about my staff. There were approximately ten people in the department at that time, and they were all very good at their jobs. They worked well together, and I liked each of them personally. But now none of us had anything to do.

For the first time, I thought about the real consequences of how I had spent my sixteen years with the Fruit Company: what I had learned and how I had used it, whom I had benefited, and whether the good outweighed the bad. It was a depressing exercise. I decided I didn't want to spend the rest of my life doing the same things.

The more I thought about it, and the more I looked at the events around me, the more certain I became that public relations was helping to screw up the world. In back of almost every bad situation, every lie, every injustice, I could see the hand of the PR man pulling the strings, making things happen, covering things up. Public relations had taken over the government, the prisons, the protest movement, even the ecology. I was riding across the East River on my way in from La Guardia one afternoon and I saw the huge smokestacks of Con Edison belching pollution: the stacks were painted the colors of the American flag, and I knew instantly that a PR man had been responsible. I was looking at the phone directory one day and I began to study the distribution of the nation's area codes: why, I wondered, was 212, the area code for New York, an entire continent away from 213, the code for Los Angeles? And suddenly it came to me that there was probably some other reason for it but it could be the telephone company had deliberately designed the system so that if you made a dialing mistake, it would be a costly one. And it wasn't just the big companies that were doing these things; everybody had become his own PR man, and everywhere I looked it seemed as if image and style had taken the place of substance. The nation was operating on the principle of a commercial for Arpège. I read that the President of the United States had told a staff group, in discussing the War on Poverty, "Promise them anything, as long as we don't have to pay for it." Public relations had brought us the world of 1984 fifteen years ahead of schedule, complete with Newspeak and Doublethink. It was the new era of the hustler, the huckster—and of the Release for Every Occasion.

The night before I turned thirty-five, on March 8, 1969, I couldn't sleep. I thought of my family and my office associates, and I kept trying to find the balance between what I owed them and what I owed myself. I knew that, in the long run, the answers to my problems did not lie in any future I might make at United Fruit. At that time in my life I could look forward, at least in theory, to another thirty years of work.

The next morning I went in to see Jack Fox and told him I was quitting. I had no idea what I was going to do with myself, but at least my decision would give me some time to make up my mind. At first, Jack didn't think I was serious but when he realized I was, he said it was time we had a long talk.

He started out by reminding me how important public relations would be to United Fruit in the months ahead, when Black had completed the deal and began to run the new company. Fox said he would have a hard enough time integrating the old company into the new operation, and he didn't want to have to live through the experience with a key position vacant, a position that Jack felt Black might fill with one of his own people—specifically his nephew. I realized I had a responsibility to Fox, not only because he had brought me a long way in the company, and not just because I liked him enormously as a person; if any of my thoughts about team play and pulling together meant anything, this was a good time to prove it. Besides, Fox reminded me, I had an inside seat on one of the largest shows of its kind in corporate history, and I owed it to myself to ride it through to the end.

Chapter 10

A QUESTION OF IMAGE

AT ABOUT the same time that Black was signing with the Fruit Company in Boston, an equally historic event was occurring on the West Coast. César Chavez and the United Farm Workers Organizing Committee were signing a labor contract with the California growers of most of the nation's table grapes, after years of bitter struggle. Our management knew that the Fruit Company's lettuce-growing operations would be particularly vulnerable, now that Chavez was looking for new worlds to conquer. And the growers themselves knew it as well, so they signed up with the Teamsters Union instead, in an effort to block him.

The Teamster contracts were all "sweetheart" deals which paid lip service to the principles of unionism while favoring management at the workers' expense. Chavez heard what the growers had done, and he was furious. He arrived in the Salinas Valley shortly after the signing, set up headquarters practically on our doorstep, and demanded that the United Fruit Company be the first to rescind the agreements that had been signed with the Teamsters. Naturally he wanted the company to sign up with his UFWOC instead.

To that point, the negotiation had been conducted on a local level, and Chavez had no friends at all among the local growers. The Fruit Company's representatives flatly refused his demand, so Chavez got in touch with Jack Fox, who was still nominally United Fruit's president. He told Fox that things were either going to change fast or they were going to get very hot for the company all over the United States. He promised a boycott of not only the company's lettuce, but its bananas, its Baskin-Robbins ice cream, A&W root beer and anything else with either a United Fruit or a Chiquita Brands label on it. Chavez then put a little muscle behind the threat: within a few days of that telephone call, local UFW sympathizers began to picket United Fruit Company headquarters at the Prudential Center in Boston, and they passed out handbills that warned passersby not to eat scab lettuce or scab Baskin-Robbins ice cream, and to stay away from A&W root beer. Chavez was very thorough, and clearly a man of his word. The marchers also picketed some of the area's major chain stores. Fox began receiving cards and letters from people who promised to buy no more Fruit Company products until Fox signed with Chavez.

Chavez did not limit his attentions to Boston, or to Jack Fox. He had one of his leading New York backers, Anne Puharich, call Eli Black. Anne, whom I met later, is a professional champion of the radical chic, and the walls of her fashionable Central Park South apartment are decorated with collages of pins and banners from the causes to which she has given her support. Her call was effective.

Eli Black called Fox and told him to negotiate with Chavez. Fox said that there was no profit in bargaining from weakness with either UFW or the Teamsters, and that they should stand firm as long as Chavez continued to play the game of intimidation. He told Black the company should be willing to risk the strike which Chavez had threatened, that they should accept the boycott, and that they should meet strength with strength. He pointed out what he felt were the long-term hazards of dealing with UFW: that it was disorganized, not a union in the true sense, that it was operated by Chavez more in the style of a religion, and that the demands would probably escalate with the company's concessions. But even more compelling, in purely practical terms, was the fact that about 90 percent of the Fruit Company's banana transportation was handled by Teamster carriers, and if the Teamsters ever decided to use the very same techniques which Chavez had threatened, the company could be completely paralyzed overnight. Fox pointed out that the Teamsters had not attempted this kind of leverage at any point in their negotiations, but that Chavez had used that threat in his opening move.

Black did not agree. He told Fox that the company could not afford to take a UFW boycott, fair or not, legal or not, prolonged or not, because of the effect it could have on the already questionable United Fruit public image. On the more positive side, he told Fox to consider what a dramatic impact it would have on that image if a mighty organization of United Fruit's size and wealth were to sign a labor contract with this little Mexican-American. The argument hardly convinced Fox, but Black was adamant and he was also the boss. So Will Lauer was sent out to Salinas, California, to meet with representatives of both unions. Jack Fox himself went out and so did I—but all of us knew that Eli was in charge.

Will Lauer is a superb negotiator; he is tough, smart, patient, and fair, and he has tremendous physical endurance. A few days later, Will succeeded in getting the Teamsters to rescind their contract.

There were two powerful factors which Will Lauer was able to combine to the Fruit Company advantage. First, he knew that the Teamsters were anxious to keep a low profile while the future of Jimmy Hoffa, then a prisoner of the federal government, was subject to the good opinion of the public. And second, he knew that if the contracts were ever tested in court, they would fall apart: the workers had never been polled or even consulted—the Teamsters had negotiated the contract directly with United Fruit's local management, without any reference to their supposed constituency. (In that respect, it should be noted that UFW worked on exactly the same basis, and that until the H. P. Hood Company signed with UFW orange pickers in Florida some time later, Chavez had never gone to the workers with a poll to determine that he was, indeed, their legal representative.) So the Teamsters backed off, but not without a lot of resentment and hard feelings.

Lauer's next job was to sit down with César's lieutenant, Dolores Huerta, who had been trained by the militant labor theoretician Saul Alinsky. (César, too, was an Alinsky graduate.) Neither Lauer nor Huerta had much use for their considerable skills at the bargaining table, because Eli Black had already decided what he wanted the contract to say, and it was just about everything UFW had asked for. So both sides signed with little further ado.

The Teamsters national headquarters had agreed to the recision of our original contract, but when that agreement was relayed to the rank and file it didn't go down quite as smoothly as might have been hoped. The Teamsters have always been a force to be reckoned with on a local or regional basis, but one of the problems Hoffa and Dave Beck before him had with the union was in getting its various locals to act in concert on a national level. The Salinas Valley is about as far as a Teamster can get from Washington, D.C., without drowning, and the news was greeted with outrage. Where their own interests were directly involved, it seemed to me the California wing of the Teamsters couldn't care less if Jimmy Hoffa had stayed in jail the rest of his life. Once we had signed with César, when our troubles should have been at an end, they were, in fact, just beginning.

The Teamsters Local came out in force. They threw a picket line around the Fruit Company's property, they refused to let the field trucks roll either in or out across that line, and they began to make threats against both the company's property and its personnel. I was out there for about four weeks while the tension was at its height.

Meanwhile, back in New York, the management was insisting that we put a PR "face" on the situation which implied that the Fruit Company had come to the party of its own free will, that we were in bed with UFW because we really loved them and what they stood for—even though there had been enough publicity attached to UFW's earlier demonstrations so that any American over twelve years old knew that César had fired one across our bow and now had the same cannon pressed firmly amidships. So the negotiating team had to deal with the pressure from New York on one side and still avoid embarrassing the national Teamsters Union on the other. It was one tough situation to straddle: our new owner's view of public relations versus the possibility that the Teamsters might be pressured by our actions into calling a national strike against United Fruit. After more than six years, and after several shootings and extensive property damage and the loss of millions of dollars in crops, the UFW-Teamsters battle still rages.

Not all of our public relations efforts during that period were defensive, and not all of them were as depressing as our experiences in the Salinas Valley.

On the more positive side, for example, was MAS, the Middle American Sports Foundation.

The idea started a year before Black's raid, when I discovered that no Central American nation had ever won a gold or silver medal in Olympic competition. Statistically, this impressed me as being so improbable that I began to look into the situation in detail. I found that most of Central America's sports heroes were foreigners to those countries. And yet, five hundred years earlier, the Incan relay runners were among the fastest men on earth; they could do a mile in 6½ minutes, in the thin air and rugged trails at up to three miles above sea level. They were able to provide the Lord High Inca with fresh seafood every day, even though he lived 130 miles from the ocean. They carried messages as far as 1200 miles in five days—about twice as fast, over that same distance, as the mounted couriers of the Roman Empire.

I told Fox that I thought we should organize MAS, which would send some of America's best professional athletes to Central America for face-to-face meetings with their fans, with students and instructors and coaches from all levels and in as many cities as possible. The tours were not to include company towns; the idea was not designed as an alternative to the round of golf pros and movies for the entertainment of our employees. Fox agreed, the board agreed, and we were off.

That year, a series of 64 clinics were conducted throughout Middle America by some of the most famous names in sports.

Jack Fox and I even made the circuit ourselves, along with Bill Russell and K. C. Jones, getting the endorsement and support of the presidents of each of the six Middle American countries for the MAS program.

For a couple of years, MAS was pure gold. It attracted a lot of favorable attention to the company, engenered a lot of goodwill, and took United Fruit into areas where it had never been before. It was the beginning of the end of an era that both Fox and I looked at as the bad old days. By the clinics and tours, and by sponsoring Middle American participation in such athletic events as the Boston Marathon, we were reversing the low profile, look-the-other-way philosophy that had characterized our efforts, or lack of them, for the previous two decades. We were starting to tell our story—and we were telling it louder and more often than our critics were telling theirs. And we knew that if someday MAS could help produce a Honduran Roberto Clemente, we would have won ourselves important goodwill while contributing visibly to the morale of our host nation.

If we needed further evidence that MAS was working, it came in the reaction of the division managers. They hated it. It was just about the same response one might expect from the division commanders in Viet Nam if Bob Hope had decided to take his show to the people in the cities rather than the troops in the field.

A year later, MAS was reviewed by Eli Black and Phil Fuchs, and the company withdrew all support and let MAS die.

The passing of MAS meant far more to me than merely the end of a professional accomplishment in which I had taken pride. I had come to feel, during those few years under Fox's leadership, that the company had attained a kind of moral watershed in which the excesses and indifference of the past were being balanced by a commitment to a new, responsible direction.

United Fruit Company had earned the title, *"El Pulpo,"* because it deserved it. The company, and the business climate in which it operated, reliably mirrored the variable, highly adaptive values of the American government. In the beginning, a boatload of bananas came into Boston and created a business where none had existed. It was a modest, even humble start for a new form of business organization: the multinational company. United Fruit had come into existence without any ethical anchor. Its loyalties, where it had them, were directed to power, to money, to growth, and certainly not to the nations in which the business had its roots and from which it derived its profits. Within three decades of its founding, United Fruit had become a government unto itself, in many instances more powerful and larger than the host countries in which it operated. The values of the era allowed the company to take without giving back in reasonable proportion. It allowed growth without sharing of the wealth, without the creation of meaningful local opportunities, without changing its style or direction when conditions warranted such change. United Fruit bought protection, pushed governments around, kicked out competition, and suppressed union organization.

In word and deed, United Fruit mirrored American economic and political determinism. When Theodore Roosevelt wanted the Panama Canal, America got the Panama Canal. Our interests there were protected by the United States Marines, who were used to make sure Colombia couldn't put down the revolt that made Panama a separate and cooperative republic. Presidents Monroe and Coolidge read the same doctrine into history: they protected continental neighbors against a marauding world; they sent troops to protect marauding U.S. interests against our victim neighbors. For the most part, all that was seen of these efforts north of the border were the benefits. But at the other end of the telescope, the United States Government and the Octopus whose interests and policies that government nurtured were seen as one and the same: brutal, monolithic, oppressive.

Through the decades, the policy of the American government abroad had wavered. It drifted from the peaceful commitments of early Pan-American congresses to the bare divisiveness of 1928 Havana Conference. But through this conflict between the efficiencies of capitalism and the ideals of democracy, America blandly assumed—because Americans at home saw so little of the consequences of their deeds—that the actions of the past in Central America could be washed away at any time with words, and that Yankee conduct would again be trusted by all Latin Americans merely because we said once more that it should be.

At about the same time that MAS was getting under way, I told Jack Fox about another idea to which he also gave his approval and support. This time the product was a film, and the title was *Yanqui Go Home:* it was to be the first honest public look the company had ever taken at its operations in the tropics. We had done lots of films in the past, of course. The emphasis in *Yanqui* was on the word "honest."

The most recent predecessor of *Yanqui Go Home* was a movie I helped produce back in the early sixties, entitled *Treasure of the Tropics. Treasure* was the philosophical descendant of Ed Whitman's Living Circle advertisments: the treasure was Green Gold, a bounty Columbus never dreamed of, and the most enlightened company in the hemisphere, United Fruit, was down there to mine it—luckily for everybody.

I can't believe that *Treasure of the Tropics* or any film like it ever convinced an audience of anything at all. In fact, looking back, I can't believe I had anything to do with it; but I did. I recall doing such things in the course of making that movie as taking three dozen freshly laundered T-shirts in various sizes with me to the tropics, so that only clean, sparkling field laborers and shining, carefully rehearsed kids passed in front of the camera. I made sure we used as few close-ups as possible, regardless of the subject, and even though kids all over the world go barefoot in warm weather, I carefully avoided shots of anyone without shoes. There was even one scene in the movie where we faked a blowdown of one of our plantations. We got everything from window fans to airplane engines, and pointed them at the edge of one of the banana farms. We had carefully nicked each plant to make sure it would fall, then we smeared some vaseline over the camera lens, played some sprinklers in front of the trees, and turned on the fans and engines. It was a nice, artistic scene.

Treasure did absolutely nothing for United Fruit. It was a favorite at ladies' clubs and American Legion halls, where the audience was predisposed in the Fruit Company's favor and the movie just confirmed what they already believed. It went over very well in the Catskills, too, where resorts kept using it as an inoffensive and relatively scenic excuse to turn out the lights. (I recall that Grossingers, in particular, ordered the film again and again.)

Yanqui was conceived as a film that would reach college students and that would directly address all of the issues that *Treasure* so carefully skirted.

The film was to be in three parts. The first section would be the critical case against the Fruit Company, and it would trot out every negative thing that had ever been said, whether it was true or not and whether it was fair or not. It quoted some of the company's severest critics as well as some of the most thoughtful: *Fortune*'s devastating article from the 1930s, John Gerassi, Arevelo, Asturias—anyone who had a bad word was given a hearing. The second part dealt with how the company had portrayed itself through the years, culminating in highlights taken from *Treasure of the Tropics*—the contrast between parts one and two were startling. The third portion, which comprised roughly half the film, was concerned with looking at the company as it really was.

The main points we wanted to make were that the company had changed—that there had been a watershed in the 1950s, and that the change was continuing into the future; and that the company itself was aware that it still had a long way to go.

We were right in the middle of producing *Yanqui Go Home* when Eli Black took over United Fruit. In the course of reviewing some of my department's activities, I mentioned the film and he asked to see a print. I explained that it had not yet been totally edited, but a day or two later I was about to show him a rough cut. I watched him closely during the projection, and I knew the film was in trouble. When Eli heard or saw

something that he thought was dangerous, he would physically
withdraw: his lips became tight, his hands and feet drew inward toward his body, and he gave the impression of literally
shrinking in size. He said nothing until the film was ended, then
told me he had some serious reservations. He began making
a list of people to whom he wanted me to show the film before
it was edited in final form and printed. The list included Kaplan
and a number of the men he had brought with him from AMK.
Most of them had never even been to Latin America and knew
next to nothing about our operations there.

So I resisted. I told him that *Yanqui Go Home* was a professional effort to give the company some credibility with an important sector of its national public, and that I was not about
to let men who had no knowledge of either the company or
public relations meddle in my area. For the next several days,
Black tried most of the stratagems at his disposal short of actually
commanding me or firing me, but I would not move. The film
was too important a factor in the direction the company would
go, and in where I would go as well: I absolutely refused to
return to ten years earlier, when I had been either too young
to know better or too ambitious to care. I did agree with Black
that he could show it to anyone he wanted, which was entirely
his prerogative, but I was not about to allow those people's comments to change the film's effect. Black finally gave in, still with
uncountable misgivings, and allowed the film to be completed.

The victory was short-lived, but *Yanqui Go Home* survived
long enough to get the highest ratings possible from film re-
viewers and to receive hundreds of bookings and favorable
publicity for the company as well, ranging from feature stories
in the *Boston Globe* to plaudits from *Business Week*. It was
called a whole new approach in sponsored industrial films.

Not *all* of the reaction was favorable. I remember the comments the film got from Harvey Johnson in particular. Harvey
was the former Fruit Company supervisor of the farm at Laurel
in Costa Rica when I had my adventure with the derailed
motorcar, and he was now in charge of the company's entire
tropical operations. He told me he hated the movie. He said
he had never seen a company sell its product on television by

knocking it. I explained that the film was not a TV commercial and was not selling a product, and that a public relations film was not the way to "sell" the idea of United Fruit Company anyway. Harvey remained unconvinced.

Eli Black remained unconvinced as well, and eventually he decided the film was too "dangerous" to continue showing. Before that decision was reached, *Yanqui Go Home* had helped precipitate at least one more crisis—a crisis from which neither Eli nor I would recover. But that was still three years in the future.

One hot Friday evening in July, 1970, my telephone rang just as I was about to leave my office. The call was from Washington, D.C., and the Latin voice on the other end identified the caller as a man I had met a few years earlier in Honduras. He said he was the acting press secretary to the president of Honduras and it was clear from the tone of his voice that he had no time to waste on pleasantries. He said that he was calling me at the request of his government, and that it was imperative that I come to Washington immediately. He knew the schedule of flights, and he wanted me to take the next plane.

Ordinarily, my immediate interpretation of such a summons would have been that the Fruit Company was in some new kind of trouble in one of its tropical divisions, and the government was about to do something drastic. But the tone of his voice convinced me that this was not a threat but an urgent request for help.

My speculation was prompted by political problems in Honduras. I knew that she was at war with Salvador, and Honduras was taking a heavy beating from the American press. I drove directly to Logan Airport and flew to Washington.

The first few minutes of our conversation confirmed my guess. I was assured—and I believed—that the Salvadorians had fired the first shot and were carrying the burden of aggression. They were also getting some excellent advice in the area of press and public relations. Every time they attacked, they managed to construct the action as a defense or a retaliation for some far more reprehensible act, real or imagined, by the Hondurans. Their press releases and news stories drew heavily from the lexicon of our own Pentagon which at the time was strained so mightily in explaining the American actions in Viet Nam. The Salvadorians had the advantage of knowing where the action was going to take place before their adversaries found out about it, and they managed to engineer a small mountain of sympathetic publicity in most of the North American media. They had even advanced the fiction that their war of aggression was the result of a riot which had followed the defeat of the Honduran soccer team in Salvador a few weeks earlier. The Hondurans were being beaten up, which was bad enough, but what hurt even more was to be miscast in the role of bully. They wanted my advice on press relations.

I had never handled the PR for a war before; it was exciting and I got right down to business.

I was honestly sympathetic with the Honduran position; despite the overtones of comic opera, I knew that people were getting hurt and some were dying—and I felt that if Honduras wanted to turn the tide of the war, they were first going to have to turn public opinion.

The Hondurans then began to tell me their own version of the events that had led up to the opening of hostilities. They said that the Salvadorian allegations were totally false, that there had been no connection between the loss of the soccer game and the firing of the first shots. What happened, they claimed, was that some "Salvadorian pig" had urinated on a Honduran woman, and that was what had started the whole thing. I told them I thought the soccer story was better—besides, it was the kind of thing you could mention in print and on the early news.

They told me they had turned to me because the United Fruit Company "had the best public relations in the world." It occurred to me that implicit in this compliment was the mandate that I come up with a better story if I didn't like the one they had just dished up. I agreed to help, but for the time being they would have to make do with the one about the "Salvadorian pig" peeing on the woman.

The first night I provided them with the names of a number of key newsmen in this country and in Latin America to whom

I felt they should take their version of the facts. I advised them to avoid rhetoric and exaggeration, that they should concentrate on conveying credible information systematically and fast. I explained that they were going to have to combat the highly professional Salvadorian press and that the slightest suspicion of propaganda or falsehood in their efforts would bias the media against everything else they said and did. I did not say they had to deal in truth. I recommended that they organize a system for issuing dispatches on a regular basis, even when there was no real war news. I pointed to this country's success in balancing news from the battlefield with news from the conference table, and I suggested that a program of peace initiatives be reported in detail as a part of every press release. The next day I had a breakfast meeting with the ambassador and later in the day I showed them how to set up their news bureau and helped to get it started and made a few phone calls for them.

I told them they needed to get about ten American journalists to visit Honduras and that I would arrange to get a five-thousand-dollar fund together to be used for their travel and expenses to and from Honduras. Surely their reports would make a difference in the propaganda war. The Hondurans liked the idea so I drafted a telegram to the president of the Inter-American Press Association and the president of the Overseas Press Club from the president of Honduras.

> The Republic of Honduras is greatly concerned over the inadequate and often erroneous reporting in the North American press in recent weeks. Reports of genocide, rape and other crimes against humanity are completely erroneous and are propaganda intended to cloud the real issues. In the interest of truth and fair play the Republic of Honduras extends an invitation to any accredited journalist to visit our country and see for himself what the facts are. To facilitate those journalists who do not have the necessary funds to visit our country we are offering the IAPA a five-thousand-dollar grant to be used for travel and expenses to and from Honduras. A similar grant is being made

to the Overseas Press Club. Please cable your member-
ship and advise them of this offer.

> *Osvoldo Lopez Arellano*
> *President*
> *Republic of Honduras*

The telegram was approved by the president of Honduras
and went out over his name exactly as I had drafted it. The
five-thousand-dollar grant came from United Fruit.

The Hondurans were grateful, and I promised to give them
any more help they might need as events progressed. Over the
next several weeks, in Boston, I followed the news of the war
in the papers and on television.

During those few weeks, slowly at first but then more surely,
I saw the Honduran cause reported more sympathetically. It
started with a few relatively neutral stories on the war, and
then some suggestions that a particular incident or skirmish was
not the fault of Honduras but of Salvador. And as I saw that
my suggestions were paying off, I became more and more caught
up in the excitement of what was happening. The Hondurans
had been calling me fairly regularly to try out new publicity
tactics or to ask for my ideas; now I found myself thinking of
the war with growing enthusiasm as my side began pulling
ahead, and from time to time I would call them with new suggestions for further widening the gap. The war I was fighting
was the war of the press. I had started losing sight of the war
in the jungles of Honduras and Salvador.

One day, when the war seemed near to its end, I made a
final telephone call. By this time, the man who had called me
initially had returned to his country's capital, and I reached him
at the Presidential Palace in Tegucigalpa. We chatted for a
moment, and he said that everyone there felt Honduras was
very near to bringing the hostilities to a successful conclusion.
I asked him if he would be interested in one final suggestion—
an idea I was certain would finally break the back of the Salvadorian public relations effort and discredit them once for all.
He said he would be very interested indeed. The idea, I told

him, was to place some Russian weapons in the hands of dead
Salvadorian soldiers, and then to announce the "discovery" of
these weapons to the press, with pictures, at the next news conference. Chinese weapons would be even better. I even had
some ideas for where they could be obtained.

The response at the other end of the line was a moment of
awed silence; then he said he would pass the suggestion along
to his people.

Within just a few hours of that telephone call, reality caught
up with me. I began to think of what it could mean if they were
really to follow my suggestion, and I felt rotten.

Besides, we had already accomplished everything we were
after. Why should Honduras jeopardize all it had gained?

As I thought about the possible consequences of the suggestion, I also started to question my own motives. There were two
elements to my participation of which the Hondurans were still
unaware. The first was that when the Hondurans called me
down to Washington that first time, I was already smarting
from a very skillful and successful attack which the Salvadorians
had mounted against United Fruit. As soon as the war had
started, Salvador had alleged that the Fruit Company was supporting the Hondurans, which we decidedly were not, and that
we were behind much of the Honduran aggression. This press
campaign was simply the smoke screen behind which the government confiscated our Tropical Radio operation and put an
end to our shipping operations in Salvador, and it was used as
the excuse for kicking us out of the country. So I was predisposed in favor of the Hondurans even before they got in
touch with me.

The other factor in my participation was my discovery, shortly
after my trip to Washington that Friday night, that Salvador
was getting its public relations advice from a Norte Americano
as well: a former high-ranking official in the United States Department of Defense was down in Salvador, advising the government what face they should put on every move they made.
I soon began to picture myself in a game of chess with an unseen opponent, and the more I tried to anticipate his next move,
the more I came to think the same way he thought. The phony

weapons ploy was not my own invention: our troops in Viet Nam had been doing it off and on for the better part of a decade and it was used in Guatemala in '54. I saw this same American advisor behind the whole series of lies that had led to our being kicked out of Salvador, and I was determined to beat him at his own game.

I was just about to call back Tegucigalpa to tell them I had had second thoughts about my suggestion, when I heard that the Organization of American States had arranged a truce. For the time being, the war was at an end.

Now there is no way to tell whether Honduras would ever have used my stratagem. I'm still grateful that I didn't happen to think of it a day earlier.

At around the same time as the Honduras-Salvador War, another kind of war was taking place off the coast of Ecuador. The Ecuadorian Government had recently extended its maritime borders to the two-hundred-mile limit, and when boats of the American tuna fleet refused to recognize the new territorial claim, Ecuador's navy forced them to shore and seized the boats and their catches. As a result, I read one morning in *The New York Times* that the Longshoreman's Union was boycotting Ecuadorian cargoes on ships entering New York Harbor. Longshoremen are quite patriotic, as they have shown more recently with their refusal to load wheat to Russia.

At first I was delighted. The boycott meant that no Ecuadorian bananas could be unloaded in New York City, which would ease some of the competitive pressure on United Fruit. In fact, I had even played with the idea of helping organize such a boycott just two weeks earlier—until I realized that it would be illegal for the Fruit Company to become involved in restraining our competition. The longshoremen had the same idea without my help, so we were going to get all the advantages of restraint of trade with none of the risk or stigma.

A few hours after reading the story, however, I discovered that a load of Ecuadorian bananas was at that very moment about to enter the Panama Canal for the long trip north—on board a ship of the Great White Fleet. There had been a slight gap between our own sources of supply and the market demand in New York, so we had purchased some bananas from Ecuador. We decided to reroute the cargo to Japan.

That particular ship was the largest and the newest in the company's fleet, and just a few weeks earlier I had attended a reception at the Algonquin Club for the Chairman of Kawasaki Industries, in whose yards the ship was built. I remember one of the Fruit Company's executives, a Texan, telling me of his impressions of the trip he had made to Japan while the ship was under construction. He was oblivious to the fact that several of the distinguished Japanese visitors were following our conversation with interest. "They build this fuckin' bamboo scaffolding all around the fuckin' hull," he said, "just like in *The Bridge on the River Kwai*. Then they swarm all over it, thousands of them, some of them with no shoes, each with some little job to do, something to rivet or weld or paint or hammer or measure"— I looked over at the Kawasaki executives as the Texan continued, and they all smiled broadly and looked right back at me, waiting for him to continue "—swarmed over it—just like a bunchafuckin-monkies."

Kawasaki got its revenge when one of the new ships reached midpoint in the Pacific. I got a call from Captain Charlie McAuley at my home at about ten-thirty, two or three nights after we had changed the ship's course. He said it had sailed into a typhoon, and that a huge crack had appeared in the forward deck, right to the waterline on both port and starboard sides. The next morning we got word of what we both imagined to be the ship's last transmission: they were taking on water faster than they could pump it out, the ship was breaking up, and the end seemed only moments away. The radio signal was weak and getting weaker.

Despite it all, the ship survived. The captain discovered that the seam in the deck closed right up as soon as he signaled the engine room for reverse. So he sailed to Midway Island—about nine hundred miles—the same way I had returned to our farm in Costa Rica by motorcar some fifteen years before: backwards. Perhaps someday he will become Director of Public Relations.

In the early months of 1972, I spoke with Dick Severo, the new Latin-American editor of *The New York Times,* based in Mexico City, about a story on United Fruit. Ordinarily, I would have steered clear of someone in Severo's position. But he was new in his assignment and relatively inexperienced: he had been an urban news reporter, and had little background in politics, economics or business. I banked on the likelihood that he would be favorably impressed by what he saw. There were two reasons I felt we needed a story at that time. The *Yanqui* film had recently been released, and I wanted to support it with as much favorable company publicity as possible. The second reason was that Eli Black, like most chief executives, liked shiny things, and nothing was shinier than a feature story in America's leading newspaper.

I suggested to Severo that he visit the Honduran Division, which was the company's tropical showplace. He agreed and I made the arrangements. I made sure he got all the literature available, saw all the right things, met the right people. I learned in subsequent conversations with both Severo and his New York editor that he had been favorably impressed and that we were going to get a pretty good story. I did not know in advance, however, and neither did Severo, that the story would appear on a slow news day and start with two columns on the newspaper's front page. After learning that it had been scheduled for publication, I told Eli Black.

When I finally got my copy of *The New York Times* that April morning, I could hardly believe my good luck. Not only were we on the front page, but Severo wrote the best story United Fruit had ever received. He said that we had lived down the legacy of a bygone era and had evolved into the one of the most socially responsible companies in the Western Hemisphere. I'm sure Severo believed everything he saw, and I'm sure he believed everything he wrote. I'm equally sure he didn't see very much.

The part that frightened me was that Eli Black believed it too.

When I spoke to Black in his office that morning, there was no question that the article pleased him. He was smiling, buoyant and expansive, and there were several times when he reached

across from his chair to mine and patted me approvingly on the
arm, a form of benediction he reserved for people he really, truly
liked and who were either in terrible trouble or who had just
demonstrated that they were capable of doing something a-b-s-o-
l-u-t-e-l-y b-r-i-l-l-i-a-n-t. But he made it clear that he felt the
article reflected the company as it really was—that there was no
finagling, and no luck, involved in getting such a story into print.
He said that it was about time, that we had it coming to us.

Someday, I thought, *The New York Times* might do a story
on Eli Black himself. I knew it would make interesting reading.

He was born Elihu Menashe Blachowitz in Poland in the
early 1920s and came to this country with his parents at an early
age. He lived and went to school in the Lower East Side of New
York City.

While he was alive, *Who's Who* merely listed Black's name,
address and title as chairman and chief executive officer of
United Brands. Eli believed that less is often more, and besides,
he did not want to call attention to the time he had spent as a
rabbinical student at a Yeshiva, or to the fact that he was an
ordained rabbi.

Black was particularly conscious of his religion. He made a
point, whenever possible, of being home before sundown every
Friday, he observed the Jewish dietary laws to some extent and
he regularly participated in synagogue services. A few years ago
he backed a publishing venture whose charter was to preserve
the Jewish traditions while at the same time modernizing them
and making them more relevant. The Prayerbook Press has been
highly successful, but I am certain that Black did not invest in
it to make money; rather, he was backing his convictions, and
the success was incidental. I am also reasonably sure that if the
Press had lost money, he still would have continued to support it.

For a short time after he left the Yeshiva, Black led a small
congregation on Long Island. But he wasn't happy. He talked
very little about that period in his life, but I often had the feeling
that his discontent derived from the fact that a rabbi exerted
little real influence in the practical world and no power. He told
me that he had become a rabbi because it was the family busi-

ness, just as many Catholic boys become priests, or doctors' sons follow in their fathers' footsteps. I remember Richard Nixon once making the comment, "I would have made a good Pope." And I am certain that Eli Black felt the same way about himself. But the Rabbinate lacked the hierarchical organization of Catholicism—and its potential career goals. Black's father was a rabbi, and possibly Eli's view of his own future as a rabbi was colored by the relatively low religious status achieved by his father, who was a ritual slaughterer. I remember seeing such rabbis going about their business in the meat markets of Brooklyn when I was a boy: small, dark, bearded men, alien in appearance, anachronisms from another world.

During one interview with a reporter from *Time* magazine Eli learned that the forthcoming article would mention his descent from a line of ten generations of rabbis. He protested: "I don't want that in the story."

"But it's news, Mr. Black," the reporter said. "My editors wouldn't let me take it out."

Black put up his hands to close out the reporter's response. "No, no, I don't want it in. Say I come from ten generations of intellectuals and scholars. Forget the rabbi business."

But however Eli felt about the status of his first calling, there is no doubt that the Talmudic training had a profound effect on his view of the world. It had given him the mental discipline to see a problem from all sides. He was contemplative, and I seldom knew him to make a decision that was either hasty or impulsive.

So after three years as a rabbi, Elihu Blachowitz changed both his profession and his name.

He first went to work for an investment banking house and then he went to work for Julius Rosenwald, the financier. In short order he became one of Rosenwald's "bright young men" (the phrase is Black's own), and he helped his new mentor put together the equity package for the sale of the Empire State Building. As a reward for his services, Rosenwald gave him a fractional share in the transaction and from then on, Eli told me, he did not have to worry about money. Afterward, Black began to examine carefully his role in the sale, and he told me that he

came to the conclusion he was every bit as bright as Julius
Rosenwald. That led him to the conclusion that, "If Rosenwald
could do it, I could do it too," almost the exact conclusion he
drew from comparing himself with the great expert on mergers,
Jimmy Ling. So he began looking seriously for new worlds to
conquer.

In 1954, he found what he was looking for. He was invited by the financial interests controlling AMK Corporation to
take it over as president; he was still in his early thirties. Originally, AMK was the stock exchange symbol for American Seal
Cap Corporation, a five-million-dollar sales company that made
lids and liners for glass bottles. The acquisition of John Morrell
Company was still thirteen years in the future. Black built his
business slowly and methodically, diversifying, strengthening the
company's financial base, and eventually abandoning the bottle
cap business in favor of more fertile fields. By the time he swallowed Morrell, Black personally had gained ownership of 10
percent of the AMK Corporation's stock—enough of a bankroll
to enter the fastest game in town. He started conversations with
the management of Libby, then with Johns-Manville, then with
the Great American Holding Corporation, all with the object of
acquiring them. For a number of reasons, those talks never led
anywhere (one of the reasons was his preoccupation with the
prospect of acquiring United Fruit), but clearly Black saw himself as well along the road to becoming the builder of a conglomerate.

He was gracious in company, and he prided himself on his
manners. Black believed that his strongest point was his ability
with people. He once told me that no one could handle people
the way he could. He realized that he didn't have the charisma
of a Jack Fox or a Mayor Lindsay or a César Chavez, and
charisma was a quality he greatly admired. But he had something
else, something that to him was even more important. He was
very good at winning people's confidence.

Except for the last year before his suicide, he lived simply.
I visited him at his home in Westport, Connecticut, where he
lived before the move to the bigger house, and found it pleasant,
modest, tasteful. There was a painting studio for his wife, and

there was a swimming pool. Lots of books were on the walls, despite the fact that Black's business life must have left him very little time to read for relaxation. A short time after my visit, he bought a larger house very near the one I saw. He kept the old house and his daughter lived in it. He also kept an apartment on Park Avenue and another in Boston. He rode in a chauffeur-driven black Cadillac. The Blacks had a son as well as the daughter, both in their twenties.

He didn't smoke, and he usually drank Fresca or sometimes quinine water. He had no hobbies, had little interest in athletics as either a participant or spectator. He dressed conservatively, wore no jewlry, had a plain black leather band on his wristwatch. He gave the impression of a man whose pleasures were mainly of the mind.

Black's taste in art, as in furniture, ran to the modern. He favored the rectangular abstractions painted by his wife Shirley, although his collection included works by Avery, de Kooning, Hartley, Basking and Rivera. If Black could have had his way, Shirley Black's name would have ranked with theirs. She had had a very successful showing of her works, but Eli deserved much of the credit for their profitability: he made certain that his friends in the investment community were invited—and he also sent invitations to the officers of his companies. At one opening, shortly after the acquisition, all the Fruit Company officers who were in the country at the time put in an appearance, and all of them except three—Jack Fox, Dick Berry and me—bought a painting. A lot of those same men found themselves out of work shortly after that show. More than one told me he wished he had saved his money.

But E. M. Black, the man who was so good with people and who was ordinarily so careful in his manners and his choice of words, had another side to his personality. It was a side that most people never saw. I had my first glimpse of it when I resisted his demand that I submit *Yanqui Go Home* to editing by people I felt were not qualified, but that was only a hint, a preview of coming attractions. It was not until Eli started his battle with WNET, Channel 13, in New York City that I was to see that other side.

Shortly after *The New York Times* article appeared in the spring of 1972, I received a telephone call from one of the producers of a show called *Free Time,* which was on public television, originating from Channel 13 in New York. He told me they were planning to do a show on the social responsibility of large corporations, and that he had seen *The New York Times* story on the Fruit Company. He wanted me to provide someone from United Fruit to debate on the company's behalf. I learned that other *Free Time* guests had been Jane Fonda and Tom Hayden and Abbie Hoffman and I began to get a feel for what kind of a show it was.

My immediate choice from the company was Victor Folsom. Vic was the former general counsel and a director of United Fruit—the only director, as I mentioned, not to approve the company's takeover by AMK. He was now retired and living in the West, but he had more knowledge of the company, more cool and more TV experience than anyone else in the company. He would have been ideal. I took the idea to Eli Black. I barely finished explaining the situation to Black when he told me that he, himself, would appear.

It had never crossed my mind that Black might think himself capable of defending United Fruit in a national TV debate. I tried to explain the risk he would be taking, particularly when we still didn't know who was going to be speaking for the other side. He was unshakable, so I went back to my office and called Channel 13. Of course they were delighted.

The show was to be aired live on a Tuesday, but by the middle of the previous week they still had not found an advocate for the opposition. Finally, around Friday, they decided that their man would be Juan Saxe-Fernandez, a professor of sociology at the University of Mexico, a Costa Rican by birth. As soon as I heard this, I started calling around to find out what I could about him. I spoke with the head of the department of sociology at Boston University and all of our public relations consultants in the tropics. I hired a researcher to develop any information she could, and by Sunday we had a pretty good book on him. We found out that Saxe-Fernandez was about thirty, a Socialist, and had written a couple of books on Yankee imperialism. I told all this to Black, and was even able to give him some of Fernandez' writing. I began to prime Black with information about the company, and I produced a seven-page memorandum highlighting United Fruit's history. It presented the Disney version of the Guatemala episode, the early days of the company's formation and growth, our noninvolvement in politics, the extent of our land holdings, labor relations, statistics on wages and benefits, education and health care, the company's economic contribution to the areas in which we operated and some of the more persistent myths that he might be hearing that Tuesday night—along with some rebuttals for disarming them.

The shooting was scheduled for ten o'clock at Channel 13. Eli went to the ballet earlier that evening and arrived at the studio a few minutes before ten. He met Saxe-Fernandez for the first time two minutes before they both went on camera. Standing beside him Black looked every inch the mogul, and Fernandez looked like a frail peon, shy and vulnerable, with a mismatched jacket and pants and a rumpled shirt that was open at the collar.

Within the first few minutes of the show, Black knew he was in trouble. Fernandez scored a couple of blows, but what hurt far more was the moderator's obvious partiality to Fernandez' point of view, and his antagonism to Black's. Eli not only had to deal with a tough and experienced fighter, he also had to ward off a few blows sent his way by the referee. The United Fruit Company was an easy target, and the moderator had clearly decided the case in advance of the evidence. Black made up his mind early in the show that he had to become more assertive if he wanted to stay in the fight. Toward the end he fell into a couple of obvious traps, and at moments he became overbearing in his insistence on being given equal time. He said at one point that he had spent "countless hours" discussing the Fruit Company's role with the President Figueres of Costa Rica; as soon as I heard that, my stomach did a figure eight and the moderator landed on him with undisguised glee. Did he think it right, Black was asked, for the head of a company to have that kind of access to the head of a sovereign nation? It was a tough question to answer, and Eli didn't have much of a comeback. His overall performance was acceptable, but his opponent had touched some vulnerable areas. After the show his daughter summed up what had happened that night: some people came to the program with a bias in favor of United Fruit, and some came to the show with a bias against United Fruit—and there was nothing in the debate to cause either side to change its mind.

The debate lasted about thirty-five minutes, which was a few minutes longer than we had expected, and then we left the studio. It was only the next day that we discovered there had been a second part to the program. Bob, *Up the Organization*, Townsend, the late Stephen Hymer, a professor from the New School, a civil rights lawyer, and a blue-collar worker from the General Motors assembly line in New Jersey sat around for the rest of the hour, talking about the social responsibility of large companies. Several references were made to Eli Black and the appearance he had just made on that same program. One of the comments cited "the Eli Blacks of the world"; the tone was generally uncomplimentary but moderate. Black was enraged.

He flew to Boston and confronted me with the situation. He told me the whole thing was my responsibility, that it was my fault that I had not done my "homework," that I had failed him, that he would either forgive but not forget or forget but not forgive—I don't remember which. His mouth was distorted, his face waxed and waned between ashen horror and purple wrath, and he used language which I had never heard from him before. He said I had allowed him to be trapped, that I had not appraised the situation sufficiently in advance, and that the moment he had set eyes on Saxe-Fernandez he knew he had no chance at all of coming out ahead.

I pointed out to Eli that he was the head of one of the most powerful corporations on earth, with assets of over a billion dollars. In addition, he personally was a millionaire many times over. People generally won't find his great power and wealth all that sympathetic, regardless of whom he happens to be standing next too. I asked him to think of how Lyndon Johnson or Richard Nixon must feel, unable to pick up a paper or tune in a radio or television news broadcast without seeing or hearing some slighting reference to his performance and his character.

That seemed to slow him down for a minute; I think he found the comparison flattering, and I could see him turning it over in his mind. But when the minute was up, it was more of the same. He told me he wanted apologies in public from Channel 13. He said several times that he wanted revenge. I had never in my life heard anyone say seriously that he wanted revenge.

There was no public apology or private one either. There was no revenge. After a few more spasms, the incident was filed in Eli's memory bank where I knew it was available for instant retrieval any time he wanted it.

Then in June, Eli got a thoughtful postcard from the folks at Channel 13, saying, "We thought you might like to see the show on which you appeared . . ." and letting him know that it was going to be repeated in the fall. They knew he didn't want to miss it.

They were wrong. Black wanted very much to miss it. He called me down to New York and told me to "kill it" or get the objectionable parts edited out. He said he wouldn't take no for an answer.

I called the station and tried to get in touch with someone from *Free Time,* but they were all gone for the summer. I spoke to the Channel 13 lawyer and told him that Black did not want the show to go on. We talked about it for a while, then the lawyer said he wanted to listen to the tape and would call me back. An hour later he told me what I already knew: that there was absolutely nothing about the show that was libelous or that in any way infringed on Black's rights. I asked if Black could rebut the show if the station chose to run it, and he said no to that as well. He assured me that public television was sensitive to the requirements for equal time and fairness and that they were on very safe ground in flatly refusing Black's request.

The show was aired, although in a later time slot than originally scheduled. It was so late that Eli Black may very well have been its only viewer. But a viewer he was, and the next morning he called my office in a rage that made our previous discussion seem trifling.

One of the reasons for his new anger, it turned out, was that he had tried to reach me at home when the show ended, well after midnight, and he had been told that my telephone had been disconnected. I had just moved into a new house, and he had called my old number. I told him that I had given the new number to his secretary several days earlier, but that only seemed to agitate him further. He told me he would be in Boston that afternoon, and that he would call me to his office as soon as he arrived.

He did. He called so soon after he got in that by the time I entered his office, he still had his hat and coat on. If anything, he seemed even angrier in person than he had sounded over the telephone. There was more of the language of a couple of months earlier, and we generally traveled over the same old ground we had covered at least twice before.

Then, in tones that labored for control, Black opened Phase Two of our meeting with the statement that he was not going to fire me. I knew the game was finally over.

From that moment on, I just had no stomach for my job. I was to stay with it as a consultant for another fifteen months before submitting my final resignation, but my twenty-year commitment to the company was fatally bitten that day in September, 1972, almost four years to the day since I first heard of Eli Black.

Costa Rica, mid-1950s. *Left to right:* Mrs. José Figueres, President Figueres, Vice-President and Mrs. Richard Nixon stopping for a banana break at a Fruit Company plantation. That bulge in Figueres's hip pocket is no banana—it's a .45. (*Foto Carrillo*)

All-expense-paid press junkets in the early 1950s were an important part of United Fruit's public relations strategy. This one, in 1953, took top editors and publishers on a tour of five countries visiting United Fruit divisions and capital cities. They did a great deal to influence public opinion and alert Americans to the "Red menace." This picture was taken at the airport in Tegucigalpa, Honduras. *From left to right:* Richard V. Lindabury, N.Y. *Herald Tribune;* George Chaplin, editor, *New Orleans Item;* E. S. Whitman, United Fruit's PR director; William Gray, editor of the International Edition of *Life;* U.S. Ambassador to Honduras, John D. Erwin; Martin O'Neill, *Time;* Robert Lund, industrial editor and managing editor of Detroit News Bureau, *Journal of Commerce;* Gaynor Maddox, NEA Service, Inc.; Dan Kidney, N.Y. *World Telegram and Sun;* Peter Celliers, foreign editor, N.Y. *Daily News;* Robert P. Vanderpoel, financial columnist, *Chicago Sun-Times;* and Sergio Santelices, Latin American editor, International News Service.

Edmund S. Whitman joined the Fruit Company shortly after World War I, as a timekeeper in Honduras, and became the company's first vice-president in charge of public relations in the late '50s. "Whit" and Edward L. Bernays, the "father of PR," set United Fruit's public relations strategies of the '40s and '50s. The film *Why the Kremlin Hates Bananas* was his pride and joy. When Thomas Sunderland joined United Fruit, Whitman resigned nine months later because of ideological conflict.

Thomas Elbert Sunderland, president and vice-chairman of the board of directors during the '60s. One of Sunderland's first decisions was to take the film *Why the Kremlin Hates Bananas* out of circulation and destroy the prints. Although he resigned from his post in 1969, Sunderland remains a United Brands consultant.

The title frame from *Why the Kremlin Hates Bananas.*

United Fruit workers load a banana ship at Puerto Armuelles, Panama. Under the golden peel, the bitter taste of trouble.

J. Arthur Marquette was in charge of the company's steamships and pier operations for many years, which included handling the details of United Fruit's involvement with the CIA in the Bay of Pigs invasion.

What does a banana have to be to be a Chiquita*?

It's sort of like passing the physical to become a Marine.

The banana's got to be the right height. The right weight. The right everything.

Right off, it has to be a good eight inches along the outer curve. And at least one and a quarter inches across the middle. It has to be plump. The peel has to fit tightly. The banana has to be sleek and firm.

It has to be good enough to get through a 15-point inspection. Not once,

but three separate times.

Occasionally, though, a banana comes along that's got everything going for it—except maybe it's a smidgen under minimum length.

We should pull it, we know. But our inspectors have hearts, too.

Which is why you may sometimes find a Chiquita Brand Banana that isn't quite eight inches long.

Come to think of it, though, you sometimes find Marines named "Shorty," too.

Chiquita® Brand Bananas.

*Chiquita is a registered trademark for United Fruit Company's brand of bananas.

A product with appeal. In this case, the appeal is to a copywriter's slightly prurient sense of whimsy. *Life* didn't think it funny, but a lot of magazines were too polite to admit they got the joke so they ran the ad.

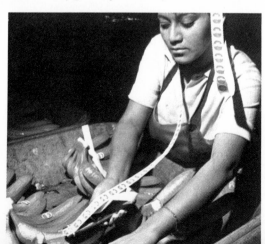

By applying tiny blue Chiquita stickers — over one billion of them each year—the company was saved in the early '60s.

Bananas used to be shipped on their stems until the industry converted to boxes.

Ed Toland, known as "the man who had everything," was treasurer of United Fruit until several of the company's abortive acquisition attempts provoked a sense of failure and caused his resignation in 1968. It was not long after that he jumped to his death from the 22nd floor of the Yale Club in New York City.

The man in the middle, talking to two United Fruit executives, is Herbert C. Cornuelle, who was president at the time Eli Black took over United Fruit. The occasion was a conference of United Fruit executives from all over the world, called together in December 1968, to hear the news that the United Fruit directors decided to merge with Black's AMK.

Left to right: Eli M. Black, John M. Fox, and Robert Raymond, New York Stock Exchange stock specialist, taken on July 1, 1970, the first day the United Brands Company was admitted to trading on the New York Stock Exchange. Black bought the first 100-share block. (*Wagner International Photos, Inc.*)

(*Donald MacKay*)

Eli M. Black, the new conqueror, lands in San José, Costa Rica, in 1970, to visit United Fruit's plantations and to attend receptions in his honor. *Left to right:* Señor Gronblad, United Fruit executive in charge of protocol in Costa Rica; John M. Fox, the deposed United Fruit chief executive; Eli Black, the winner of the tender battle; Morton H. Broffman, an AMK director, subsidiary president and strategist in the takeover; and Richard C. Johnson, senior vice-president of United Fruit. (*Laboratorio Color Flex*)

Harvey Johnson, a young-old banana cowboy whom Eli Black liked and kept promoting to the point where at one time he was in charge of all banana production, the fleet of ships, and all terminal operations.

Phil Fuchs, Black's nephew, was employed by the company for most of his business career. His last job was handling the company's public relations.

Eli Black in Washington for the second inauguration of Richard Nixon. On the evening before, he hosted a dinner in Washington for the ambassadors of the Central American countries and their wives. Seated next to Black are: Mrs. Joseph Jova, Charles Meyer, Assistant Secretary of State, Shirley Black, and U.S. Ambassador to Jamaica Douglas Fletcher.

Bob Gallop, United Brands' general counsel and longtime friend of Eli Black. He resigned from the company after a heated exchange with Black, just a couple of months before Black committed suicide.

Ed Gelsthorpe, a top-flight executive, hired by Black in the summer of 1974 from the Gillette Company where he had been president. Gelsthorpe, a professional manager with an impressive business record, quickly took command and provided the leadership the company needed. After only a few months, Black became torn between his concern for the needs of the company and the possibility that Gelsthorpe would turn in a star performance that would underscore Black's own failures.

Eli Black in one of his favorite poses.

Chapter 11

TRANSFORMATIONS

WHEN A COMPLEX organization begins to fall apart, it doesn't all go at once; it isn't like a bomb in the cellar or a plane crash. It happens in bits and pieces, a fissure here, a missing part there.

The process starts with the people. They become angry. Or frightened. Or restless. They take longer lunches. They change their work habits; those who worked long hours now work less; those who took it easy begin to show up on time and leave later. They talk a lot about the man at the top.

There was a lot of talk about Eli Black. About his poisonous personality. About the way he manipulated people. About his indifference to the human consequences of his acts. And most of all, about his incompetence. "What the hell were we so afraid of?" one Fruit Company executive asked me one day. "We thought he was some kind of genius."

"A lot of people still think he is," I said.

I doubt if any of the criticism ever reached Eli. But he could see it in the faces of the operating management, and especially in the attitude of the employees from the tropics. The old diffidence was gone. In its place, more and more openly, I was beginning to see contempt.

But if Black was the victim of sniping, he was also a fair marksman in his own right. A lot of the old management—

even those who had honestly transferred their loyalties to Black after the takeover was complete—became the victims of his attacks.

It was an especially bad time for Jack Fox, who had been assigned a place in the back seat once Black began running the company. Jack had spent almost all of his adult life building things and making them work. Now he found himself with little authority, almost no responsibility and cast more and more in the role of scapegoat. The new management had to blame someone for the company's poor financial showing in the time since Black had launched his attack, and although the attack itself was largely responsible for the slump in morale and earnings, the traditional target in such cases is the former management.

Black was very critical of the acquisitions and diversifications that Fox and Cornuelle had completed before the takeover. The acquisitions had been more extensive than Black, on the outside, had calculated; once he gained control of the company he found that most of the legendary one hundred million dollars in loose cash that had made United Fruit such an attractive prize in the first place, and which Black had cited earlier as holding the key to a doubling of the company's future profitability, was simply not there. Fox and Cornuelle had either spent it or committed it to investments or capital improvements just exactly as they had told the shareholders they had. Earlier, Black had chosen to ignore these denials, but now that he was in control of the company, he was forced to explain the situation to the shareholders. Two obvious possibilities were ruled out immediately: Black was not about to admit that he had seriously overpaid for the company (after all, he still had the usual option holder's reasons for wanting to keep up the price of the stock), and he was not about to admit that Jack Fox had been telling the truth all along. So instead he began attacking the quality of the acquisitions Fox and Cornuelle had made. In a series of quick sales and divestitures, sometimes at bargain basement prices, Black set about trying to restore some of the company's liquidity.

Certainly not all of the acquisitions predating Black's arrival were without their problems. Some of them had started to go sour from the beginning, and others showed early signs of deterioration once they came under new management. But the banana business was also showing new weakness, and most of its problems were a direct result of the takeover: things dragged on too long while everyone held their breath, and no one was really minding the store. To blame all of these problems on Fox was neither honest nor fair. I knew that Jack had made his decision to stay on with the new company for a variety of complex reasons—but the most compelling was simply loyalty. He had an enormous psychological investment in the company and in his job, and he was not the kind of man who quickly turned his back on threats or in the face of new opportunity. It would be impossible to miss this quality in Jack's character, and I soon realized that Black not only recognized it but that he was taking advantage of it almost daily. It was a galling, demeaning experience for Jack and for those of us who watched it.

On November 9, 1970, in a letter to "the men and women of United Fruit Company," Black wrote, "It is seven weeks since I became chief executive and chief operating officer of the Fruit Company. I didn't write to you any sooner because I did not want to engage in the usual platitudes or vague promises."

He went on to point out that 1970 had been a difficult year due to hurricanes and floods and an acquisition program that did not pay off. He also cited overhead and staff that were "completely out of proportion to realistic requirements." He said that the new management had moved to dispose of certain losing or marginal operations, and that costs had been reduced by ten million dollars by the termination of nearly four hundred people.

The letter closed with the statement: "Obedience in an organization is easily achieved—very often it can be commanded —loyalty, however, must be earned and won. My object is to win your loyalty and enthusiastic cooperation by providing you with a strong and effective leadership."

Loyalty. Enthusiastic cooperation. Leadership. Coming from Eli Black, the words sounded like wishes. And a lot of the employees thought they were funny.

It was becoming increasingly more difficult for me to write the kind of stuff Eli wanted and was paying me to write. I had a particularly tough time with the next to last annual report I produced for United Brands. What could I say that would sound like Eli Black and still quicken the reader's pulse and strengthen the shareholders' sagging confidence? One dreary January afternoon, Eli called me to his office to discuss another matter and after we finished he casually asked me how the annual report copy was coming. Before I had a chance to respond, we were momentarily interrupted by his secretary bringing in the afternoon tea. As she placed his cup in front of him, I glanced at the teabag and suddenly there it was—one of those one-liners compliments of Salada. I don't remember the exact quote but it was some trite saying to the effect that "progress requires change." So, out of a combination of desperation and devilment I told Eli the annual report was coming along just fine and that we were going to focus on the fact that "progress requires change." Eli thought that sounded just dandy and those words found their way into his annual report letter, printed one hundred thousand times and distributed all over the world. It was a rotten thing to do and very unprofessional too, but what I was being asked to do was also rotten and unprofessional. I recall that at the time I almost wanted to be caught, to be exposed for putting the words of the teabag into the mouth of our chairman, to be fired for doing it. But, Eli never glanced down at his teabag and never knew how much he owed to that unknown writer of teabag wit and wisdom.

Following the 1970 cutbacks and divestitures, Black made improvements in the employees' pension fund; the changes didn't cost him anything, but they gave people the impression they were getting something better than they had had before. He came up with a stock option plan and a stock purchase plan. Those didn't cost him anything either.

At the same time, other key managers of the company were resisting Eli. They were busy working on their résumés, making new job contacts or restoring old ones, even plotting half-heartedly among themselves about ways of getting rid of Black and Kaplan. Many began drinking more than they usually did and sleeping less. Much of the energy previously directed to the job was now going elsewhere.

In many ways, Eli's problem was similar to that of the company: both were being judged by performance rather than by empty promises or platitudes. And in both cases the performance was showing the makings of real disaster. Eli could not run the company, and he was proving it. He could not delegate responsibility, and he wouldn't accept criticism. It was an environment that was tolerable only to those who were even more afraid to leave—or who were willing to knuckle under. Increasingly, Black found himself surrounded by managers who were as incompetent as he.

That incompetence, coupled with the lack of a moral anchor, was to set the company adrift on a meandering, unguided course that would culminate in Eli's suicide and the company's exposure in massive graft and corruption. If Eli had possessed the vision and wisdom to supply that moral anchor, the corruption probably never would have occurred. But even lacking the anchor, if he had had the simple competence to surround himself with men who possessed the skills which the company itself institutionalized in the first fifty years of its history, the corruption most likely would never have been exposed.

But he was unable to manage power and all the money, fame and flattery that went with it. Instead, feuding, greed, hostility and bitterness filled the void Eli Black created.

In 1970, the first year after the takeover, the company showed a net operating loss of two million dollars. This figure was thirty-three million below earnings in the year prior to the takeover. It was also somewhat less than the bonanza Black had cheerfully projected while still on the outside looking in. One of his worst problems was one he never mentioned to the employees or the shareholders or the financial world—and one of which he, himself, may have been only partly aware: he had to run the company at the same time that he learned the business. This kind of on-the-job training is not only difficult and demanding on the trainee, but it is costly to the company and extremely risky. Black seemed to understand only part of the risk: it was obvious that if he succeeded in turning United

Fruit around from the straits in which his raid had placed it, he would be in the strongest possible position with the company's management, its employees and its shareholders; I don't think he gave much thought to the alternative if he should fail.

Black was a victim of his own mystique during those early months. He met frequently with the rest of the Fruit Company's management (with Fox safely shunted off to a siding), but a lot of those managers held him in awe, partly because they feared for their jobs. Black got very little backtalk in those days, but he also got very little straight talk. In fact, he was told only what people thought he wanted to hear and in some areas where the truth would have been uncomfortable he heard very little. As a result, his expectations became more unrealistic at the same time the real situation was deteriorating dangerously. Black was telling what he thought was the truth when he made his optimistic early forecasts for 1971, but the intelligence on which those forecasts were based was usually incomplete and often wildly inaccurate.

By April of 1971, the truth became inescapable. About a year later, Black told me of what he had been feeling during the annual meeting, which took place during that month. He said that all he could think of was Harold Macmillan, who once had been asked by a reporter how he could appear so cool and unflappable during times of great crisis. Macmillan had said, "Unflappable—perhaps on the outside but you should see it flapping on the inside."

Until that time, it was the closest Eli had come to admitting to me that he was scared.

Although there is no way of telling whether he calculated the risks in advance, it would be safe to guess that Eli was aware of what his failure cost him by the time the first year was out. The awe he had first inspired disappeared, and a lot of the fear along with it; in their place were beginning to appear the signs of disillusionment. The management knew Black was vulnerable, and they had learned that he could not do their jobs as well as they themselves could.

Black's efforts at cost reduction went beyond divestiture. In his letters to shareholders, he spoke of "cutting out the fat, but not the muscle and bone," shopworn terms from the butcher's idiom which one might suppose he inherited with the acquisition of John Morrell and Company and had used with its shareholders there as well. He ended the new product research previously initiated under Fox. He put an end to the company's projects in aquaculture and mariculture. He stopped all experiments with rice and corn crops in Central America. And in areas where he did not call a halt to such activities, he often asked for a slowing down which was tantamount to killing them.

The company's cash position was way down, and its debt, of course, was enormously increased by the package of financial paper Black put together in buying it. In time, the debt was so great that the company had to earn forty thousand dollars every working day just to make the payments on that debt, before it could turn a penny in profit.

The company was now in debt by almost the same amount as its book value before the takeover, when United Fruit really did have one hundred million dollars in the bank. All this, despite the fact that the acquisitions made the surviving corporate entity about three times as large as United Fruit had been on its own.

Not all of the former Fruit Company staff stayed on for the new game. One early loss was the man who, ironically, had been most responsible for the company's decision not to resist Black from the beginning. Every time anyone raised a voice of protest, Herb Cornuelle had dispatched it with an epigram. He kept telling us things like "it didn't matter whose name was on the stock certificates," meaning that it didn't matter whether the company had one shareholder or fifty thousand. Yet, as soon as it was all over, Herb was the first to bolt. He let us know that he had accepted the presidency of a company in Hawaii. It was the Dillingham Corporation, whom he and Fox had courted so ardently on the Fruit Company's behalf. His decision to leave hurt many of us including Jack Fox. It also left a serious hole in the management.

The day Herb left Boston, I offered to drive him out to the

airport. On the way, he grew reflective about his seven years with United Fruit, and his pensive mood continued inside the terminal as we waited for his flight to be announced. Before United Fruit, Herb had been with Dole Pineapple Company, by non-Hawaiian standards a relatively small company. He told me that he had come to Boston to see if he could "make it in the big time." And he said he had discovered that there is no big time.

"You're wrong, Herb," I told him. "There is a big time and we were in it. We just didn't have what it takes to stay."

Cornuelle didn't like that. He had played and lost; now I felt he was trying to convince himself the game had never taken place. Five years later, in November, 1975, Herb and I met in the Algonquin Club and I told him I was writing this book and planned to go into his role in the takeover. Herb understood and then quietly said, ". . . believing Eli Black and not trying to fight him off were the biggest mistakes of my business career. I think about them a lot."

Another divestiture Black attempted during this period was the Panama division. Del Monte Corporation was ready to buy it, and the sale would have satisfied the Consent Decree that had been hanging over United Fruit for so long. But the Panamanian Government resisted. They told the company that if it tried to pull out there was a good chance that United Fruit's entire Panama holdings would be expropriated before the sale to Del Monte was completed. So the negotiations with Del Monte shifted from Panama to Guatemala, where all our troubles had started.

I felt the reasons we went back to Guatemala to satisfy the conditions of the Consent Decree were the same reasons we had gone there in the first place: it had a weak, permissive and corrupt government, and the company's social responsibility to the country was not likely to be made the issue that it had been in Panama. It worked; the company's Guatemalan operations were soon sold to Del Monte, following, I was told, the promise of a bribe.

In the early sixties, about ten years before Del Monte became interested in United Fruit's Consent Decree problem, Aristotle Onassis approached the company and offered to buy its two Panama divisions. He wanted them because he felt they were viable and potentially very profitable properties, but more than that because they were to be his first step in a plan to get control of the Panama Canal. If he could accomplish this, he would automatically have some degree of control over the Panama Canal. His idea was to give himself some preferential Canal treatment with respect to tolls for his huge fleet of oil tankers and possibly even fix excessively high rates for his competitors and his archenemy, Niarchos. It was a wild scheme and he never shared many of the details with the company or its intermediaries. The company turned him down for a number of reasons, principally because United Fruit did not want Onassis as a competitor in the banana business. Onassis could have pursued it further through the courts but he never did. One reason I suspect he didn't was that around that time Onassis became distracted by another major project—Jacqueline Kennedy.

"In a contest such as this," Black told writer Chris Welles after winning control of United Fruit, "strategy and aggressiveness are very important. But often you win not because of your own abilities but because of the other side's mistakes." He was speaking of Zapata. He could easily have been speaking of United Fruit.

On December 21, 1970, in a letter to shareholders, Black said, "I am confident that 1971 will be a turn-around year for the company."

In 1971, the new company showed a loss of twenty-four million dollars, the largest in its history.

I was certain at the time, and I remained convinced, that the decline in earnings, quite apart from Black's overpayment for the company and regardless of the new accounting practices, was due in large measure to the struggle he had precipitated within management for control of the new company's direction—a struggle he had guaranteed against throughout the takeover from his first conversation with the Morgan Guaranty Bank. Black's style of management was completely contrary to everything that had gone before. His surrogates, particularly Kaplan, became minutely concerned with details of all the other executives' operations, and they constantly second-guessed them, overruled their recommendations, dismissed their experience as irrelevant, ignored them and demeaned them in ways that were sometimes subtle and sometimes not. There had been very little in the way of a management team to begin with, but Black's and Kaplan's chaotic style threatened to demolish what little there had been.

The year 1971 saw a major restatement of the company's financial position with the introduction of accounting procedures which until then had never been used by United Fruit. Company accountants "wrote up" the assets, in effect diminishing the large goodwill account and giving the appearance of having gotten more for the investors' money. As *Unaccountable Accounting* was to observe later, "Spring brought forth the appraiser's wisdom."

Also that spring, Black and I had a long talk about the company's position and its prospects. He stopped by my office at about six o'clock one evening and stood at the window, his hands clasped behind his back, watching the lights come on across the Charles River in Cambridge.

"You know, Thomas," he said, "I'm finally coming to realize something very, very important. About this company. About the people I've been listening to."

I got up from behind my desk and crossed to his side of the room. There were two chairs beside where Black was standing; I settled into one and waited for him to continue.

"Everything I've heard—from the management—from the operating personnel—has been wrong."

"Not everything," I said.

"Everything," he repeated. "When little pieces of the truth are buried in exaggerations or lies, they might just as well be lies too."

I nodded. I knew exactly what he was talking about, and that the only hope for change had to begin with his recognizing the problem.

"Every time someone asks me for a forecast," he said, "I turn around and ask someone else. I ask in the divisions, and the people I talk to don't even hear the question. They think I'm really asking 'How are you doing your job?' So the answers are just what you'd expect. 'We're doing just fine, Mr. Black. Things have never been better, Mr. Black. The last quarter was an atrocity, but we've got it turned around.'" He sat down wearily in the chair beside mine, pushed his glasses up and rubbed his eyes. "Damn."

"When you don't give people room to say anything else, Eli . . ."

"I know, I know," he interrupted, "that's not the point. The point is . . ." He put the glasses back in place and studied the back of his hands for a moment, searching for the words. "The point is, when someone in the tropics lies to me—or someone in my own management team withholds the truth because he knows it will hurt—hurt him, hurt me, what's the difference—then I turn around and repeat the lie. To a shareholder. To a reporter. To people in the financial community. People who trust me. People who know my word is my bond."

"You've been giving some pretty optimistic forecasts," I said.

"And I'm going to be called to account for it," he said. "It's time to face reality. The company is in deep, serious trouble."

"Hearing you say that, Eli, is the best news I've had all day."

He looked at me obliquely. It was clear he didn't know what I meant.

"You have to face the facts before you can change them," I said. "Every time I hear you say all our problems are behind us, or that it's the fault of the previous administration, or that our troubles are due to an act of God, I shudder. You've been describing the future like a dream—not the way it is now or is likely to be, but the way you want it. And more and more of what you say about the past sounds like an alibi."

He noddel slowly. The conversation depressed him, but he was coming to grips with the facts.

"Thomas," he said, "something has got to be done about it. Something decisive." He slapped his knees for emphasis and stood up. "Something decisive," he repeated.

"It's got to come from you, Eli."

He walked out of the office, then reappeared a moment later at the door. He was smiling. "We should talk more often, Tom." Then he left again.

I finished the work on my desk, packed my briefcase and headed home. For the rest of that evening and again the next morning I thought about the things we had discussed. And I kept coming to the conclusion that even though it was up to Eli to take the initiative, there were areas in which I could be of help. For one thing, the time was probably right for me to repeat my offer to take a hand in the wording of his public pronouncements about the company's immediate future. Certainly any written statements could be more deliberate and moderate than they had been in the past. I also had some thoughts about how to open some of the channels of communications that until then had been blocked because management and the operating personnel feared reprisals for their candor.

But when I called Eli's office at midmorning, I was told he was not in. Maury Kaplan had been placed in charge of the company. On the spur of the moment, I was told, Eli Black had decided to take a long vacation.

He was gone for a month.

By the time he returned, the situation was almost beyond the point of salvation. Many of the former Fruit Company holdovers who were strong enough simply swam away from the sinking hulk, rather than risk being pulled down in the undertow which they felt was coming.

Mel Levine, former executive vice-president, quit. Will Lauer, former vice-president of personnel and labor relations, quit. Chuck Hulsebosch, the former treasurer, quit. Len Wilson, former vice-president in charge of planning, quit. And so did several other key men.

Captain Charles McAuley, head of the company's shipping operations, dropped in on one of his fellow executives one day

looking pale, shaken and physically ill. The fleet was a tremendous expense item, and Charlie was under constant scru-
tiny. He had just come out of an especially bad session; his face
was florid and he appeared to be hyperventilating. A friend advised him to go see Joe Miller, the company doctor, who diag-
nosed Charlie's condition as the possible precursor to a heart
attack. He was taken immediately to Peter Bent Brigham Hospital and three hours later suffered a severe coronary; even with
the advantage of an advance warning, he nearly died. Shortly
afterward, still in his fifties, Charles McAuley retired.

George Howard was one of the Fruit Company attorneys. He
hated the idea of the merger and began looking for another job.
I met him in the garage beneath the Prudential Center one
morning back in about March of the year of the takeover.
George had been a pilot in World War II and had been shot
down over occupied Europe. Just as he landed, a German soldier
had shot him in the head; it took away one eye and did some
ghastly things to his sinuses, but he lived. When I saw him in
the garage that morning, he was standing rigidly beside his car,
stiff-legged, his feet spread and his arm on the car roof for support. His face was gray and he was in obvious pain. One eye
had always given the impression that he was weeping, or about
to weep, but now I saw that his entire face was covered with
perspiration. I asked him what I could do to help, but he told
me that it was already passing. He said he had had attacks like
that before, that it was something to do with his back.
I suggested he go see the company doctor, but by that time his
pain was clearly subsiding and he began to relax. He said it was
nothing a doctor could help. A few weeks later, George died of
a heart attack.

Most of the former Fruit Company board was replaced. Some
were pushed, some jumped. At this writing, only one man remains who was a United Fruit Director—George Peabody
Gardner, Jr.

It was also apparent that Black began having trouble within

the ranks of his own AMK organization. Of all the officers listed in the AMK 1968 annual report, only two were still with the new company thirty-six months later. A particularly serious loss was Morton Broffman, the former president of John Morrell who had been with AMK for many years prior to Black's run of acquisitions. Broffman had served as Black's number two man until the takeover of United Fruit—but another Black protégé, Maury Kaplan, was elevated to that position once the Fruit Company acquisition was completed. Shortly after Black named Kaplan chairman of the executive committee, Broffman quit. (Herb Cornuelle told me that he, too, had taken Kaplan's appointment as a cue for his exit: he said that he found himself dropping from the number two position in United Fruit under Fox to the number five position in the new organization under Black, Kaplan, Broffman and Fox.)

Broffman was well liked within United Fruit; he was quiet, intelligent and poised, a good listener, and he knew the food business. By contrast, Kaplan was just the opposite: a poor listener who often fell asleep at meetings. He was strictly a numbers man who knew very little about the business. If Black had appointed Broffman in Kaplan's place, the company's future would have been unquestionably different.

And so, most likely, would Black's.

I finally decided to leave United Fruit in the summer of 1971. The event that brought on the decision to leave happened several weeks before, in late spring.

I was aboard a helicopter between Newark and LaGuardia. Because of traffic we had been routed across the southern end of Manhattan, and I found myself looking down at the familiar sights of years ago—the West Side Highway, the piers, West Street, where I had spent some of the most important years of my life. We passed over the company piers and, like the company itself, they were in the process of being dismantled. All that remained of Pier Three were some twisted boards, dust and rubble. We swung inland over the tip of Manhattan and I looked east toward Brooklyn where I was born and north at the cluster of skyscrapers in the evening haze.

When I was a boy, I had nightmares about those buildings. They were mountains that I could not climb. They had no footholds, no doors. They just rose straight upward, almost without end. I knew that my only way out of the nightmare was to get into them to reach the top. But I felt I never could—they were designed to keep me out.

As I looked down at them, from the helicopter that day, they were nothing, just parts of the landscape, no longer challenging or overwhelming or frightening. I began to think that the important parts of my past—the company, the city I had grown up in, my ambitions—were all dead—that important, irreplaceable parts of myself were gone forever. By the time the helicopter landed, I was deeply depressed.

I went into the nearest bar and for the first time in my life got drunk.

I woke up the next morning at the airport motel and took the shuttle to Boston. Over the next several weeks I began to sort through what had happened and where I was going. Finally, in mid-July, I went to see Eli Black and told him I was through.

Eli exploded. He stood up and shouted at me. "This is a mistake! You're making a big mistake!"

I didn't answer, but something on my face must have slowed him down.

"Thomas," he said, "this is not the way to get more money from me. If you want more money, the way to get it is to ask like a man."

"Eli . . ." I started.

"You just walk in and say, 'Eli, I need more money.' Not, 'Eli I'm going to quit.'"

"I don't want more money," I said.

He looked at me without comprehension for a moment longer, then sat down heavily in his chair. "Well, then," he said, "you must be sick. Mentally sick."

He even went so far as to give me the name of a psychiatrist he felt could help me. I did the best I could to convince him I wasn't sick. Next he offered me the job of heading up one of the operating divisions. Again I said no.

Finally he suggested I take a trip around the world. He told me he had just done it himself and it had worked wonders; in fact, the trip had been suggested to Eli by his own psychiatrist, and he had no doubt it would be just as good for me.

"That's a good idea," I said. "I'm not going around the world, but I will do something I've never done in my life—I'm going to take a real vacation."

"Good, good," he said, genuinely happy. "You'll straighten right out. You'll see. Take along some cheap novels and stick your feet in the cold ocean once in a while. You'll see."

I took off the entire month of August and spent much of it in Maine trying to decide what I wanted to do with the rest of my life. I even read a couple of cheap novels and put my feet in the water. When I came back I went to Eli again and told him again that I was quitting.

I told him that I was planning to start my own PR firm. He glowered.

For the next several weeks Eli Black had very little to say to me and I found myself doing most of my business with him through Maury Kaplan. It was easy to understand his attitude.

First of all, my resignation came during the middle of a rush to the door by most of the company's officers. I was of use to Black. I was good at my job. I knew the company as a whole better than any other person. I was a young promising officer whom he didn't want to lose.

Looking back from that date, over the previous dozen years, the company had had thirty-seven officers.

Twenty were fired.

Only three retired and only three were still there.

Eleven quit, ten as a direct result of the takeover. The eleventh was Ed Toland.

The process of selling off the assets continued into 1972, 1973 and 1974. Black sold seventeen percent of Baskin-Robbins. He sold the A&W Canadian operation. He sold land in the tropics. He sold the Guatemala division to Del Monte. He sold the freeze-dried food operations. He sold the remaining eighty-three percent of Baskin-Robbins. He sold Revere Sugar. The effect of each of these moves was to produce cash.

The company began to repurchase some of its debt, a technique often used by builders of conglomerates who are trying to fatten profits without increasing productivity. The company made a successful offer to exchange its 5½ percent hundred-dollar convertible debentures, issued to help finance the takeover, for ten dollars in cash and a new sixty-dollar nonconvertible debenture paying 9⅛ percent interest. The offering reduced the company's debt by fifty million dollars, which meant an extraordinary gain in 1973 of about thirty-eight million dollars—based on the Accounting Principles Board's new ruling that a reduction in liabilities generates a profit. It is worth noting that the thirty-eight million dollars generated was more than the company's net income for 1972.

In describing this "fiscal fairy tale," *Forbes Magazine* exposed the gambit in detail: "But if United Brands Chairman, Eli Black, hasn't exactly been a roaring success in the food business, he is pretty good at arithmetic . . . he was, in effect, laying out $13.5 million now for a chance to save $50 million in sinking fund payments over a weighted average of 15 years. Big deal. If United Brands were profitable enough to earn 9% or so on its invested capital, Black could achieve the same result by buying banana boats: $13.5 million in current dollars invested at 9⅛% compounded has exactly the same actuarial value as the $50 million in 15 years. Furthermore, he doesn't even start saving that money until 1980, when sinking fund payments begin: and he doesn't get it all until 1994. But thanks to APB 26, he shows all that gain this year.

"Yet the $20 million after taxes are really very future dollars, and worth only a fraction of that amount today."

About a year later, *Forbes* followed up its story on "Eli's Magic Act," this time listing the company's paper under the title, "Junk Bonds." The *Forbes* pieces bothered Eli a great deal.

In a July, 1972, interview with Dave Gumpert of the *Wall Street Journal*, Black told the reporter that the company had a "very complicated capital structure." He asked Gumpert not to print the remark, but he went on to explain that it was his intention to simplify that structure. In the context of the interview, the off-the-record comment was a plea for clemency: Black was asking the reporter to be patient, to be understanding, and he was letting him know that Black found the maze he had inherited just as bewildering and impenetrable as the reporter did. It was a classic parallel to the kid who has murdered both his parents asking the court to be lenient on the grounds that he is an orphan. The capital structure of the company was complicated because Black himself had made it that way, and not because he acquired it in that condition.

In the first three years after the acquisition of United Fruit, Black went through two treasurers, three controllers and two vice-presidents of finance.

Another reporter for the *Wall Street Journal* once asked Eli if he was sorry he had bought United Fruit Company. He thought for a moment and then answered that in the light of subsequent stock prices, he felt he had paid too much.

The 1972 annual report showed earnings equal to about one percent of the company's assets. By April Fools' Day, 1973, the stock was under $9.00 a share. A year later it was under $8.00 a share. By February of 1975, the stock was selling at a price lower than its bottom during the depths of the Depression of the 1930s, when Sam Zemurray decided it was time to come to Boston.

The new company finally came to be called United Brands. It was comprised of the original AMK Corporation, John Morrell and Company and United Fruit. By mid-1974, it had become theoretically possible for some new raider—perhaps a frustrated kamikaze pilot—to make a far more spectacular coup than Black had accomplished six years earlier. It was now mathematically possible to buy 10 percent of this far larger company for only a quarter of what Black had laid out for 10 percent of United Fruit alone in 1968. Of course, the company's debt was far larger as well.

Stated another way, the decline becomes even more dramatic. With approximately eleven million shares outstanding, it was mathematically possible for a new raider to buy almost 40 percent of United Brands for the same amount of money Black spent on his opening bid for just 10 percent of the old United Fruit.

Given those conditions, there were two possible roads for Eli to travel. The first was conservative: to face the facts and to rectify with leadership and strong management the errors, misuse of people and misjudgments that had brought the company to the brink.

The other was to pyramid. To use the inertia of motion to maintain the illusion of growth. To continue the magic act.

On February 16, 1973, I read the following article in the financial pages of the *Boston Herald-American,* and I saw the road Eli had chosen.

"TAKEOVER" OF FOSTER GRANT CO. CHARGED

By Ken Regan

LEOMINSTER—A disgruntled Foster Grant Co. stockholder told Chairman and Chief Executive Officer Edward Creiger at the annual shareholders' meeting here Tuesday that "I think United Brands Co. is here to take over Foster Grant and I protest it."

As of Jan. 2, 1973, United Brands owned 33.6 percent of the outstanding shares of Foster Grant according to the company's proxy statement.

In reply, Creiger said, "I'm not an officer or director of United Brands . . . I'm not privy to their plans."

United Brands Chairman and Chief Executive Officer, Eli M. Black attended the meeting along with three other United Brands officers. Three were elected to three-year terms on the Foster Grant Board of Directors and one, to a two-year term.

Black declined to tell shareholders what United Brands' plans were in regard to Foster Grant on the grounds that his company is in registration with the SEC.

"I'm reluctant to make many comments," he said.

However, Black did say United Brands bought the Foster Grant stock after being approached "by an old friend and one of the founders of the company." (Abraham Goodman, chairman of the Foster Grant executive committee and president of H. Goodman & Sons, Inc.)

"He approached us with the idea that we might acquire the estate of the late Joseph C. Foster (600,000 shares of the 725,583 owned by United Brands were acquired from the Foster trust) and, after an intense study of our own, we decided that this was, indeed a good investment."

Black concluded, "We are happy investors, we are pleased and we only wish the company well."

A few days later I ran into one of the United Brands officers in the Prudential Building, and the subject of Foster Grant came up. I told him I thought Eli was risking a credibility gap by repeating the same platitudes he had already used on John Morrell and United Fruit. The officer said, "Nobody remembers those things, Tom, except for guys like you. That's why Eli's up there and you're down here."

A few weeks later, United Brands had acquired more than half of Foster Grant's outstanding stock and had announced its intention to get the other half through a tender offer.

The brain drain that resulted from AMK's acquisition of United Fruit was not the only reason for lower earnings or the long drop in the price of the new company's stock. Black overstated the importance of transient natural disasters in his reports to shareholders, and the shareholders were no longer that naïve. He milked Hurricane Francelia, for example, for three years after it occurred.

Black did not invent the policy of blaming nature for the ills of management; he just revived it. Tom Sunderland and Kenneth Redmond had placed a lot of emphasis on the eco-

nomic impact of blowdowns and floods. Then Fox and Cornuelle came along with the view that acts of nature were inevitable
and that they should be accounted as part of doing business.
They believed that the company should plan around natural
contingencies, and if the balance sheet was severely affected by
such events, then it was the fault of management and not of
nature. When Black reverted back to blaming nature, a lot of
the shareholders knew he was copping a plea; they had heard it
before.

In fact, this unrealistic view of nature was one of the factors
that had cost two earlier company presidents their jobs. The
board believed Tom Sunderland placed too much emphasis on
the economic impact of disasters, and some of them took the
attitude that it was a smokescreen for the fact that he had never
been able to pull together an effective working team. They made
Fox president and chief executive officer, kicking Sunderland
upstairs into the chairmanship. (From there Sunderland more
or less drifted out of the company. When news reached him in
1968 that there was an attempt under way by an outsider to
take over United Fruit, he was one of the first major shareholders to unload a large block of stock—an act which many
people in the company regarded as depressing to morale, oppor-
tunistic and disloyal.)

But while Black was blaming others for his troubles, he was
also busy capitalizing on one of his own greatest assets: his
ability with people. He could get people to do what he wanted,
he told me; he could "handle" them. For reasons that did not
become entirely clear to me until much later, I took special
exception to that side of Black's character. For example, in the
spring of 1972, César Chavez came to New York during Pass-
over, and Black told me that he invited Chavez to participate
in a well-attended religious service. Black arranged for Chavez
actually to read some passages to the congregation. "That," he
said later, "is public relations." I quietly ground my teeth.

Even Bob Gallop, United Brands' general counsel and one
of Black's oldest business associates from the days of AMK, told
me one day that "Eli is kidding himself," with respect to Chavez.

Gallop explained to me that the objectives of labor and management are often 180 degrees apart (a fact I guess he felt I did not know), that it is the goal of labor to get the most for the workers, and that management is committed to giving the least. All the publicity and fellowship in the world are worthless when each side is going to have to represent his constituency: there are times when leaders have no friends.

Black was equally attentive to President José "Don Pepe" Figueres of Costa Rica. He felt they had much in common. Small and flamboyant, Figueres thought of himself as a revolutionary and carried a loaded pistol in his back pocket everywhere he went. When a hijacker made the mistake of stopping off in Costa Rica to refuel his stolen airplane a few years ago, Figueres personally drove to the airport and machine-gunned the tires of the airliner so it couldn't take off. He was equally direct about guerrillas and insurgents: "To keep them in prison is like keeping dynamite in the kitchen," he once said. "So we leave them where we find them." Black considered swashbuckling those qualities in Figueres which others might have considered ludicrous. And he told me that he and Figueres shared tastes in literature; he had noted during his numerous visits that they had the same titles on their shelves.

It was true that Black had made a big investment in cultivating a relationship with Figueres that went beyond mere business; his goal had been a kind of president-to-president fellowship based on personal contact, as witness the "countless hours" of debate and discussion and philosophical reflection of which Black boasted to the audience of Channel 13. Relationships like that are always two-sided, and Figueres had long been partial to men of finance; Robert Vesco, for example, is another Figueres intimate, and, I suspected, for the same reasons. Vesco has not only been granted asylum in San José, but Figueres allowed him to continue his operations there, manipulating foreign investments with immunity even though he is one of the greatest swindlers in history, following the looting of Investors Overseas Services of more than two hundred million dollars.

Similarly, Black believed that his "close personal friendship" with General Torrejos of Panama, who achieved a certain prominence north of the border recently with his attempt to take over the Panama Canal and his visit to Fidel Castro, was another corporate asset that would pay dividends for years to come.

I can only speculate on how Chavez, Figueres and Torrejos viewed their relationships from the other sides of their respective fences. I don't think one will find it in the eulogies.

In March, 1973, a young Price Waterhouse auditor assigned to the United Brands accounting read through an issue of *Unibranco*, the house organ for which I had suggested Phil Fuchs as editor. Under Phil's direction, a striking change had taken place in the publication's content: the January, 1973, issue had a cover painting by Shirley Black, Eli's wife and Phil's aunt; the lead article was "Taking Stock—A Message from E. M. Black, Chairman of the Board," set off with a picture of the author; the second article was a two-page spread on "Major Installations Visited" by our chairman and chief executive officer during 1972; all told, there were eight photographs of Eli in that issue; there was even one of Phil Fuchs, whose name appeared twice—on the cover.

The March, 1973, issue had another lead article devoted to the activities of Chairman Black—this time, his meeting with "Central American Dignitaries." The article said in part, "Upon completing his talk, Mr. Black introduced Charles Meyer, Assistant Secretary of State, who greeted the ambassadors and their wives on behalf of the U.S. government. Upon completion of his speech, it seemed as though the formal part of the evening had come to a close. However, many of the ambassadors representing their own governments spontaneously rose to tell in their own words of the new, remarkable relationship which exists today between the United Brands Company and their countries."

There were nine photos of Black in that issue, two of his wife and one of Phil. The Price Waterhouse auditor read the two issues and shook his head. "This isn't a company magazine," he said. "It's a family album."

Predictably, the more visible Black made himself, the more

he was subject to attack. Some of the sniping was simply business as usual and was directed at Black merely because he was
an inviting target. For example, because of a large contribution
by United Brands Foundation to Lincoln Center, Black was
asked to participate in ceremonies for the opening day of the
Street Theater Festival at Lincoln Center. The Street Theater
provides a vehicle and a showplace for deserving local talent in
the performing arts, a fact Eli observed at the outset: his opening
line was "Black is beautiful." Amei Wallach of *Newsday* described some of the high points. "He gave a kind of corporate
speech with big words about 'this country,' 'the democratic
process' and 'United Brands,' and disclosed that his was the
first company to recognize César Chavez and his United Farm
Workers. The audience listened impassively to all the speechify-
ing. Some rode their bikes around the plaza. Some lay prone on
the fountain. Some made a game of seeing how many Chiquita
banana labels they could paste on their faces or how many bananas they could eat."

Black gave away not only bananas but root beer and ice
cream, all dispensed free from hand-painted Costa Rican donkey
carts around the plaza. He quoted Danton, who said that eternal
vigilance is the price of liberty, and finished: "We are one of
a growing number of companies that have recognized that social
consciousness is a legitimate and vital concern of business and
industry. If our business is not to be controlled and regulated
beyond reasonable limits; if we are not to lose our rights to speak
out, publish and write freely; if we are not to have an ersatz
culture, then all of us—business, labor, government—the entire
community—must assume our full responsibilities as members
of a democratic society."

Just as predictable as the criticism was Eli's inevitable response: anger. And, beneath the anger, almost as visible if you
knew Eli well enough to look for it: the deep, rancorous hurt of
damaged pride.

There was other criticism that Black never heard. I knew
about it and once commented to another officer that Eli
wouldn't be having quite as much difficulty keeping the com-

pany together if he wasn't a Jew. The officer answered, "Well, Tom, don't you think there's some good reason why people have hated Jews for the past two thousand years?"

In the early morning darkness of December 23, 1972, the city of Managua was destroyed by three violent earth tremors which killed thousands of Nicaraguans and made refugees of many thousands more. By Christmas Day there was almost no standing shelter, no food, and little drinkable water. I knew that Black was certain to see in this disaster a public relations opportunity for the company, and I spent most of December 25 waiting for the telephone to ring. It did and we met the next day.

Black said he had an idea for sending a dozen civil engineers from the company's tropical divisions to help rebuild the roads and bridges of that city. His idea came from a doctor to whom he had spoken a day or two earlier, who was headed to Managua to offer medical aid to the victims: the doctor suggested that United Fruit take a leadership role in the relief effort, both with respect to the location and purchase of medical supplies, food and portable shelter, and the coordination of the efforts of other individuals, private and government agencies and companies. Black then said he wanted two things from me: he wanted the company to achieve the leadership role the doctor had suggested, and he wanted the publicity that would result.

I warned Eli of the dangers of grandstanding in such circumstances and told him that public opinion could easily turn against us if we were seen to be serving our own public relations interests ahead of the interests of the disaster victims. I also told him that there was no way for the Fruit Company to take the place of such established rescue and relief organizations as the Red Cross and CARE, that we had a logistical disadvantage, that we would have to start from scratch in competition with an ongoing, worldwide effort by those other organizations, and that even if we succeeded to a limited degree, it would be at the cost of diminishing the effectiveness of our competition, which I felt was inappropriate as well as politically risky.

Black listened impatiently, dismissed the objections out of hand and told me to be back in his office the following morning with a list of specific recommendations for going ahead with his plan. I felt guilty coming back with the list—but I also felt that as long as I accepted money from Eli to come up with ideas, I had to do just that.

The list was long. I had put down every idea that entered my mind with absolutely no regard to its value to the disaster victims or even whether the suggestions were physically possible. My only criterion had been show biz. I proposed that the project be named NEED for the Nicaraguan Earthquake Emergency Drive. Eli read the list carefully from top to bottom, his expression indicating growing delight, and he told me to go ahead with every one of the items on it.

It was a strange moment for me: far from being shocked or horrified, I felt instead that my cynicism and anger and resentment toward Black, which had been brewing for months, had suddenly been vindicated in full. It was a moment of surprising relief, and I left his office feeling almost euphoric without understanding why. Surely it wasn't because Black had bought my program—at least not entirely: I knew that half the ideas in the package would be embarrassing to put into operation.

There is little to be learned of NEED beyond a brief summary of its results. We spent over fifty thousand dollars on advertising in newspapers, radio and television and the return was about two to one—the wrong way. Of the roughly twenty-five thousand dollars this effort brought in, about 20 percent was contributed by United Brands itself. The advertising and publicity program was a success in Black's view, however, even though I had to keep reminding him of our original objective every few days: each ad carried a tagline identifying United Brands as the sponsor, and we were seen at our benevolent best by millions of banana buyers throughout the nation. It did, however, produce twenty-five thousand dollars for the earthquake victims. We also made a movie—at an additional cost of some twenty-five thousand dollars—showing the folks at home how compassionate we were to our less fortunate brethren south of the border. Naturally, Eli Black played himself. We wrote up the whole experience for the 1972 annual report—without the numbers—under the title, "Our Social Responsibility."

The pyramid began tottering in 1973.

Early in the year the Top Banana changed rank. The banana sales of another company—Dole—passed Chiquita for the first time in history.

Black sold Baskin-Robbins.

"We still believe Baskin-Robbins is a gem," Maury Kaplan said to a *Wall Street Journal* reporter at the time. "But the cash and notes look awfully good to us."

That spring, the FTC decided the company should get out of the fresh vegetable business—primarily the extensive lettuce operations on the West Coast.

But the "public relations" went on. One morning I received a memorandum which began: "In line with the reorganization effective January 31, 1973, whereby United Fruit Company has been eliminated . . ."

Of course, the company wasn't really eliminated. It was just another case of Eli Black adjusting appearances, working changes on the surface while the substance remained unchanged.

On September 3, 1973, *Time* magazine carried a story on United Brands. It was researched and written by Hal Moore, whom I had got to know a few months earlier and who would become a friend. The article went through several *Time* re-writers and editors, and although the result was extremely favorable, my feelings were mixed. I was pleased with it as a PR accomplishment, but I was also aware that my view of PR was coming to look more and more like Eli Black's.

Shortly after it appeared, Black called my office.

"Well," he said, "at last we have one that's not too bad."

The comment made me angry, and I asked Black what he meant. But before he had a chance to respond I mentioned similarly favorable stories that had appeared in recent editions of *Business Week*, that front page *New York Times* piece and the *Chicago News*.

"Well," he said, "What I mean is it could have been worse."

"You're right, Eli, it could have been worse—it could have been a lot worse.

"Let's look at it a bit closer, Eli. The article says that you're the guy who transformed the company. It says that you brought 'peace, harmony and profits.' It says you're an empire builder.

"Now let's consider what it left out," I went on. "When you think about it, the things that make this article really remarkable are what it leaves out."

Black said nothing.

"For example, it omits any reference to profit levels *before* the takeover. It doesn't say anywhere that United Fruit made a hell of a lot more money before you showed up than they have since."

More nothing.

"There's no reference to the price of the stock which stands at about eighty percent below its level before the takeover. There's nothing about the company dropping down to second banana in the industry. No mention of the lettuce problem. No reference to our invasion of Guatemala: this is the first major story on the company in the past two decades that doesn't bring up the Guatemala story. And it never mentions the Old Guard: Fox, Cornuelle, Sunderland, Zemurray."

Eli waited until he was sure I'd finished. I expected to be fired.

"Tom, Tom," he said. "We agree, we agree. It could have been a whole lot worse."

One of the company's better-known critics over the years has been Dr. Benjamin Spock, although some of the things he has said about United Fruit have gone wide of the mark. For a long time I kept a lengthy mental file of his errors and distortions about the Fruit Company, perhaps in the hope of someday setting the record straight. One day in late 1973, purely by chance, my opportunity presented itself. I found myself sitting beside him on an airplane to New York. We spoke of mutual friends, politics and, inevitably, of kids. The subject of United Fruit never came up. By the time we said good-bye, I began to wonder why I had let the chance pass.

I thought about it for a long time.

I knew I had changed a lot during my years with United

Fruit, and the company had changed too. I realized with a twinge of regret that at age thirty-nine, I had crossed an invisible boundary and had now spent more than half my life working for the same employer. What I was now doing, and had done for twenty years, was coasting on a decision made in another era, under vastly different circumstances, by a boy of eighteen.

Of course, that decision had been consciously renewed at various times in my career, particularly in the first months following the takeover. But during the years since Black had completed his raid, I found myself gradually and subtly losing the initiatives I had accumulated—initiatives that had meant both personal and professional growth—and with them I was losing control of the new direction my life was taking.

The thing that made it especially easy and dangerous was that the ground I was now covering was all so familiar. Gradually, without at first realizing what was happening, I found myself operating more and more in the style of the early 1950s. Reacting to perils of the company's own making. Nagged by a sense of unreality. But knowing this time that what we were doing *was* real. And that it was wrong.

The Nicaraguan earthquake promotion was wrong.

The *Time* story was wrong.

Probably Spock would have argued that the company's reaction to every public relations phantom in its history was equally wrong, starting with Lee Christmas and "Machine Gun" Guy Molony, through the invasions of Guatemala and the Bay of Pigs, right up to the war between Salvador and Honduras. And he probably would have said the machismo, the self-sufficiency, the piety, the oppression, the sleight of hand, the self-serving patriotism were all wrong as well.

In my first fifteen years with United Fruit, I could have given Dr. Spock a terrific argument. But after five years with Eli Black, I no longer could. I knew better.

For the first time, it occurred to me to wonder if Eli Black knew better too.

Eli's life, like my own, had been neatly halved. The similarities didn't end there. He had spent the first half of his life as an outsider, poor, shy, and alternately besieged by feelings of inadequacy and a fierce sense of compensating superiority. I understood that kind of background, and sympathized with it.

Eli spent the first few years of his life in the Polish town of Lublin, haunted by the burden of all those generations of rabbis and scholars who had preceded him. Just a little while after the Blachowitz family moved to America, the Germans arrived in Lublin, and in short order they set up a death camp. In three years, the camp killed and cremated over a quarter of a million people. Most of them were Jews. Most of them came from the same world as Eli Black.

I grew up in Brooklyn with other survivors of that world, and as soon as I first met Eli Black, I recognized him. It was one of the things I liked best about Eli, a combination of shyness and mortal tenacity, a meekness and a holding onto life with both hands and all his strength.

But those traits and contradictions were also things that worked against Eli in his running of United Fruit.

Probably it had something to do with his Talmudic training. In the Brooklyn of my boyhood, I never remember meeting a rabbi who was born in America. Most of them, like Eli, came from Eastern Europe, and they had an almost medieval attitude toward pride and worldliness: they had been trained in the art of self-effacement, of withdrawal, and that same training had been given to Eli.

It must have required a tremendous effort of will to change such ingrained habits as that training produced. The fact that Black was not completely successful in shedding all remnants of that part of his past doesn't lessen his accomplishment, but it greatly lessened his ability to lead men in a world where a limp handshake or an averted eye were interpreted not as signs of piety but of weakness.

Those mannerisms were the worst possible beginning to any kind of meaningful communication with the Fruit Company's Old Guard in Boston and New York. In the tropics, they were suicidal.

There is another, more subtle, aspect to that background that I recognized as well. Eli had never allowed himself to get too close to people. When he emerged from the rabbinate at the midpoint in his life, despite his best efforts, he came no closer to the new people around him than he had been to the old ones. No matter which world he was in, I suspect that Eli Black always treated most people as though they were on one side of the looking glass and he was on the other. I could even see it in the way he chose to die.

I resigned the United Brands public relations account in January of 1974. A few days later, at the height of the Arab oil embargo, when public wrath at multinationals—and especially the oil companies—was at its peak, and when food prices were also at their highest, an ad appeared in the financial pages of leading newspapers throughout the United States. It was headlined, "An Agricultural Products and Petrochemical Company Reports on a Year of Progress." In PR, that's known as positioning yourself in the market. The ad was signed by E. M. Black of United Brands.

On almost the same day, I received a large, potted plant in my new offices on Newbury Street. The note read "Wishing you every success." And it was signed "Eli."

I wrote to thank him. But both of us knew we had seen each other for the last time.

To be exact, the last time I *saw* Eli was on television—on Saturday, September 28, 1974. The economic summit meeting was under way in Washington, and a long, tedious procession of business and professional leaders was being brought before the President—and of course, before the American public— to voice their various views, in exactly two minutes apiece, on what was wrong or right with the way the country was managing its fiscal affairs. It would have made a fairly good carnival, except that after a while all the faces and opinions took on a colorless, oppressive similarity. I had started watching in the hope of learning something, but after an hour or so began to suspect that the program was the new administration's first major attempt at mass hypnosis.

Then I heard a familiar voice say, "My name is Eli Black."

I can still hear Eli's voice and see his half-deprecating smile as he launched into a heavy, labored compliment to Chairman Arthur Burns—an "ice-breaker" that was meant to make him appear human, to win points with his audience. I remembered instantly that here was a man who was very, very good with people. The compliment went on. And on. It took the entire two minutes. The moderator informed Eli his time was up.

For an instant, Eli appeared desperate. Then he took control again and turned on the semismile. "Just three points," he said. His mouth opened and closed, forming words, but nothing came over the air. They had simply pulled the plug on him. A few seconds later the next man in the procession had taken his place.

Measured in terms of his new life, Eli was even younger than I when he first heard of United Fruit.

And I am certain he reacted just as I did, fifteen years before: with awe at the company's power and magnitude and with an overpowering desire to belong, to make it his own. United Fruit gave both of us an image of ourselves we badly needed. It was one more bond that gave us our unique relationship in the company. I was nineteen and eventually was able to grow through that image and finally grow out of it.

Eli Black was forty-five.

I have one especially vivid recollection of Eli, from a photograph he showed me that had been taken on one of his trips to the tropics. He is wearing a tan, short-sleeved uniform shirt with flaps on the pockets and tabs on the shoulders. He is smiling shyly at the camera. It's the picture of a little boy, playing a role, dressed in a safari shirt.

Since Eli's death, I've often wondered if that photo could have been among his final thoughts that February morning. Was his last view of himself from the dual perspective of the methodical, deep-thinking Talmudic scholar on whom he had turned his back half a lifetime earlier, and the pockmarked, tough worldly cynic in dark glasses he was never able to become? Whichever Eli Black served as his final judge, he saw himself as a failure. And he was without mercy.

Less than five months after he appeared on TV—and almost one year to the day from the last time we met—Eli was dead.

Chapter 12

WHAT HAPPENED NEXT

ALTHOUGH I SEVERED the business asociation, I still retained close ties with the remnants of United Fruit. Jack Fox had gone to the presidency of H. P. Hood. Will Lauer stayed in Boston—with USM Corporation—and we kept up our long-standing friendship. I frequently ran into other members of the old team —George Gardner, Herb Cornuelle, Harvey Johnson, Peter Smith and a small handful of survivors who were still aboard the ship—and others who had made it to shore and, like me, were reorganizing their lives. In addition to my new public relations firm, I had opened a small printing facility in Boston's Prudential Center in partnership with Charlotte Appleton. Another friend and former Fruitero, Web Lithgow, was a partner in a couple of television ventures. Hardly a day passed during the following year in which I failed to touch, in some way, on the friendships and loyalties and experiences of more than half my lifetime.

In the spring of 1974, I read about the sudden levying of a disastrously high banana tax. Following the lead of the oil-producing countries, seven Central and South American banana exporting countries formed a cartel. Their objective was to levy a one-dollar export tax on each forty-pound box of bananas. United Brands and the other companies quickly and loudly protested, touching off what the press referred to as the "Banana War." The cartel's united front quickly divided, however, when Ecuador, the world's largest banana exporting country, backed down, leaving Panama, Costa Rica, Honduras and Guatemala to negotiate the best deal they could. All but Panama followed Ecuador's lead and lowered the tax. Panama, however, remained firm. Black suspended Panamanian operations and waited. The suspension, which lasted six weeks, caused great hardship to the Panamanian workers and further inflamed the hostility toward the company, prompting talk of a buy-out by the Panamanians. In August, Black wrote a letter to United Brands shareholders in which he said that these taxes "violated and breached the provisions of existing agreements." But he also said that the company realized Panama's need for additional revenues, and that he, therefore, intended to negotiate in order to arrive at a reasonable solution. Later that same month, the company announced that it had reached an understanding with Honduras in which a $.25 per box tax was established.

Two months later I had dinner with Harvey Johnson at his country club. Harvey was not a happy man. The sunny California disposition I had first seen sixteen years earlier had been noticeably eroded; I could see changes that had taken place in just the few months since I had left the company: the negotiations over the banana tax and the subsequent discussions with Panama had taken a toll on him. He had the reluctant stoicism of someone who is forced by events, but not by character, to grin and bear it.

He told me of a plane ride he had taken some weeks earlier with Eli Black and Bob Gallop. They had left their chartered jet in Panama City and taken a twin-engine prop plane to an island not far off the Panamanian coast, to an airport too small to accommodate the jet. For most of the day they negotiated the lowering of the banana tax with Panamanian officials, and by evening Black had grown short-tempered and impatient.

At about six o'clock, Black suddenly said, "I want this wrapped up in an hour. No more screwing around. We're going back to Boston tonight."

Bob Gallop said, "Boston, Eli? Tonight?"

Black was vehement, and so in the allotted time the negotiations were concluded and the three men left for Panama City.

Later that evening, they arrived in Panama City in a heavy
tropical downpour. They found their chartered jet, and Eli went
inside to wake up the pilot and advise him they were going to
take off in a couple of minutes. Gallop had made it clear to
Black that he was exhausted—from the strain of the flight down
and from the day's work on the island—but Black had been
adamant. He was obsessed with the idea of returning to Boston
that night, and there was nothing more to be said.

Gallop looked at Johnson as they stood under the wing of the
plane in the blinding rain. "Who needs this?" he asked. "I've
made enough money. I have what I want in life. Just tell me,
who needs this?"

The rear door of the plane opened, the two men got in, and
they found that Black had already taken over three of the seats—
he was stretched out in comparative comfort on what amounted
to a bed—and so they rode the entire trip to Boston sitting up
as Eli Black slept. A few hours later they were in the company's
boardroom, and Eli began the meeting by telling a story about
his father and a small, locked box he kept on top of his bureau
with the key right alongside it so that anyone could open it.
It was a long rambling story that Eli seemed to delight in telling
but Harvey said no one else in the room got the point and didn't
kow how to act when Eli finished telling it. Eli laughed finally—
so they did too.

"Why do you stay with it, Harvey?" I asked. "You could do
anything you wanted. You could have a real life."

He shook his head and I had seen the expression a few
thousand times before—on the faces of other men who had given
a lot of years to the company and who couldn't admit that things
had gone *that* bad—on my own face in the mirror until the beginning of that year. "It's just a few more years to go, Tom," he
said. "I've just got to stick it out for another few years to retirement."

In the late summer of 1974, in order to ensure the lowering of the banana tax, United Brands officials agreed to pay an official of the Honduran government over a million and a quarter dollars, with the pledge of an additional million and a quarter more to come when the fix took effect.

By fall of that year, several of the officers of United Brands were beginning to detect changes in Eli Black's personality. Ed Gelsthorpe, the new senior vice-president whom Eli had hired after he left Gillette where he was president, said that often Black was "disoriented"; he noticed he was beginning to slur his words and lose track of his thoughts and objectives. Don Meltzer, the company's chief financial officer, saw Black "stagger from the room" as he went from one meeting to another on a particularly busy day.

There was talk that Black was using addictive drugs. After his death his family and his two physicians acknowledged that he was taking Seconal, which acts as a central nervous system depressant, but they deny that it was having an adverse effect. The day he died, the medical examiner found traces of Seconal in Black's body.

In November, 1974, Black asked George Gardner to resign from the board; Gardner refused. First, there was the matter of pride. Also, he had an investment of over twenty years with the company. But as much as anything, George Gardner had an important financial stake in United Brands. And a man like George Gardner was not about to surrender responsibility for the management of that investment to a man like Eli Black.

The relationship between Black and Gelsthorpe, which had started in July, began deteriorating before the summer's end. The two clashed frequently, usually in private but sometimes quite publicly. As Black became more openly concerned with the company's financial problems, he had to turn over more operating responsibility to Gelsthorpe—but Black relinquished the power grudgingly. He seemed torn between a concern for the needs of the company and the possibility that Gelsthorpe would turn in a star performance that would further underscore his own failures.

In short order, the conflict deepened as the United Brands management became aware of Gelsthorpe's skills. It was clear that Gelsthorpe provided the leadership that the company needed: he had operating experience, made decisions based on reason, was a good listener, and could be persuaded to another view—virtues that Eli lacked.

Black began to complain that he was being cut off from information. He began to listen to people who told him that his generals were plotting against him.

Near the end of 1974, it became apparent that losses would be around seventy million and Black was forced to sell off the company's interest in the operation he had once described as "the jewel in the company's crown." Foster Grant was turned over to a German plastics firm, at a profit to United Brands of thirty million. United Brands' debt service was then so enormous, and earnings so poor, that he had no choice. An article in *Business Week* on January 13, 1975, quoted "a former executive of United Brands" as saying: "One of the things he does best is buy and sell companies. But after Foster Grant, there isn't much left for him to sell." That "former executive" was once Eli's closest friend. Even when Black died, Eli was unaware of the source of the quote and still considered the man an ally.

The debt leverage game had caught up with Black at home as well. His new home was heavily mortgaged and virtually everything else he owned was similarly pledged or had declined in value—especially the approximately three hundred and fifty thousand United Brands shares he and his family owned. He was in, as they say on Wall Street, "for everything." And at that point, Black alone knew it.

On December 27, 1974, there was a board meeting. On the agenda was the approval of an agreement with Panama which Gelsthorpe had negotiated. The discussion that followed culminated in a bitter and destructive exchange between Eli and another of his longtime friends, Bob Gallop.

Bob, who was the company's general counsel, took a firm stand in favor of the Gelsthorpe proposal for settling the Panama problem. Eli, who had previously given his approval to the Gelsthorpe solution, suddenly reversed himself. Now, he said that it was too facile and expensive, and there was a strong implication that Gelsthorpe was merely trying to advance his own career by currying favor with the board, regardless of the cost to the company.

When Gallop finished his defense of the Panama agreement, Black looked at him bitterly and the two began a heated argument. According to one board member, Gallop shouted at Black, "There is no place in the company for the two of us." To which Eli replied, "When are you leaving?"

Gallop denies this version of the exchange. According to him, Black said that if he felt so strongly about the agreement he should retire, whereupon Gallop said, "Why should I? I haven't done anything wrong. You should resign!"

Word of the exchange traveled fast. Some people in the company viewed it as a point of no return in the deterioration of Black's control over the company and his own life. Several executives felt it was the most significant event since Eli took over United Fruit.

A few weeks later Gallop did indeed give up both his directorship and his position as general counsel.

After that meeting Black became convinced there was a plot: Gelsthorpe; Gardner; John Taylor, president of the Banana Group; Don Meltzer, his financial vice-president, and several others including some board members who had been Black loyalists, were seen as the nucleus of the conspiracy. Over the New Year's holiday Black decided to fire Gelsthorpe and Taylor at the next board meeting, in early January. He talked it over with his public relations consultants who replaced me, Ruder and Finn, and they advised him against it. They pointed out that the two top executives were the only remaining management with real operating experience, and that the firings would be coming right on top of the huge operating loss for the year, the Foster Grant sale and the resignation of Eli's friend and associate of

long standing, Bob Gallop. They advised Eli that it would be
"bad PR."

By the turn of the year, Eli's critics both inside and outside
the company had divided into two camps. One group felt that
only major surgery could save the company. The others felt the
situation was already fatal.

The list of company problems was long and formidable: it began with the decline in profits since Black's takeover; the decline
in the prices of the common and preferred stock and the value
of the bonds and the warrants; the elimination of stock dividends; the cannibalization for cash of such profitable operations
as Baskin-Robbins, A&W of Canada and Foster Grant; the dramatic decline in the company's banana market share; the management's inability to deal with Latin-American problems and
their creation of many new ones; the inability to hold top-level
people; the enormous debt burden; questionable accounting practices and the bribing of Latin-American officials. Several investment bankers, groups and individuals looked over the company
with a view to acquiring it. But it no longer made financial sense
and one by one they all dropped out.

Those of us in the first camp realized that if the company was
to survive, it would have to be without Eli Black.

About the middle of January, 1975, I received a long-distance
call from an old friend from the Midwest who had terminated
a long association with Black just a few weeks earlier. The purpose of the call was to set up a meeting with me at Boston's
Logan Airport for seven o'clock the next evening, a Tuesday,
before continuing on to New York.

The friend was a professional consultant and had been close
to Eli's business operations, and probably knew Eli and his way
of operating and as many of his secrets as anyone. But a few
weeks earlier, for no substantial reason, Eli had ended the consulting arrangement.

We met in the cocktail lounge at Logan, and as I listened,
I began to get a better feel for what was happening to Eli and
to the company.

"He has some personal papers of mine. I gave them to Eli a few months ago because I had asked him, as an old friend, to give me some personal advice. Now I want them back."

"That's not worth a trip to New York is it?" I asked. "Wouldn't he just mail them to you?"

"That's the problem. He won't. I've asked him three times to send them, and he finally told me last weekend that he just wasn't going to do it. He says he doesn't want to give them up because it will mean an end to our friendship."

I nodded. "It doesn't sound as though there's much friendship left."

For the next several minutes, I heard the details of how Eli had terminated the consulting contract. It was a textbook case of all the qualities in Eli which had turned dozens of friends, over the year, into enemies: the assumption of an authoritarian manner without warning or explanation.

"I didn't ask you to meet me because of the papers; I'll handle that myself. But there's another matter where you can be of real help. I have a friend in the Midwest who is interested in taking over United Brands."

"Your friend doesn't need my kind of help," I said. "He needs a doctor."

"He needs a front man. Someone who can't tie him to the takeover, but who has credibility in his own right. If the deal doesn't go down, he doesn't want anyone to know he made the try. If it does, he wants to have the advantage of surprise.

"He wants to see if he can pick up a block of shares—almost 10 percent—being held by one family." Because I knew the family, I was asked if I would contact them the next day in order to feel them out.

I agreed to make a call and we were to talk by telephone the next night. About midmorning on Wednesday, I placed my call. The man I was after was in the Orient and wouldn't be back for at least a week.

Late that night, at home, I received the call I had been promised. The voice on the other end was shaking badly, and within a sentence or two it cracked. "Oh, Tom, my God, I've never seen anything so pathetic in all my life."

I had been prepared for just about anything else, but not this. "Pathetic?" I asked. "What's pathetic?" I fully expected to hear something altogether new, something in no way connected with Eli Black. For some reason, perhaps because the whole conversation until now was so unexpected and incongruous, I found myself fighting the strong temptation to laugh.

"Tom, you've got to forget everything I said to you last night. I never said any of it. I don't want to do anything to Eli but try to help him. I don't want to force him out, to hurt him, to be responsible in any way for taking the company away from him. I just want to help." Some throat clearing and then, "Oh, my God, I've just never seen anything so pathetic."

Finally I said, "Does this mean you got your papers back?"

That did the trick. The tremors stopped, there were a few resolute coughs, and in a voice that was almost composed, "No. I don't care about the papers anymore. Let me tell you what happened. I called Eli at the Pan Am Building to say I was in town, and told him why. Eli asked me to meet him after business hours—he had appointments right up to six, but said we could get together at around dinnertime and talk privately for as long as we liked. I agreed, and we met at about six thirty.

"From the beginning, Eli made it clear that he had no intention of giving up the papers. 'If you take them, I know it means I'll never see you again. I can't face losing another friend.'"

He then started to list all the friends who had "deserted" him. It was a long list. After each name, he provided a little biography of the relationship—how it had flourished and how it had died. Some of the biographies contained some very revealing footnotes. Bob Gallop, for example, according to Eli had become a millionaire many times over, and then had turned his back on Eli and walked away—once he had gotten all he could from knowing him. Maury Kaplan had done essentially the same thing. Tom McCann did the same—only he wasn't a millionaire—but he could have been if he had wanted "—if he had stuck with me."

At this point, my friend took a deep breath. If I were ever going to give in to the temptation to laugh, this would have been the place. But the story was beginning to have some of the same effect on me that the actual events had had on my caller.

Eli's ragings continued. "Tom McCann has problems worse than Job. His children are on drugs. His wife is suing him for divorce. He's lost all of Charlotte Appleton's money in that crazy printing company. He's lost all of his own money with Web Lithgow in those television productions. . . ." Eli went on and on. The thought never entered his mind that his listener might know that what he was saying was all fantasies or all lies.

"He's ready to kill himself," Black concluded. "He's turned his back on me and look at him now! Look!"

My friend repeated the conversation verbatim into the phone. It had just ended minutes before. "We've got to help him."

As I listened, I recalled a passage I had recently read by Erich Fromm: "The lust for power is not rooted in strength but weakness."

During the next several days, I gave a lot of thought to that telephone conversation. And in the course of it, I also thought back to how my attitude toward Eli had gone through so many changes in the years I had known him.

At first, I thought of him solely as a corporate raider, an outsider who was breaking up the Old Boys' Club for which I had spent most of my life prepping. I had resented him because he was a spoiler—but also because he meant change in a system I once thought was so strong and self-contained that change could never touch it.

And it was largely because of my recognition of that resentment—and of its causes—that I took another look at Eli once I had the chance to know him as a man.

To my surprise, there had been qualities in Eli Black I had actually come to like. For all his strategizing and planning and manipulation, there was a side of Eli Black that was as good and ingenuous and vulnerable as in any person I've ever met. I thought of Eli's game of "Look at Me, Look at Me—What Do You See?"

It was January 18, 1973, the day after Nixon's Second Inaugural. Eli had called me at home and asked me to meet him in his apartment at the Prudential. It was a Sunday and I was about to sit down to a chicken dinner with my family.

"That's no problem," he said. "We'll have dinner in here. Bring in a couple of sandwiches with you. Just hurry up and get in here. There's something I want to show you."

Eli met me at his apartment door. He never looked better: healthy, confident, beaming. He opened the door and then stood back. "Well?" he said, expectantly.

I looked him over very carefully before saying, "Well what?"

"Look at me, look at me—what do you see?"

"You look like you got a little sun, Eli," I said.

"Yes, but that's not it. Guess again."

"It's the suit." I said.

"No, no, no. You're not even warm. It's a new suit—but it's not the suit. Look closer." He tugged at the cuffs of his shirt, and as more of the sleeve emerged from the jacket, I saw the familiar gold and blue pattern of the Presidential Seal.

"I see," I said. "Those are the President's cufflinks you have on."

"Great!" said Eli, delighted with my reaction.

He told me he had spent the previous evening at the Inaugural Ball in Washington. I asked him if he had actually seen and talked with the President.

"Yes," he said, and his eyes were filled with an almost dreamlike look of pride. "And—" he added, "I—even—shook—the—hand."

For the next three hours, Eli talked on and on. Very little was expected of me: he was so full of the excitement of the past day and night that any listener at all would have done as well; I nodded now and then to show that I was still with him, but it was a monologue rather than a conversation.

"Henry Kissinger was there," he said. "You know, I'm never able to look at Kissinger without thinking how similar we are. I mean, we're alike in the very important ways—things relating to character, strength, and intelligence.

"Kissinger's great asset is not his grasp of the basic motion of history—in fact, I don't believe he has any more of a feel for the long-term significance of current events than any other Secretary of State.

"But his greatest strength, as mine, is one single skill."

Eli looked at me for the obvious question, but I merely looked back noncommittally and waited for him to continue.

"Our greatest strength is people. Both of us are very, very good with people."

Twenty minutes later, Eli told me that his own long-term objective in life was to become Secretary of State. There is no point in having that kind of skill, he said, unless you put it to the ultimate use.

"Look at me, look at me," Eli said one summer afternoon. I had seen him that same day at least three times, and now he had stopped at my office, closed the door and turned in a full circle as he spoke. "What do you see?"

As usual, I looked him over very carefully from behind my desk. "You're letting your hair grow out?" I asked.

"Cold, cold," he said. "Not even close." He turned another circle.

"You're taking ballet lessons!" I said. It was around the time he was most closely involved with Lincoln Center. Besides, I didn't have the slightest idea what he was aiming at.

"You louse!" he said. "You louse! I've lost almost twenty pounds."

I had to laugh. Nobody had called me a louse since I was a kid in Brooklyn. "Gee, that's great, Eli. How'd you do it?"

"Simple," he said. "I have a system. A foolproof system. It's called not eating."

He thought a moment longer. "You know that new wonder drug for dieters? It's a sulfa drug. Sulfa denial."

I kept telling myself that those recollections didn't balance out against other kinds of memories I had of Eli—about the other, far less attractive side of his character. I thought about the group we had come to call the "Plumbers" because of its similarity to the White House "Plumbers" unit: a department, staffed by former FBI men, intelligence agents, security and law enforcement men. Ed Gibbons inherited them when Tom Warner left and Ed told me how shocked he was when he found out their backgrounds—he was expecting that the department would be made up of men who were nothing more than accountants. I know of one instance where the Plumbers "audited" one of Eli's closest friends and found that he had filed double and sometimes triple expense records—one each with the Fruit Company, United Brands and John Morrell—for the same set of figures. And he had taken as a business reimbursement some personal outlays that had nothing to do with the company. There were also some kickbacks, nepotism and assorted bits of "dirt." Eli had known about these things and some say Eli encouraged him in precisely the techniques that the audit revealed —it was a form, he said, of indirect compensation in lieu of increased salary. And then he had used the audit to trap his friend in the act and force his resignation when he decided he wanted him out.

He also audited calls on executive's telephones without their knowledge or consent.

And he kept a "book" on many of his officers and upper management against the day one of them might step out of line. The longer and the closer the association, the fatter the book.

And when he couldn't get a book on me or trap me in an audit or listen in on a compromising telephone conversation— he simply made up some facts about my family and my business life to satisfy his special sense of justice and told them, apparently, to anyone who knew me and was willing to listen.

Somehow I reached the conclusion that there was a kind of balance there after all, that the Eli Black I had seen in bits and glimpses was still a part of the Eli Black so many of his associates had come to fear and hate. And I came to the conclusion that I owed something to them both.

I also came to the conclusion that I owed something to what remained, after seven ruinous years under Black's stewardship, of the company where I had spent so much of my life. Around the middle of January, I spoke to a couple of my former associates, who had also left the company, about the past and the present problems and about Eli and the future. We all felt for the people in the company who were suffering and in a way we felt we still shared in some of the responsibility.

I began to outline an idea. It was simple and direct: I saw it as a way out for the company and as a face-saving alternative for Eli Black. There was an ambassadorial opening in Costa Rica, and I proposed that a group of us take steps to try to get the job for Eli Black. A tall order but if it could be pulled off, it would be good for the company; good for Eli, and it wouldn't have hurt U.S.-Costa Rican relations. Chances are it wouldn't have helped them either, but Eli certainly wouldn't have been any worse than most ambassadors. There were just two years left, under Black's contract with United Brands, before he qualified for early retirement. Remembering his comments about Henry Kissinger, I felt an ambassadorship might appeal to Eli and hoped that he would see it as a first step to bigger things at State. If Black wouldn't take the offer for its own sake, the company could sweeten the pot by paying his full salary for the time he was away—half a million dollars would be a small price to pay for getting him out. Of course, the pay would switch to retirement benefits in twenty-four months, so Eli would never come back to the company.

They liked the idea because it was humane and had a chance of working although, admittedly, it was a long shot. It also took advantage of a rare opportunity—all the other ambassadorial openings were in such posts as Bangladesh, Bulgaria, Fuji and Western Samoa, and of all the countries on earth where Eli was most likely to feel at home, Costa Rica would be at the top of the list. I recounted all I could remember of Eli's long admiration for Pepe Figueres—including the reference he had made in the ill-starred debate on Channel 13.

But the board of directors would also have to be ready with a crowbar if the leverage provided by the carrot failed to be sufficient. I suggested that steps be taken to line up all the directors on the board who realized Eli had to give up control.

We felt that someone should be selected from within Black's original entourage to deal with those board members to determine where they stood. We all agreed that Mort Broffman was a likely candidate for that task even though I had serious personal misgivings about him. Mort was out of a job at the moment, and I wondered whether he might see in this confidence an opportunity for self-improvement that would prove too powerful to resist. But on the other hand, I felt that relations between Broffman and Black had been strained since Broffman had left the company.

I tried to think through the various ways it might go. At worst even if Mort went to Eli and told him of our conversation, it would solve the communications problem: what better way to let Eli know than to hear it from Mort. I had not talked to Mort in over a year but I planned to call him the next day.

Then a strange coincidence occurred: Morton Broffman called me. He invited me to lunch at his Beacon Street apartment on January 20.

It was just Mort and his wife Louise and myself. By the time we were finished with the soup and got started on the tuna fish sandwich, I realized that Mort was cautiously feeling me out. He let me know he was aware that there were various groups, both within and outside the company, who were actively interested in removing Eli from his job. And he guardedly indicated that he, too, felt that Eli should step aside.

As I left, he told me that the next day, January 21, he was meeting with one of Eli's old associates from the AMK days who was currently still a director of United Brands and who, according to Mort, had expressed "great concern" over the state of affairs.

Two days later, on January 23, Broffman visited me at my office and I decided to tell him about the possible ambassadorship. By then I realized that our conversation could be transmitted to Black within the hour—but I also felt that it might be one of the gentlest ways for Eli to hear of the idea. Broffman said the idea appealed to him because "it would not hurt Eli." He made it very clear that he felt Eli should be removed and replaced but also that he did not want to be a part of anything that would hurt Eli in any way. We agreed to meet again the following week.

One week later, on January 30, Jack Fox, Dick Berry (a former vice-president of the company) and I met with Broffman at the Algonquin Club. We discussed the situation in more detail including the idea of Mort's rejoining the company once Black was out. Mort listened attentively, nodding all the way. He said he thought it was right in every respect. He thought it was humane and fair and "viable" and he agreed to approach some of the directors with whom he was friendly to feel them out.

We all shook hands after lunch. I told Mort I'd be looking forward to seeing more of him in the days ahead. He and Jack went off together, as an extension of the plans made by phone, to enjoy an afternoon of tennis at an indoor club a few blocks away. I went back to my office.

What Mort Broffman did not tell us was that forty-eight hours earlier, on January 28, just one week after his meeting with me in my office, he met with Black at his office in Boston. At that meeting, they discussed various attempts they thought were then afoot to wrest control of the company from Eli.

They also discussed some of the operational problems of the company and the executive management mistakes Eli felt he had made. The meeting wound up with an agreement that Mort would rejoin the company either as president or some similarly substantial title to head up operations. Eli was to remain on as Chairman of the Board and Chief Executive Officer. The employment contract was said to have been for a five-year term at an annual salary in six figures. At one point, Eli told Broffman, "We should have had this talk ten months ago." After the meeting, that same day, Eli told a mutual friend that he had "patched it up with Mort" and that Broffman was rejoining the company.

For some reason, Mort neglected to tell us of these events when we met two days later. I haven't seen Mort since that day at the Algonquin Club, so I don't know whether he ever told Eli of that meeting and the possibility of the ambassadorship. I hope he did because if he did, Eli might have seen it as one last, reasonable choice in a world where his options were fast disappearing.

Seventy-two hours before his death, Black telephoned the man who headed one of the families from whom he had won

I heard about the call from Don Meltzer, United Brands' vice-president for finance. Black was desperate and said that he needed a million-dollar loan. The request was refused.

Eli made an appointment with Mort Broffman for the following week to firm up Mort's reemployment and to further their plans for resisting the takeover and saving the company. But his time had run out. Black knew he had fallen far short of success in almost every area that mattered to him. The former rabbi was embroiled in bribery and corruption. The great achievement of his business lifetime, United Brands, was struggling to stay afloat in a sea of debt. His directors were in revolt, his management had lost respect for him, his friends had deserted him, his personal finances were at least as bad as those of the company, his ability to win people's confidence had disappeared, and he had nowhere left to turn.

When Eli jumped, the first police officer on the scene was Sgt. Howard Bender.

"The upper part of the body, the head," Bender recalls, "was exposed and that was in very bad shape."

Black's remains were lying on the northbound lanes of Park Avenue, and by the time Bender arrived, traffic had already backed up several blocks. Cars at the scene were slowly detouring around the mess in the roadway and continuing on their way, but the traffic snarl kept growing.

Meanwhile, on the forty-fourth floor, Black's driver, Jim Thomas, had broken through the locked outer doors of the company's suite and, with other employees including Burke Wright, a vice-president, had entered Black's office. Even before they saw the smashed and blood-flecked window, they had a clue to what had happened: as the door opened, they could feel the rush of cold outside air and hear the sounds of the street below.

Thomas stepped over to the hole and looked down. He saw the crowd gathering around the Park Avenue ramp, and he saw the shattered body. A few minutes later, at street level, the police asked him to make the identification.

"He was in the lobby area," Sgt. Bender said later, "and Mr. Black was out in the roadway. He didn't make what they call a positive identification. But from his dress he knew it was he."

According to homicide detective John Duffy, Black's clothes—and the contents of his pockets and briefcase—were about all they had to go on. "The head had been split, it went from front to back, right down the middle and back."

Sgt. Bender called for the Fire Department, the position of the body was marked on the roadway with chalk, and Black's remains were placed in a green rubber bag for a trip to the morgue. The fireman sprayed a hose over the place where it had lain.

Another policeman said, "It's a hell of a thing to do. Jumpers don't care. They don't think of anyone down below. With the traffic he could have taken any number of people with him."

At the morgue, Black's body received a perfunctory medical examination. No incisions were necessary; the internal organs were accessible through the torn and shattered torso. Small traces of Seconal were found in the stomach.

In his briefcase was a scrap of paper with the words "early retirement—55." It was the nearest thing there was to a suicide note.

The body was buried at Beth El Memorial Cemetery in Norwalk, Connecticut. The stone reads simply, "Eli M. Black" in English and Hebrew.

❧ Chapter 13 ☙

LAST THOUGHTS

SEVERAL DAYS after Eli jumped to his death, Don Meltzer told me that the SEC was conducting an investigation into the affairs of the company. He explained that this was a routine investigation that the SEC always performed following the unnatural death of a major corporation executive. A few weeks later it came to light that the SEC had uncovered the bribe of an official of the Republic of Honduras.

What is still not clear is precisely how the SEC first learned of the bribe—some insiders feel that the SEC uncovered it in the course of its investigation; others feel that it was a result of a tip from the State Department; and still others feel that it came from someone inside the company who wanted to precipitate a crisis for United Brands.

United Brands agreed to cooperate with the investigation but requested that any information turned over to the SEC be held confidential. The company sought to enlist even the State Department's help to ensure that confidentiality, alleging that the revelations could have a serious adverse affect on U.S. relations with Latin America. When the *Wall Street Journal* got wind of the story, the company was forced to issue a statement which said that Eli Black had authorized the payment to an official in the Republic of Honduras to win a reduction in the Honduran export tax on bananas. The payment had been made in September through the company's European subsidiaries. It had involved a numbered Swiss bank account and other cloak-and-dagger elements. But it was obvious that the handling of the bribe had been inept.

It was also revealed that officials of United Brands made payments in Italy of more than three quarters of a million dollars to ensure the company's competitive position in Italian government-controlled markets. In January, 1976, the company signed a consent decree with the SEC and is still under investigation by the U.S. Attorney's office in New York and possibly a Senate Sub-Committee. United Brands has retained a law firm just to coordinate the activities of the three or four other law firms retained to defend it. Midpoint in its investigation, the SEC charged the company with a continuing effort to conceal "the true scope and extent" of its payments to foreign government officials. The company asked the court to stay the proceeding in the SEC suit until the New York Grand Jury completed its investigation, but the SEC charged that there, too, "the true purpose of the company's request was stayed as to further prevent disclosure of the full facts and circumstances surrounding its payments of monies to government officials in Italy and Honduras."

Some of the men mentioned in this book are targets of these various investigations and, if Eli Black were alive, he undoubtedly would be among them. General Oswaldo Lopez Arellano, the Honduran Chief of State was overthrown for his alleged involvement in the United Brands scandal, and his Minister of Economy, Abraham Bennaton Ramos, was charged with negotiating the bribe and also removed.

The disclosure of the bribe shocked many people inside the company and outside. Such publications as the *Wall Street Journal* and *The New York Times*, which just a few weeks earlier had been extolling the virtues of Eli Black, now had to report one of the largest cases of corporate abuse of power in the annals of American business. The public disclosure further divided the company's board. Some of the directors were willing to tell what they knew even though it tarnished the name of Eli the controlling interest in Foster Grant only two years earlier. Black, while others rushed to Black's defense by saying that he knew very little about it, or that it was a case of extortion, or even that other members of the board and management used the knowledge of the bribe to blackmail Eli and force him to step aside. Black's immediate family also felt that some directors had been using their knowledge of the Honduran payment to pressure Eli into resigning.

In addition to the shock and the grief Eli's death caused his family, it presented them with another problem, too, because his personal financial affairs were not in good order. For one thing, his widow, Shirley Black, was entitled to no benefits under the company's retirement plan. Had he lived and worked until his normal retirement, Eli's estimated annual benefits upon retirement would have been $105,000. The directors took pity on Mrs. Black and voted to pay her his salary for the balance of the year following his death. They also authorized payment to her of a pension in the amount of $45,000 annually for life. But in April, 1976, the company announced that the pension to Mrs. Black as well as any further payments of deferred compensation accrued under Eli's employment agreement were suspended pending resolution of claims on behalf of the company against Eli in respect of the payment of the bribe and receipt of an accounting for approximately two hundred thousand dollars of cash advances made to Eli since January 1, 1970, for business expenses. As of this writing, those expenses had not been identified, and government investigators are probing deeply into the matter to try to learn why Eli needed all this money in addition to his large salary.

Regardless of the cleaning job they did on Park Avenue, the high-pressure hoses of the New York Fire Department were not to wash away the mysteries attached to Eli's passing. Why did he jump? Why did he need the one million dollars for which he asked seventy-two hours before his death? What became of the money earmarked for the Honduran bribe? Who was to inherit Eli's job? What was to happen to his family? What was to happen to the company?

EPILOGUE

IN CLOSING this book, I am also closing a chapter of my life. And, in the course of telling you about United Fruit, I have had to tell you more about myself than I had intended to.

I believe the private enterprise system still provides the best opportunity for a man or woman, regardless of how little they may have in the way of education, experience and background, to grow and develop and even perhaps have an adventure or two along the way. I am a product of that system. I'm not a numbers man, and the only way I could describe the company was to describe my personal experiences—what I thought of them, and how they changed me. I hope my failings as a mathematician have not inadvertently slighted some of Eli Black's genius. But if they have, they have. A company is more than numbers. In fact, I'm not sure that numbers have much to do with what a company is really about.

Once you get to know it from the inside, you realize that a company is a living organism, just like a family. It is related in some delicate and complex ways to all kinds of other organisms around it: to the constituencies I spoke about earlier in this book. It has ages, and it has a spirit. It can be made great by the right leadership, or it can be made mean and sinister by the wrong kind of leadership. Or, it can simply grow old and die.

One good way to kill off a company is to approach it as though it has no life, no age, no spirit, no constituencies that matter. In other words to approach it as Eli Black did, as though it were nothing more than numbers.

People have to be made to understand as well the effects of an Eli Black or a Jimmy Ling on the companies they take over, not only in terms of the loss of billions of dollars in the value of stocks, but of people. They have to face the fact that there is no such thing as a free lunch, not even at the corporate racetrack.

It was the consumer who paid for all those airplane rides Jimmy Ling took in his private jet. The price of Wilson meat had to be a little bit higher than if he had stayed on the ground. The price you paid for your kid's Wilson catcher's mitt had to reflect the cost of those joyrides. The price you pay for Chiquita bananas or a Morrell ham for a long time to come will reflect the amount that AMK overpaid for United Fruit Company, back when Eli Black took his joyride in '68 and '69.

If, however, the consumer refuses to pay, then it has to come off the other end—the worker pays in deferred wage increases, lessened fringe benefits or even the loss of his job.

Someone always pays.

INDEX